SMASHING
THE
PATRIARCHY

SMASHING
THE
PATRIARCHY

A Guide for the 21st-century Indian Woman

SINDHU RAJASEKARAN

ALEPH

ALEPH

ALEPH BOOK COMPANY
An independent publishing firm
promoted by *Rupa Publications India*

First published in India in 2021
by Aleph Book Company
7/16 Ansari Road, Daryaganj
New Delhi 110 002

ISBN: 978-93-90652-88-4

3 5 7 9 10 8 6 4 2

Printed in India

For my daughter
Aria

CONTENTS

AUTHOR'S NOTE

In a complex cultural and techno-social world where a million ideologies intermingle, ambiguities are unavoidable. The lines between subjectivity and objectivity are blurred here. The curious case of postfeminism exists in this space of ambivalence, as does this book, and I. While I do not proclaim to offer solutions to fix the quandaries concerning the 'f' words[1]—feminism, femininity, femaleness—I do hope that this book will help further complicate these concepts for the reader, and provide an alternative look into how contemporary women perform their elusive fs.

The narrative of this book is centred on the bold voices of millennial (and some Gen Z) women[2] from varied backgrounds and their lived experiences. Some of these women call themselves feminists, others don't—but they're all smashing the patriarchy one way or another. What I've sought to do is explore what challenges these ladies face based on their femaleness, how they overcome them, and what they consider (post)feminist acts in their everyday lives. As you read their interviews, please remember that these women and I possess different subjectivities. While our reflections on various issues may have influenced one another in the course of our recorded conversations, leading to a collective reflexivity[3], this does not mean

---

[1]Gender theorist Stephanie Genz introduces her book *Postfeminisms in Popular Culture* with a chapter titled 'The f-words'.

[2]Of various castes, creeds, communities, and sexualities. I don't specify each one's identity, as for most these identities are among the many they have. Only when someone considers a specific identity important to their everyday life do I mention it.

[3]As Professor Maithree Wickramasinghe points out in her book *Feminist Research Methodology*: 'What I call collective reflexivity can be seen as a reaction to the influence of postmodernist realizations that the authorial self is unstable, and therefore meta-

they agree with all my opinions. The same applies to the knowledge experts I've interviewed on various transdisciplinary subjects, who concur with me on various points but also disagree on several others. The treatise that surrounds these conversations, enriched with quotations from academics and thinkers I haven't personally spoken to, is not the result of any specific style of feminist research or methodology. Honestly, this book is a jumble of theory, pop culture, and personal opinion, and, depending on your ontological standpoint, you may derive tangible or fluctuating meanings from it.

It's essential to note here that my idea of postfeminism draws from good old feminist theories of all shades from all around the world. I'm deeply indebted to the generations of badass feminists who fought for our rights. My thoughts stand on the grand platform they've built. I take immense pride in calling myself a feminist, post or otherwise. Feminism is among the few ideological spaces that are self-critical and resilient in India, willing to listen to dissenters. Any criticism I mount in this book against it is to do with its increasingly limiting definitions of itself—where feminist activists/theorists say and write things that are at odds with the current female discourse. 'The vocabulary of Feminism today is unfortunately more disengaging than engaging.' This phenomenon is not confined to India, of course. It is true of feminism worldwide. Feminist idol Germaine Greer has called #MeToo a 'whingeing' movement while the iconic Gloria Steinem has made multiple transphobic statements. There seems to be a discord between feminist ideology and the women whom it seeks to represent. This is not to imply that all older feminists think in outdated language and all younger women are super woke. On the contrary, I find that postfeminist thought always existed alongside earlier feminist narratives, albeit on the fringes. Now, as young women break gender norms through unorthodox and inventive means, it's important that we update feminist lingo to make it less judgy and expand its scope.

---

narratives need to be de-centered in favour of the multiple and often contradictory voices (polyvocality) of the researched.'

This isn't a conventional work on Indian feminism. I am not an expert on feminist policy, activism, or women's legal rights, and my understanding of feminism is not rooted in the work of the Indian academia. Also, I must confess that I did not learn about feminism in a tidy, linear manner. As a millennial who grew up freewheeling on the internet, I've latched on to feminist ideas from hither and thither. Sometimes, I've gone back to Indian proto-feminisms for inspiration. In fact, one of the reasons I was attracted to postfeminism, as a term, is its hyperreal underpinnings. In cyberspace, postfeminist thought travels transnationally, influencing women from completely different backgrounds. At the same time, its meanings constantly metamorphose and its praxis becomes exclusive to every woman. It would seem then that there's nothing tangible about postfeminism. But such is its nature. 'There is no *original* or *authentic* postfeminism that holds the key to its definition', writes Stéphanie Genz, and suggests we analyse postfeminism as 'a network of possible relations'.

You should also know that my conception of postfeminism is at odds with the largely negative connotation it holds in mainstream Anglo-American circles. Feminist scholar Imelda Whelehan mockingly wonders whether postfeminism is an 'identity crisis'. I'd say yes, it is, and this is not a bad thing. The fact is that as feminists, we are looking into the contradictions of our beliefs and actions, which is critical for self-realization and progress. Hiding our weak spots to win in theory is not going to help the feminist cause. Postfeminist women, on that count, live real lives filled with contradictions. Most are #brutallyhonest about it. Ambiguity is the space where the most nuanced answers can be found. And in postfeminist flexibility exists the potential for tangible cultural change and social transformation. Perhaps even a tiny prospect to decolonize feminism. I intend to rescue the battered term postfeminism through this book and look at women's lives through a multicoloured filter.

India is so vast and its women so diverse, no book can claim to include everyone. Despite my conscious effort to broaden the scope and amplify diverse voices, there are many cultures and parts of India whose women I couldn't include for lack of time. The women who populate this book are largely from urban and semi-urban spaces, though a few interviews with women from rural backgrounds have been included as well. Now, you may very well ask me: *since you're against appropriating socio-economically underprivileged women's issues, why does your book include their voices?* I spoke to these women not to locate their oppression for analysis' sake, but to understand their ways of seeing the world, to know what battles they fight, and learn how they smash the patriarchy. Because more than any other class of women, they speak truth to power.

There are five chapters in this book; the first of these is 'On Beauty'. Traditionally, feminism has been wary of the concept of beauty. But beauty is a complex and contradictory condition where pleasure counterbalances shame, and hope contests pain. Living in a society that's still in the clasp of racist beauty standards means that women are not only dealing with their own personal insecurities, but also with those of their chauvinistic culture. In this chapter, I examine how young women resist the bias perpetuated by the mainstream entertainment, fashion, and beauty industries, from inside and out. I explore why women pursue or reject beauty standards and the real-life repercussions of their choices. I also look at fashion as a form of self-expression. How do women use it to reclaim their own image? Can it turn gender stereotypes on its head and visually play on socio-political complexities? Underpinning all this is an examination of how race, caste, class, religion, and sexuality remain focal points in Indian society's prejudice against the female form.

'Ishq in the Times of Tinder' considers the conundrum that is love. In this chapter, I investigate what women want (and don't want) from partnerships. What are the factors that influence who we get off with? What we talk about when we talk about sex has changed radically online and offline, and women these days not only seek pleasure from their partners, but are finding ways to pleasure themselves. In a country that has always spoken about female sexuality as a tool of male pleasure, contemporary women are rewriting the narrative, laying out boundaries on what constitutes pleasure and what doesn't. I take a deep dive into the actual acts that constitute sex to understand our queer desires. What does consent mean in twenty-first-century India? I also go into how failed love takes a toll; what happens to women's minds when they're mired in exploitative relationships. Finally, I discuss kinkiness and how it's the next step in having gender-equal sex, and good sexual and reproductive health.

In 'Women at Work', the third chapter, I focus on how young, hyper-informed (and tech-savvy) women have shifted work culture across industries. How have our work cultures changed following #MeToo? I find out how women shrewdly circumvent office politics to achieve their end goals, while dealing with everyday sexism and gender-bias, redefining fempowerment. I take a look at women's conflicting desire to be simultaneously considered equal and different to their male colleagues. I talk to women about the motherhood penalty and discover how they reinvent themselves after gap years. What sort of discriminations do women face based on factors other than their gender and how does one's relationship status, sexual, or social identity affect their workplace relationships? Also discussed: (post)feminist advocacy for working women, 'ambition gaps', and what constitutes work—how do homemakers contribute to the economy?

'Demystifying the Feminine,' the fourth chapter, deals with the feminine—is it an eternal concept or a patriarchal myth? How do women across the socio-cultural spectrum define femininity; how do they perform their gender? I explore the relationship between the female mind and body, only to discover how profoundly they are interconnected. I take inspiration from ancient, medieval, and pre-modern Indian femininity here, and briefly foray into how visual media represents the feminine and the effects of colonialism. I delve into the idea of transcendence, centred on women's thoughts and their experiences of the sublime in art and in life. This chapter also contains my thoughts on female narcissism, our androgynous selves, and why women should look for all the answers within themselves.

In the last chapter, 'Society, Sanskar, and Choice', I investigate the idea of female respectability along two tangents. One traces society's conception of honour and the backlash dissenting women face when they go against the norm. The other considers the 'empowered woman' and the criticism that conservative women are subjected to for making choices that are anathema to traditional feminism. I look into how women are fighting orthodoxy to reclaim their lives. I also explore religiosity and consider how women of faith pursue self-empowerment through their beliefs. This is followed by an inspection of (caste- and creed-based) identity and its influence on women's choices and politics. Finally, I explore the paradox of choice, what constitutes success and where postfeminism draws the line.

Then, there's my 'Conclusion: The Future is Female'. Pretty self-explanatory, that.

INTRODUCTION

I: Shifting the Paradigm

Ours is a toxic time, and a toxic place, filled with vile masculinity. Every woman in India has to navigate the country's millennia-old misogyny on a daily basis. She is discriminated against at work, casually molested on the streets, imperious men mansplain things to her and sexually assault her under the guise of assumed consent, fundamentalists troll her and threaten to kill her for speaking her mind, acid is thrown on her face when she rejects a man's proposal of love or sex. And, of course, there is always the threat of rape[1] hanging over her head.

The only way forward, it would seem, is to permanently transform into our Kali avatars[2] and reduce the patriarchy to ashes. But, alas, life isn't one-dimensional. A woman often has to take on multiple avatars to navigate her complex everyday life and negotiate relationships

---

[1] A woman was raped every six hours in India in 2016, according to the National Crime Records Bureau. But when Thomson Reuters declared India the most dangerous place for women in 2018, the National Commission for Women (NCW) was up in arms. Surely, there must be other nations worse off, no?

[2] Collective outrage engulfs our nation when the media spotlights gory details of gang rapes. Women and girls turn into their Kali avatars and demand a society where they can safely live their lives. But outrage can't last forever. People have to get back to their routines. Time passes. More women are assaulted and murdered, most of whom are Dalit or Adivasi, but this doesn't cause outrage in racist India as much. (Remember Hathras?) Police refuse to file FIRs against powerful men. The judiciary takes forever to convict, if at all. As of 2018, our parliament and legislative assemblies host more than forty-eight MPs and MLAs with registered cases, for perpetrating crimes against women. India's rape culture, meanwhile, persists across socio-economic strata. Clearly, women's safety is not a priority of the establishment.

with the opposite sex at work, at home, and in bed. Every woman inhabits a unique structural reality, where her race, religion, caste, class, and sexuality determine her privileges (or lack thereof), while her ideology decides her politics. Each one fights her own battles, in her own quirky way, performing a nuanced version of femininity[3] that reflects her fantasies, aspirations, and desires. This may involve rebelling outright against the tenets of conventional womanhood, but also entails the audacity to leverage her gendered social position to her advantage. Theorists consider space to be critical in understanding identity as performance, and the contemporary Indian woman is situated in an especially convoluted space. To win against hydra-headed patriarchy every day, she has to constantly reform her strategy. Be crafty. Subvert the idea of femininity to take back the power.

Oh, but, *fem·i·nin·i·ty*, some may scowl. Why must we talk about it now, what does it have to do with empowerment? This noun that has shackled womankind since time immemorial? It must go. To be free, to go beyond gender binaries, we must dissociate the female body from femininity first. While there's no denying the existential complexities inherent in performing feminine subjectivities, I believe that disjoining womanhood and femininity is a Sisyphean endeavour. Over many dark millennia, Brahmanical patriarchy has conveniently painted the ideal of femininity as selfless and glorified women's capacity to suffer[4], calling it divine. As a result of this, femininity, in our minds, is now a synonym for passivity, subservience, and dependence. But femininity, allow me to holler, can be both sensitive and fierce. It is the source of all creativity, sensuality, and

---

[3]Twentieth-century philosopher and existentialist Simone de Beauvoir famously said that femininity is a performance, that '[o]ne is not born, but rather becomes, a woman'. Women imitate socially defined ideas of femininity to become *women*. In the twenty-first century, I believe that self-conscious women often manipulate traditional femininity to achieve their modern goals.

[4]Mahatma Gandhi considered women's ability for self-sacrifice superior to assertive intervention, while Rabindranath Tagore wrote: 'Woman has to be ready to suffer. She cannot allow her emotions to be dulled or polluted.'

intuition[5]—buried ideas from a time when the sacred feminine was dethroned[6] and forced to acquiesce to phallocentric patriarchy.

Before I go any further, let me untangle this academically loaded word[7] a bit. In the gender-egalitarian world of our dreams, a biologically essentialist view of gender which connects femininity to femaleness is considered abhorrent, outmoded, and problematic. Most academics prefer to use the politically correct term 'female sexuality' when talking about the idea, and, therefore, it's incumbent upon me to explain myself. Please note that when I use the term femininity, I'm not talking about the socially constructed standards of the same that are imposed on women everywhere.[8] I believe that femininity is a complex and prismatic phenomenon that's constantly transforming within each one of us,[9] irrespective of our sexual orientation or

---

[5]Ancient wisdom allows us deconstructed modern people to catch a glimpse of the quintessential nature of femininity and its celebration in times bygone. Many cultures worshipped the sacred feminine and considered it to be the source of life, the giver of balance, and promoter of unity. On the other hand, femininity was also associated with the wilderness, reflecting a woman's inner wild nature.

[6]Not a conspiracy theory. Several Indologists trace the origin of India's goddess cults to Harappan times. The archetypal divine mother seems to have been the civilization's principal deity, which finds a continuation in Dravidian folk religion—still centred on ancient matriarchal wisdom with the goddess as mother. Meanwhile, Mother Earth is sacred to most tribal cultures across the subcontinent. It appears that when patrilineal and patrilocal groups from the Eurasian steppe migrated to this land, pop culture shifted—with the masculine principle being held supreme in keeping with their beliefs, and the feminine being demoted to the position of (fair) consort. The idea of 'Brahmanical patriarchy' didn't just come out of nowhere.

[7]In case you're wondering: I mean femininity, of course.

[8]Which in India is not a monolithic stereotype. Brahmanical patriarchy (as exemplified by *Manusmriti* and even the *Kama Sutra*) has codified different versions of femininity for women based on their caste and ethnicity. This means that while an upper-caste woman is expected to be delicate and sexually virtuous, a lower-caste woman is stereotyped as tough and amorous. As a result, women from different castes/creeds have to fight different battles with society to reinforce their own version of femininity.

[9]The masculine (purusha) and feminine (prakriti) principles 'are a duality in unity', holds ecofeminist Vandana Shiva, drawing from Vedic philosophy. 'They are inseparable complements of one another in nature, in woman, in man.'

gender identity.[10] It doesn't always exist in isolation and melds with masculinity to form newer expressions of androgyny, all within the same individual. (Being bisexual myself, I can personally vouch for this matter.) Through a spectrum extending from femme to butch[11], and beyond binaries, it manifests in a rainbow of sexualities and genders. Femininity is and always has been a source of transcendental power.

Undoing the Patriarchy in Our Heads

In the masculine world that we live in, femininity is code for vulnerability. We are expected to downplay our feminine side lest we be pigeonholed as irrational, hysteric, or worse, weak. To appear capable in our professions, we are required to bring out our 'mannish' side. Think logically, wo(man). Don't let your mind wander. After all, patriarchal superstructures have been built on a solid foundation of masculine thinking. It isn't an accident that even our most enlightened forefathers[12] considered women to be less objective than men. Since the beginning, male liberal thinkers (like their unenlightened antecedents) upheld the intellectual priorities of men over women. When women did philosophize, their thinking was dismissed[13] for deviant intuiting (because even the norms of thinking were gendered). It's no surprise then that women had been effectively banished from the world of science until not long ago, because they were not considered suitable for plain logical pursuits, what with their susceptibility to feel grief, regret, guilt, compassion, etc. Even today, feminine qualities are

---

[10]Be we asexual, hetero- or homosexual women, gender non-conforming, fluid or transgender, or men, there's a trace of femininity in each one of us. Whether we suppress it or celebrate it is a personal choice, but we can't deny its existence.

[11]While femme and butch identities were originally adjectives used within the lesbian community, now even straight women identify themselves with these terms—and express their sexuality so.

[12]From Aristotle and Kant to Rousseau and Freud, male thinkers wrote off women as inferior beings prone to feminine thinking.

[13]While female philosophers like Gargi and Maitreyi were lauded in ancient India, as was Akka Mahadevi in medieval times, by early modernity, women were not considered suitable to acquire or create knowledge.

dismissed as flaws in people of all genders.[14] Feminized skills, on the other hand, are undervalued across industries (and at home). In my humble opinion, gender equality is doomed unless femininity regains its position of power in our minds.

This is not to say that all women are inherently more feminine. On the contrary, I think female masculinity equally defines our gender identities and sexualities. However, even as the patriarchy says that femaleness must denote femininity, it simultaneously curtails all feminine expressions that challenge hyper-masculine hegemony. This has created a double bind for women, whereby they aren't allowed to fully galvanize the faculties of their masculine or feminine aspects. A woman has to confine herself within the parameters set forth by religious, social, or cultural codes. To do away with these conventions, many women's libbers have radically rejected femininity and redefined gender over the years. They fought for women's rights as human rights and created avenues for women to step into the corridors of power. Unfortunately, these aren't truly egalitarian spaces where women can simply exercise their free will. At the door, standing guard, are benevolent patriarchs with ogling eyes. Be it in the establishment or the anti-establishment, every woman still has to deal with feudal mindsets and its associated sexist biases at every stage (Avarna women and those from minority communities are especially targeted, both subtly and overtly). All traces of femininity are assumed to be subtle invitations for male attention. Female masculinity, meanwhile, is seen as perverse. So, what should women do? Bury our female consciousness altogether? Suppress our sexualities and be gender-neutral in our thoughts, words, and actions?

---

[14]Take intuition, for instance. The 'ability to perceive or know things without conscious reasoning' (as defined in Webster's New World Dictionary) has been dismissed as unscientific. Effeminate men and emo women have been sidelined for ages because masculine, usually male, bosses only go by hard facts or cocky arrogance. But recently, through its own attendant rational reasoning, male-controlled corporations have decided that emotional intelligence is a key business leadership skill—and intuitive thinking is now considered a form of high intelligence. I suppose we are to consider our strengths as flaws until the patriarchy decides otherwise.

A two-year study, published in 2019, found strong implicit bias in various scientific fields. This is one of several studies that show that even overtly noble domains like STEM and social sciences can be unconsciously sexist, because a distinctly masculine culture predominates these disciplines, and inside most people's heads: science = male. As a result, not all brilliant women are promoted to the positions they deserve. Gender pay gaps persist. Female researchers are also less likely to be awarded for their contributions, because the establishment tends to value, acknowledge, and reward male scholarship[15] more. Meanwhile, in the world of the liberal arts, when women write profound literature, deliver transcendental performances, or create intense visual art that is centred on feminine subjectivities,[16] their oeuvres are immediately gendered and segregated as women's work. They are never lauded as the universal standard that all must now aspire to. Can it really be that female creativity is limiting, or are patriarchal yardsticks predisposed to commend male vision? In fact, neuroscientists[17] have found that women's brains are hardwired to seamlessly blend logic and instinct. It then follows that a woman is inherently capable of groundbreaking creative enquiry and profound expression. Then why hasn't she been celebrated as much? It seems to me that as long as dominating men hold authority, they'd reify the idea that masculinity is the universal and that femininity is 'the Other'.

---

[15]Known as the 'Matilda effect': 'women's research is viewed as less important or their ideas are attributed to male scholars, even as a field becomes more diverse', declares a study published in the Harvard Dataverse.

[16]Unconsciously or deliberately, it doesn't matter. When a woman produces something, her work is either viewed as feminine, or as rebelling against the feminine, but always somehow linked to the feminine.

[17]According to a study led by Professor Ragini Verma at the University of Pennsylvania, women's brains are highly connected across the left and right hemispheres (where the left does logical and right does intuitive thinking), while men's brains are typically more connected between the front and back—meaning that women are hardwired to instinctively combine logic and intuition, while men are liable to be more focused on a single manner of thought at a time. However, in a book titled *The Gendered Brain: The Neuroscience That Shatters the Myth of the Female Brain*, cognitive neuroscientist Gina Rippon argues the opposite case. Neuroscientists remain divided on this matter.

For men (liberal or conservative) may very well believe in gender equality, but their Absolute[18] will still secretly remain masculine; femininity will forever remain an addendum, the inferior.

In order to challenge the patriarchal notion of gendered difference, we may very well take the popular route of arguing against cognitive sex differences altogether, instead reasoning that any dissimilarity is socially constructed. While this idea may be groundbreaking, in theory, it doesn't help solve the puzzles of reality. Honestly, even though every individual is unique in how they think or what they're good at, there are certain enigmatic aspects of sex that cannot be reduced to social conditioning. Women *feel* a certain way. They perceive the world differently, and there is value in that difference. Why should we, as women, give up on that and work towards neutralizing our minds? If you, however, choose to go down this path, be warned. Neutralizing isn't always neutral, often it's masculinizing.

Kicking the Patriarchy off Our Bodies

As a woman, there's no escaping the penalty at every step for being female bodied. At workspaces, educational institutions, and even at home, women are expected to get on untiringly alongside men irrespective of the natural processes of their bodies[19]. These expectations range from the seemingly benign, like asking them to hold their bladders longer than possible[20] and making them work in freezing office temperatures pre-set for the comfort of male colleagues, to seriously sexist practices like consigning women's physical ailments

---

[18]In philosophy, the Absolute signifies the supreme truth or the ultimate being. In theology, the Absolute is an attribute of God. In both cases, it is about transcending everyday existence and seeking the eternal.

[19]Thanks to years of women's rights movements arguing the case against gender differentiation, men have come to believe that women have to put up with the same working and living conditions as men if they want to be a part of the man's world.

[20]Women workers in several industries go for long hours without bathroom breaks, that is, assuming there's a bathroom available in the first place. They are consequently at a major risk of developing genitourinary diseases.

to the realm of obsessive imagination[21] (because man-made modern medicine has only just started figuring out women's bodies and its physiological differences). When a woman possesses physical might comparable to a man or performs female masculinity, she's denied her womanhood[22] altogether because then she's considered too manly. Whether a woman's physical dynamics are consistent with society's idea of femaleness or not, she's nonetheless tied to her body. Menstruation, childbirth, PCOS, fibromyalgia, and menopause (to name some) are drastic physical events that take a toll; while for trans folks, the physical journey of transition, if they choose to go through it, is arduous. Our body routines cause a considerable amount of psychological stress in each one of us, but society doesn't consider it real. And we often push it under the carpet ourselves, consigning mental wellness to oblivion. While it is true that women have a higher threshold for pain than most men, this doesn't mean that they have to work against the flow of their bodies to prove to the patriarchy that they're equal[23]. Delinking ourselves from our female bodies (and minds) in order to demystify femininity might work temporarily, but this method won't bring the emancipation we seek. Perhaps, for that to happen, we must reappropriate the pains of our gendered bodies, focusing the spotlight on the realities of our existence rather than hiding them away.

The female body is also a site of immense pleasure. I don't mean an object of pleasure for men, but that a woman's body seeks erotic

[21]Diseases such as endometriosis (when uterine tissue begins growing outside the uterus) or fibromyalgia (a chronic pain disorder) are often regarded with suspicion and their symptoms are disregarded as exaggeration. Meanwhile, several women are misdiagnosed after having a heart attack—because women's symptoms are different to men's—and this neglect often leads to their death. Women with autism often aren't diagnosed at all because the tests to identify it are skewed towards men.

[22]Santhi Soundarajan, an Olympian, was stripped of her Asian Games silver medal in 2006 because (outdated) gender tests branded her a man.

[23]By this, I do not suggest that all women possess the same hormonal make-up. With every passing year, the medical fraternity finds that the levels of androgen and estrogen which determine the maleness and femaleness of human bodies are not as stable as originally envisaged. This means that every woman's body is unique—following its own rhythm.

Smashing the Patriarchy

gratification. One that narcissistically admires/detests itself. Women aren't naturally inclined to be sexually passive—they are active agents who pursue their sensual wants. Clearly, the patriarchy is petrified of female sexual power. Perhaps it has an infantile fear of every woman's pussy, a secret fascination with the vagina's potential to create life combined with a beastly impulse to violate the sexy/ugly female body that bears said vagina. Patriarchy can get pretty perverse. In its benign form, it overprotects women precisely because it knows what the vilest men think. In its malevolent form, it seeks to brutalize, then relish female suffering. But here's the catch. Never mind that it's usually men who indulge in violent acts of carnality, it's the women who are condemned for their vanity and conceit, for giving into evil temptations of the flesh. Women are expected to employ their sexual energies in only one of two ways: serve as submissive wives or saintly women[24]. Whenever a woman dares to resist the patriarchy[25] and seeks pleasure in her own body or in another woman's body, or uses her sexual capital[26] to seek power and influence—inside[27] or outside marriage—she is deemed unworthy. Vilified as promiscuous and wanton.

Now, in a society where men freely exhibit their narcissistic

---

[24]Like Sita, wife of Rama, who took the Agni Pariksha (trial by fire) to prove her chastity, or like Kannagi, wife of philandering Kovalan, who burned the city of Madurai as revenge for the unjust execution of her husband. Or like the saints Meera, Avvaiyar, and Karaikal Ammaiyar, who subverted hegemonic structures and wrote poetry devoted to the gods. But, to do so, they chose to abstain from having sexual relations in the real world altogether.

[25]Ancient, medieval, and pre-modern Indian texts are filled with instances of women who transgress. Only, patriarchy has rewritten their stories to make them examples of what good women shouldn't become. Take Surpanaka, for instance. A strong-willed, independent woman, a widow, who happens to desire. Initially, she's attracted to Rama, who rejects her and asks her to approach Lakshmana—who insults her and cuts off her nose. In popular versions of the Ramayana, Surpanaka is depicted as a dreadful demoness and seductress. But really, she is a wronged woman, and a survivor of sexual violence.

[26]Coined by Dr Catherine Hakim from the London School of Economics, sexual or erotic capital includes qualities like beauty, sex appeal, social grace, liveliness, social presentation, and sexual competence.

[27]This applies to married women, too, for wives who sexually entrance their husbands are considered manipulative.

swagger and sexual aggression, how can a woman play sexual politics? Should she perform a show of stoic modesty and restrain herself from demonstrating her sexuality completely? Or should she strategically use her feminine (conceit, charm, and cunning) and masculine (arrogance and aggression) qualities to attain positions of power and hold her sway? In a violent land like ours where sexual harassment laws are mere words on paper, the idea of women using their sexual capital to any advantage may appear unthinkable. But I beg to differ. Patriarchy has continually eroticized and traded the female body. It has forbidden every expression of female sexuality that doesn't fit its purpose. To disrupt this arrangement and gain agency over their own bodies, women must represent their *selves*. Queer the narrative. Reclaim their gender identities and wear it on their sleeves. Redefine sexual politics in the streets, in the boardroom, and in the bedroom. Confound the patriarchy by turning gender stereotypes upside-down and deploy their female sexualities to their individual benefit[28]. Do pardon me if all of this offends you. I'm aware that I'm advocating for women to be shameless. To be guiltless. Perhaps, even a bit narcissistic. Instead of all this, you may say, we should win over the patriarchy with our nurturing love. Well, been there and done that—for centuries. Time for a change?

Going Beyond Victimhood

In our postcolonial consciousness[29], the discourse of woman as victim is the central belief around which the advocacy for gender rights revolves. This approach can be (and has been) useful when

---

[28]I'm sure some of you are thinking that this sort of feminism reeks of privilege (more on this later). Clearly, only a woman with some form of socio-economic patronage can afford to play sexual micropolitics in her everyday life without dire consequences. While there's no denying the peril inherent in performing femininity (or masculinity), it's important to concede that all sorts of women already use their sexual capital at work and home.
[29]Historian Lata Mani suggests that while reconstructing Indian history, British colonialists painted a picture of our women collectively as victims, in order to legitimize colonial intervention into native affairs. This outlook, it would seem, has stuck. Globally, women from the 'third world' are seen as an oppressed lot, who are in immediate need of rescuing.

one demands constitutional justice in an inequitable society, sure. However, it also inadvertently brands women as eternal sufferers and perpetuates the idea that Indian women's lives are infinitely regressive. That all our foremothers lived pathetic docile lives through ancient, medieval, and pre-modern times. Only when the honourable British Lord Bentinck abolished sati did the notion of women's empowerment dawn on Indian soil. That's nonsensical. Powerful women exist not only in our myths but throughout precolonial history[30]. Indian women have challenged and destabilized the patriarchy, individually and collectively, and have *survived*. So, how do we reclaim the resistance of our foremothers?

Welcome to the twenty-first century. Today's young Indian women have unequivocally declared that they shall suffer no more. They have already ended their victimhood and are now assertive survivors who turn their perceived weaknesses into strengths. Conscious of their sexist realities, their globalized minds constantly decode the everyday nuisance of discrimination. To rise above it, some break away from tradition altogether, while others choose to hang on to their inherited cultural identities[31], recontextualizing it for modern times. This quest to balance conflicts of ideology and identity isn't a new phenomenon, obviously. Women must've explored it all through living history and dealt with it as they see fit. But as historian Rebecca Solnit writes, '[t]he history of silence is central to women's history.' Consequently, we don't know what women thought in the past exactly, as most ancient, medieval, and early modern texts in India about women are either prescriptive or

---

[30]From Nangeli, the nineteenth-century Ezhava woman who dared to cut off her breasts to protest a derogatory breast tax to fifteenth-century Punjab's Heer who fought to love as she wished to Razia Sultana in the thirteenth century, who defied all odds to become the first woman sultan of Delhi to the mythical Draupadi from the Mahabharata, who strove to avenge the wrongs meted out to her—India abounds with narratives of brave women who fought against patriarchal hegemony, with their bodies and their lives.

[31]One's ethnicity, caste, creed, language, and a million other factors intermingle to produce a person's cultural identity. However, in a country rife with identity politics, some identities are more politically contentious than others.

written by men, barring a few lucky surprises.[32]

Today, thanks to the internet, many young women have found a new space to dauntlessly voice their opinion irrespective of context and create their own narratives. A space where they are entitled to unapologetically be themselves. Curate a lifestyle and attitude that reflects their micropolitics. As digital natives, millennials (and Gen Z who are many steps ahead) understand the power of the internet. Through tweets, images, videos, memes, comments, and essays, they constantly defy the patriarchy. Through social media campaigns like #MeToo[33], #TimesUp, #WhyLoiter, #PrideNotPrejudice, #QueerIndia, #HappyToBleed, #IWillGoOut, #DalitWomenFight[34], and #SmashBrahmanicalPatriarchy, they have changed the manner in which activism is done. In this visceral mode of activism, their virtual bodies become 'sites of dissent'. This is a generation of women who speak for themselves, and stay true to their personal experiences and identity, despite what the critics say. And as they increasingly become aware of their digital rights, they're reclaiming the internet from sexist trolls who lurk in every corner online, as they do in real life[35]—by talking back, telling them off, and calling them out.

This new age of female digital disobedience has shaken up the patriarchy like never before. And it comes at a good time, too, because masculinity is now in a crisis. Around the world, hyper-masculine

---

[32]In the words of the eighth-century Tamil Alvar poet Andal, in the verses of the fourteenth-century Kashmiri mystic Lal Ded, and in the seventeenth-century Mughal princess Jahanara Begum's personal diary, we hear women's voices.

[33]The first wave of India's #MeToo really began with Raya Sarkar's Google spreadsheet. The hashtag #MeToo, however, was first used by journalist Arathi Renjith when she accused activist Rupesh Kumar of attempting to molest her. Since then, it has been used widely by urban women to record their experiences of sexual harassment in cyberspace. Allegations against harassers have been mounting across industries, especially in entertainment, journalism, and art.

[34]This unites Dalit activists around the world who highlight caste-based discrimination and sexual violence faced by Dalit women. The website dalitwomenfight.com has links to various strategies through which they break the silence regarding caste apartheid.

[35]There are more men on the internet than women in India. In 2016, there were 70 per cent men and 30 per cent women, according to Statista. However, things are changing quickly. According to a new report, 26 million new female users got on the internet in 2019.

Smashing the Patriarchy

men are fighting to the death, paying little heed to balance and justice. All our aggrandizing wars, skewed social schemes, ecologically destructive practices, and short-sighted economic policies are a direct result of patriarchy. It's unequipped to run the show and now its time is up. Moreover, petitioning the patriarchy to share power with women is useless. Take the Women's Reservation Bill[36], for instance. The Indian establishment has still not passed it after all these years of being a democracy. It has, however, passed several paternalistic acts for the welfare of women, like the Medical Termination of Pregnancy (Amendment) Bill, 2020. It stretches the upper limit for termination (from 20 to 24 weeks), but requires women to take permission from the Medical Board for late-term abortions, encumbering them further with bureaucratic process while paying little heed to their bodily agency. It's pretty obvious that while the patriarchy may make some beneficent commiserations every now and again, the power dynamic remains the same. Men give and women receive. The same old social contract. Young women are running out of patience with this iniquitous arrangement at home and work, and their path to equality, or rather, to absolute power, is a subversively individual pursuit.

Reimagining Feminism

It's crucial to remember that not all young women identify as feminists. And if they do call themselves feminists, they don't all toe the feminist party line (so to speak). Because not everyone agrees entirely with all the principles of traditional feminism.[37] Consequently, their digital disobedience has shaken up the idea of feminism in India, too. Because, before the internet, feminism was a preserve of those who had academic access to Western feminist theory and those who actively fought on the ground for gender equality alongside social

---

[36]It is supposed to give 33 per cent of seats in the Lok Sabha and state legislative assemblies to women. It has been talked about for more than twenty years, but no party has passed the bloody bill. Also, why not 50 per cent?

[37]Obviously, women's studies and movements are a combination of ideologies. Yet, certain varieties of feminism are more self-righteous than others (read leftist feminism).

justice. Calling oneself feminist in that era was often contingent on receiving validation from either of these groups. And the popular version of feminism among these well-meaning women was socialist or Marxist. Fast forward to today, and women of all kinds claim #feminism—each one defining her own idea of empowerment.

In fact, the upsurge has prompted several feminist critics to condemn young women for using feminism as a pop-aesthetic without fully understanding its tenets. Feminist icon Urvashi Butalia[38] said of millennial feminism: 'But their kind of feminism has come from social media involvement, and is often focused on individual rights …it's also in some ways lonely activism, because they *are* doing things, they *are* gathering on social media, but there isn't the sense of a whole movement behind them.' This raises the question: what's wrong with seeking individual rights?

After all, not every young woman can be expected to devote her entire life to conventional activism that fights for feminist justice, equality, and reform.[39] However, this doesn't mean that by pursuing self-empowerment, women don't contribute to the feminist struggle. Remember that in Indian society, even the most individualistic woman has to deal with a number of patriarchal people. Her idea of empowerment may involve an emphasis on her own self-esteem, but it also inevitably centres on micropolitics in her everyday life. She's bound to change perceptions (at home, work, in society) and pave paths for other women. On the other hand, every other millennial and Gen Z woman does do #activism, highlighting the causes she believes in, contributing to social change in the little ways that she

---

[38]Whose grit I admire deeply and am personally indebted to—for bringing Indian feminist theory to the uninitiated (like me). Her publication houses, Kali for Women and Zubaan, have produced an array of trailblazing feminist works.

[39]Interestingly, many social justice warriors who do devote their lives to these causes have gone beyond political feminism altogether, to universal love and mindful advocacy. Like activist Sukhnidh Kaur, who raises awareness about important social and political issues, but through a prism of love and healing. She approaches every issue from a personal point of view, making her activism seem more rooted. Not at all like she's trying to tick ideological boxes.

can. But that's still selfish, some may say. This sort of individualistic politics can't be called feminism because it isn't collective.

Traditionally, feminism has centred itself around struggle and resistance. So, it theorized issues that affected womankind as a collective and strove to actively organize around these. However, 'collective' is a complicated term—every woman fights a different battle based on her positionality. In any case, after all these years of collective feminist struggle, the lot of womankind has improved a little bit, I think. And we have reached a space where women are at the brink of breaking out of the shackles that have fettered them. Now is the time for feminism to reimagine itself along the dimensions of power and leadership. Open itself up to allow for a new sort of heuristics to develop, where women can learn feminism on their own and apply it in their lives how they see fit. A sort of DIY project. Still, the guardians of feminism may point out that women can't be trusted to think up their own idea of empowerment, for what if they make regressive or uninformed choices?

For a generation that was brought up on a heavy dose of women's lib, a majority of young women do seem determined to undermine feminist ideology. Is this because these women are entitled? Taking for granted the little gains that decades of women's struggles have brought. Living lives in apolitical bubbles. Being calculative bitches in search of power and privilege. Inadvertently conforming to gender norms and buying needlessly gendered products. Falling for the evil tricks of patriarchy and capitalism?

Or, are they postfeminist?

Nota Bene

Postfeminism is not anti-feminist. The 'post' in postfeminism[40] implies a stage in the ongoing transformation of the feminist movement. It

---

[40]Cultural theorist Ann Brooks' book *Postfeminisms: Feminism, Cultural Theory and Cultural Forms* redefines the idea of postfeminism, which was earlier synonymous with anti-feminism. She re-contextualizes it to reflect anti-foundational movements like postcolonialism, post-structuralism, and postmodernism.

does not assume that patriarchy has been superseded, but holds that feminism has empowered women to a great extent and it is now time to renegotiate feminist politics in a contemporary framework.

II: The Postfeminist Politic

In India, most young women fumble in front of the feminist standard (the leftist-liberal one, to be precise). Their ambivalent aspirations and contradictory desires are seen as conspiracies against the sisterhood. According to the norms of feminism, the millennial who seeks equality of opportunity at work, yet performs the traditional role of wife at home and observes karva chauth is regressive. The woman who believes in gender egalitarianism but not in a socialist division of power and wealth is branded a faux-feminist for not being intersectional[41]. All glamorous actors and models are considered double-agents of patriarchy for objectifying their own bodies. Hijabis are stereotyped as oppressed even when they wear headscarves by choice, while the large section of Indian women who religiously thread their eyebrows and wax their legs are presumed to be uncritical adherers of mythical beauty standards. Women who choose to be full-time mothers are accused of being under the grip of false consciousness.[42] And anyone[43] who dares to hold a political position not endorsed by the leftist-liberal nexus is a traitor. Needless to say, it is not easy to enter the elite feminist club of excellence.

I mean, it's one thing to blame the patriarchy for subjugating women's lives. It's a totally different matter to accuse every other woman of being complicit with the patriarchy for not taking charge

[41]A term first coined by scholar Kimberlé Crenshaw.
[42]Where people think they are making a conscious choice out of free will, when they're really only conforming to oppressive cultural norms unconsciously.
[43]Actor Kangana Ranaut was excommunicated from feminism altogether for her espousal of India's Prime Minister Narendra Modi as the rightful leader of the democracy. Since then, Ranaut's politics has veered to the radical right. She often says things that are deeply problematic. Indulges in mudslinging and name-calling. But does that erase her contribution to the feminist cause? Can we ignore the fact that she is among the few women in Bollywood to fearlessly create a feminist body of work?

Smashing the Patriarchy

of her life as per a feminist framework. This attitude belittles another woman's individuality and relegates her subjective agency to the sidelines. Sometimes, I question the idea of sisterhood. Sure, we can pass the Bechdel test in real life, 'other' the men for othering us, then claim intent to raise each other up. However, we can be vicious to one another when ideological lines are crossed. If the bedrock of feminist thought is liberty, equality, and sorority[44], then we have failed miserably in understanding what those concepts mean. By caustically judging women's individual choice and subjectivity, we are losing our sisters, and feminism, its foot soldiers. Author Rene Denfeld critiques Western feminism and claims that it 'has become bogged down in an extremist moral and spiritual crusade that has little to do with women's lives. It has climbed out on a limb of academic theory that is all but inaccessible to the uninitiated.' This is true of feminism in India, too, where women constantly pull one another down for the perceived faults in their morals.

The postfeminist subject exists in this realm of alter reality, where feminism often defeats its own agenda. In fact, this postfeminist woman is the quintessential object of feminist cultural critique. She's constantly dissed for her 'double entanglement' with feminist and anti-feminist ideas. Her self-surveillant nature and self-interest are mocked. Her choices are decrypted to expose hidden agendas. But then, the postfeminist woman knows she's an object that's to be appraised—by patriarchies and by feminism. However, she doesn't like to be labelled and judged. She values her individualism. Any ideology or system that's self-righteous, she finds suffocating. So, she looks for ingenious ways to spoof 'abjectifying attitudes and conceptions of her'. As gender theorists Fien Adriaens and Sofie Van Bauwel point out: 'humour and irony are central themes within the postfeminist discourse', meaning that snarky young women everywhere laugh at what's assumed of their choices.

---

[44]Professor Elizabeth Bartlett's book *Liberty, Equality, and Sorority: Contradiction and Integrity in Feminist Thought and Practice* deals with the inherent problems of holding these three concepts together and suggests ways to balance them to form a new feminist ethic.

And their choices are extremely unpredictable, perplexing even. Indian youngsters attend protests to end sexual harassment by day, and groove to misogynistic hip-hop and item numbers by night with their baes. Arranged neo-traditional weddings are in vogue, replete with palanquins and kanya daan, and the US$ 50-billion marriage industry is booming. Even as their families look for an upwardly-mobile groom, millions of single women are online, swiping left and right in search of kinky sexual partners. There are promising gender indicators out there too. In 2016, the gender pay gap narrowed to 3.5 per cent in Indian corporates. A survey by PWC found that 76 per cent of female Indian millennials enter the workforce with serious plans to reach the top. Not only because they've been bred to be ambitious, but also because they possess the skills to make it. However, there is also a trove of contrasting information. The World Bank warns that millions of women are dropping out of the workforce. The average age of a woman having her first child is going up. But also, 25 per cent of women quit their jobs to raise children, and among them are India's most educated. What's more, these women positively acknowledge their choices and express no regret, keeping true to their Zen.

This can all be very disconcerting for the altruistic feminist. But it is only natural in a rapidly transforming world that individuals jump from one idea to another, sometimes completely contradicting themselves. No one totalizing framework can be used to understand their hyper-individual realities. It is a time of deconstructions and post-everything. Sociologist Michèle Barrett notes that 'the key thinkers of "post-structuralism" [have] mounted a devastating critique of the main assumptions on which much social and feminist theory was previously based and it has proved to be a critique from which neither has emerged unscathed.' Barrett holds that 'fluidity' and 'contingency' are the concepts we need to analyse now and move beyond blaming sexist oppression for all perceived inequities.

Whose Feminism Is It Anyway?

This is a time and space where women discursively produce conflicting meanings through their mix-and-match ideologies. They make bamboozling choices, as discussed earlier. To get on with their real-world objectives, women these days collude with patriarchies when it suits their interests and resist it when need be. A horde of educated women choose not to work outside the home and become hyper-domestic goddesses who utilize their husband/father/brother's capital to live their best lives with no guilt attached. Those who work outside the home (on their laptops at cafés or at offices) happily socialize with peers of their economic class, language, race, religion, and caste, often employing their family/friends' networks to find opportunities. The woke among them admit to these privileges, but retain them nevertheless. Capitalist and socialist ideologies intermingle unexpectedly in many women's heads, as do tradition and modernity. They may take a liberal position on one issue, but turn conservative on another. Some are nationalistic, some aren't. They take what they like from the jargon of feminism (when it serves to increase their sense of self-worth) and discard what doesn't work for them. Postfeminist women, then, are self-defining, maximizing, and ambitious subjects who practise pragmatic idealism apt for such morally jaded times.

The ideological purists among us will say that now is the time to be dogmatic. The idea of India is in doldrums. Liberal democracy is being leached away at the edges. Hindutva is eclipsing the nation's secular ethos. Islamophobia and casteist bigotry are on the rise. Dissent is being squashed with an iron fist. Feminism, as ever, should be a morally superior and humanist ideology that unites women against the ills of patriarchy, capitalism, neoliberalism, caste, globalization, eco-fascism, religious fundamentalism, and all sorts of hegemony to create a truly equitable world. Except, *woman* is not a monolithic entity, especially in 'new India' where opinions are super polarized, and identity politics and ideological warfare are rife. There are powerful women on the left, right, and centre. There is no compulsion here that all women should fight for the same sort of social or political revolution—because identities are plural and each woman espouses causes that are critical to her positionality. At the same time, feminism isn't impervious to unconscious prejudice either. In such a scenario, it's unrealistic to expect women to gather under a rigid feminist umbrella that is theoretically for all women, but in reality, excludes many based on where their political loyalties lie or how they perform femininity.

Am I then suggesting that feminists stop questioning the motives of incendiary women for the sake of solidarity? Understandably, how on earth can feminists not be at odds with those like Bharatiya Janta Party's (BJP) women wing's leader Sunita Singh Gaur, who asked Hindu men to form gangs and rape Muslim women? Clearly, Gaur is not simply a victim of regressive thinking. If anything, she's a self-empowered woman. Except, her words were held against her—she faced intense criticism, not only from the left and centre, but also from the right. Even while men who actually let Muslim women get raped under their watch sit comfortably in their regal seats sipping chai, Gaur was dismissed. Patriarchy works in convoluted ways.

Academics and activists have always termed the women's movement of the subcontinent as Indian feminisms, stressing on the plural, as not all women's movements identified with Western-inspired feminism. Islamic women's groups[45] have been at odds with secular feminists, because the latter often refuse to recognize the former's agency even while lobbying on their behalf. As evident from the Shaheen Bagh protests, Muslim women have always been capable of standing up for themselves when they see fit. The idea that every veiled woman is oppressed is preposterous but that is the notion most

---

[45]Bharatiya Muslim Mahila Andolan (BMMA) and All India Muslim Women Personal Law Board (AIMWPLB) counter Muslim orthodoxy and seek to reinterpret the Quran in more gender-egalitarian terms, because they believe that the Quran is essentially gender equal. Meanwhile, secular feminist groups have been hell-bent on issues like abolishing the triple talaq (which the government has brought about) and bringing in the Uniform Civil Code (UCC)—which both BMMA and AIMWPLB are wary of.

feminists perpetuate globally. A large section of Hindu women, on the other hand, do not subscribe to the language of feminism because it positions itself as anti-Hindu (and since the Hindu Rashtra project began, a chasm has opened up between the Hindu nationalist and the secular woman). Women from other religions too are wary of feminism for it is often conflated with atheism.

Inside the fortress of feminism, meanwhile, not all versions have proximity to power. Undercurrents of dissent have always existed. Varied groups vie to construct competing ideological frameworks for gender-development discourses inside the academia. Resident Indian feminists are distrustful of expatriate feminists. Marxist feminists are suspicious of liberal feminists. Members of the LGBTQIA+ community have been vocal about cis-het feminism's unease with trans identities (ever heard of TERF, the acronym for Trans-Exclusionary Radical Feminist?) Scepticism is everywhere. And since 2017, the fault lines of Indian feminism have become glaringly visible. It was then that law student Raya Sarkar circulated a Google spreadsheet that named seventy-two men from academia for various forms of sexual harassment. The Kafila feminists[46], including a number of seasoned academics and activists known for being anti-establishment, argued that naming and shaming men without due process was not acceptable. Young women disagreed.

Anthropologist Rama Srinivasan called this a generational conflict between feminist pioneers and millennials without patience. But this isn't the only perceived fault line. Raya Sarkar also happens to be a Dalit, and the invalidation of her list by Savarna feminists was seen by Dalit, Bahujan, and Adivasi (DBA) women as a striking instance of caste bias. This sentiment has echoed across the country among young DBA women in various movements. Many DBA feminists left the women's collective Pinjra Tod[47], writing,

---

[46]Called so because they signed a statement published on the Kafila website, asking for the withdrawal of said spreadsheet.

[47]This feminist movement battles gender-based discrimination in universities. It started a dialogue across India's academic institutions about curfews for women, sexist traditions,

'Savarna feminists…we are no longer going to be fascinated by your sisterhood circles and tokenism inclusivity. Your Time is Up too.' And, just like that, the idea of feminist sorority crumbled in the public eye, yet again.

So, in such a time, when everyone's walking on ideological eggshells, it may seem that it's best to choose the safest feminist identity: the one of intersectional[48] feminist. Every woke woman's new favourite word, sorry to say, is already passé in the West[49] where it came from (all hail Westeros). Sure, it sounds like the right thing to be, but what does it do for us in reality? Having empathy for another person's struggle is all very well, but can it be put to practical use[50] over and above showing solidarity, especially when the concerned person doesn't care for (y)our saviour complex? On the other hand, when (y)our identities are ones that were historically denied social justice, do we find solidarity with other women by radically denying them the right to speak about us altogether, thereby denying ourselves the right to speak about others?

Outside the Echo-Chambers of (Theoretical) Feminism
Every day women (of all castes, creeds, sexualities, and ideologies) engage in micropolitics on an interpersonal level in the grand sexist

---

moral policing, and higher fees for women's boarding.

[48]There are intersectional calculators online to figure out just how oppressed you are based on your identities.

[49]Jennifer C. Nash writes: In a panel discussion, 'members were invited to…determine [which] terms should be "killed"—banished from our scholarly lexicon…. Nothing generated more anxiety than "intersectionality," which was immediately declared dead…. [A] scholar voiced discomfort with "killing" intersectionality because to do that would be to "kill" black feminism, or perhaps even to "kill" black woman as object of study. The room grew quiet at the prospect of symbolically killed black women. As intersectionality slipped into black feminism slipped into black woman, the analytic moved from dangerous to desirable, from peril to promise, and the audience that had been quick to kill had been convinced to rescue.'

[50]Tell me, do all middle- and upper-class Savarna intersectional feminists redistribute their wealth and conscientiously avoid availing benefits (minor or major) from their privileged connections?

arena. From the subtle art of not giving a fuck to promptly calling out sexism, women perform diverse acts of singular resistance. But there's more to the postfeminist battle against patriarchy than resistance, because resistance is reactive to power. Women these days want to go a step further and take the power themselves. A large number of millennial and Gen Z women are looking for ingenious ways to undermine hyper-masculine hegemony. However, this doesn't mean they all refuse to engage with patriarchal structures altogether. On the contrary, many manipulate the existing establishment and defy the odds to empower themselves.

For instance, take the free market, an edifice built on patriarchal inequality. Even while leftist theorists pronounce capitalism as inherently broken, a trove of young women have astutely capitalized on consumer culture. The internet is full of female entrepreneurs selling ideas and objects to customers worldwide. From Insta-poet Rupi Kaur to cringe-pop queen Dhinchak Pooja, digital-savvy ladies know how to turn heads and get all eyes on their work. The advertising industry is full of such women. Many from diverse backgrounds have now set foot in sectors ranging from tech and beauty to art and organic farming—all profiting from capitalism. Dalit and tribal entrepreneurship are on the rise too, as women from marginalized communities begin to create capital against all odds[51]. Globalization, meanwhile, has brought a trove of job opportunities for women in varied industries, though Covid-19 and Modinomics are bringing an end to that (let's hope 'Make in India' empowers women as it promises on paper). In any case, it would seem capitalism is not the one true enemy[52]. As sociologist

---

[51]Even while leftist Dalit feminists dismiss capitalism as synonymous with casteism, a large section of middle-class Dalits see capital creation and entrepreneurship as a means to ending Savarna domination. However, it is imperative to note that middle-class Dalit women's access to investment is impeded by casteism and compounded by sexist bias at every step.

[52]Sociologist Michèle Barrett illustrates in her landmark book *Women's Oppression Today: Problems in Marxist Feminist Analysis* that the sexual division of labour predates capitalism.

Shilpa Phadke points out, the free market is a much better space for women to renegotiate their roles: 'unlike the state, where the citizen is largely a client, for the market the individual is first and foremost an actor-consumer.'[53] Money is power in today's world and most young women understand that economic independence is the means to liberty.

Now, you may very well say that all this talk only relates to the bourgeois and reeks of neoliberal free market delusion. That Indian feminism has to be collective. For the sake of the 99 per cent it has to be anti-capitalist[54], because capitalism reproduces socio-economic inequalities by selling fake dreams of aspiration. I agree with this on many levels, but not all. While it is true that the market has had different effects on various strata of society,[55] I do not think socialism or communism will end India's millennia long social imbalances. Casteism and nepotism are so deep-seated in the country, that the left is no more immune to it than the right (even as it uses utopian parlance, the left is still largely led by upper-caste and upper-class comrades). On a similar note, the fact that leftist feminism uses the same focal point for gender, class, and caste is a problem. Nonetheless, like all (moral) millennials, I'm a cheerleader for socialism, for free education, universal healthcare, and purposeful economics. But not for a moment do I buy that socialism equals gender parity. Look at Russia and China, where gender equality was once proclaimed, but gender relations remained essentially the same after the revolution (not to mention, free speech died). There's

---

[53]Phadke further goes on to ask, '[c]an the women's movement use the strategies of the market to re-sell itself to a larger audience and reclaim its right to speak on behalf of a larger constituency of women?'

[54]For example, *Feminism for the 99%* suggests that liberal feminism has failed working-class women. 'On one hand, Sandberg and her ilk see feminism as the handmaiden of capitalism.... They want a world where the task of managing exploitation in the workplace and oppression in the social whole is shared equally by ruling-class men and women. This is a remarkable vision of *equal opportunity domination*.'

[55]As of 2020, India's richest 1 per cent hold more than 4 times the wealth held by 953 million people who are the bottom 70 per cent. India is a menagerie of inequalities.

no one-size-fits-all ideology. And a woman's choice to be capitalist, socialist, communist, anarchist, or clueless doesn't have much bearing on her credentials as a badass feminist.

In India, where every woman's (hyper)reality can be radically different from another's, even when they are from a similar socio-economic background, choice becomes a central device through which to understand women's empowerment. Every major and minor deviation from the norm counts. The norm can be religious, cultural, political, even feminist. I'm sure we can all agree that most (urban) women have been exposed to feminist ideas and have inherently benefitted from women's movements. Now, when they make personal choices that are incongruous with textbook feminism, are they to be pigeonholed as feminist failures? As argued by Patricia Mann, the feminist movement has evolved into a postfeminist struggle to reconstruct relationships between women and men in everyday contexts of work, family, education, and politics. Today's women do all sorts of things to empower themselves. While some may understand feminist theory and speak in feminist lingo, others may renegotiate gender politics through seemingly unfeminist, yet canny, schemes. They may subtly transact deals with their partners after a good sex session, or play along with toxic office politics till their work gets noticed, even utilizing sexist tropes to their benefit. As writer Alka Shukla suggests: 'If patriarchy considers women to be more vulnerable, why not deploy it strategically to get what you want?...[crying] catches our Neanderthal Man from the workplace off-guard...Dick – 0. Tear – 1.'

Seems a bit reckless, elitist, perhaps even like an endorsement of patriarchal conventions, doesn't it? That brings us to a more complicated aspect of female empowerment: that of privilege. How do you smash the patriarchy when you're embedded right in it, where you consciously (or blithely) benefit from being born in a privileged intersection of patriarchal society? Do you radically disown your position, or do you smash the patriarchy carefully—distancing yourself from its regressive facets but keeping the power that comes with your position? This is where Indian feminism spirals out into a thousand directions. Because, privilege, after all, is a very relative concept.

Let's Talk About Privilege

I'm writing in English, you're reading in English—clearly, we're a privileged lot[56]. Some even call us India's fastest growing new caste (not to be taken as a compliment). At the end of the day, we're all doing locational politics here (the personal is political). Our subjective individualities are constructed socially and culturally. Not all of us are self-sacrificing saints. And no matter how we cover up our subjectivities, we're ultimately speaking only for ourselves.[57]

'Feminism is a cool sisters' club online,' derides Vandana Shukla, 'ignoring the stark reality and serious issues faced by a majority of Indian women in the real world…these privileged, urban, educated, professional women, too, are stuck in traditionalist roles even if they have modern mindsets.' The precept here is that since the struggles of rural disadvantaged women are direr than those of middle-/upper-class urban women, we shouldn't speak about the latter altogether. Dismissing the problems of privileged women as irrelevant to Indian feminism is the textbook illustration of the straw man fallacy.[58] It's philosophically sound to agree that until every woman is released from the grip of patriarchy the feminist fight has not been won, but this does not imply that to acknowledge one woman's shackles, we must belittle another's as effete. It is also crucial to recognize that merely acknowledging the problems of

---

[56]Many sanskari folk suspect that we secretly harbor anglophile tendencies and miss no opportunity to point out that English is an alien language—you know, the language of the colonizer.

[57]Now, since we're being honest about privileges and all that, I'm sure you're mildly curious about me. *What are her privileges?* I'll tell you. I'm an inter-caste Tamil, born into a family of bureaucrats, bankers, filmmakers, and freethinkers. But if you still insist on knowing what blood runs in my veins: I'm of Dalit and Iyengar descent.

[58]A logical fallacy theory where a person's argument/position is misrepresented/distorted in order to make it easier to attack it.

socio-economically underprivileged women in a sort of redemption clause to every paragraph about (privileged, urban) feminism will not make those issues vanish.

Since the beginning of (feminist) time, the Indian women's movement (spearheaded by urban Savarna women) has always fought for the poor and marginalized.[59] While we can't entirely deny the positive effects of their intervention, not much has changed. Possibly because mainstream feminism has spent more time recontextualizing socio-economically underprivileged women's issues to fit into meta-narratives for a global audience (which I suppose I'm inadvertently doing too), rather than building platforms to raise marginalized voices and further their agency (not to deny the work of exceptional NGOs and activists). After all, to effectively rage against the patriarchy from a Marxist point of view, you must show the worst of what society has systematically done to women's dignity. Now, in all likelihood, a majority of women terribly affected by the evils of patriarchy also happen to belong to DBA communities. Unfortunately, sidestepping caste to make everything about class has meant that a lot of unconscious (casteist) bias intersperses mainstream feminist conjecture. Speaking for the subaltern is inherently problematic. As philosopher Gayatri Chakravorty Spivak points out, it's important to wonder '[n]ot merely who am I? but who is the other woman? How am I naming her? How does she name me?'

Thankfully, things have come full circle now. Today, rural women can clearly speak for themselves about their own issues in their native languages.[60] Educated women from historically oppressed communities now speak in English about the intergenerational traumas that they've inherited from their foremothers, and record the

---

[59]Sociologist Srila Roy points out: 'a whole range of issues—from "eve teasing" to homosexuality—have historically not been prioritised in favour of those presumed to have greater relevance to the masses at the grassroots' in an article where she discusses the fault lines of Indian feminism in detail.
[60]Sample *Khabar Lahariya*, a rural feminist Hindi newspaper run for local women, by local women.

subtle discriminations they face every day in (liberal and conservative) middle- and upper-class urban society. This last bit has irked our greatly privileged Indian feminism, so it has now strategically turned the tables to call out English-speaking DBA feminists for their urban privilege. 'The one person Savarnas traditionally cannot stand is the Dalit who can speak,' writes Mimi Mondal, an award-winning author of speculative fiction. 'That person is therefore no longer a "real Dalit".... The "right" kind of Dalit is the body that was pulled down from the tree or fished out of the sewer, because that one is no longer squeaking.'

If leftist-liberal feminism wants to truly walk the walk, then it should let DBA women lead it from the front. They are at the intersection of the oppressions instituted by caste, class, and gender and Dalit feminist literature is the new polemic for progressive thought. At times it may seem extreme, asking the seemingly impossible of us all, but the fact that we're unwilling to change, even a little, illuminates our hypocrisies. Crucial stuff for those of us who call ourselves liberal progressives. On the flip side, the position that one can talk about an identity only if one has that identity, makes it impossible for us to integrate with each other. It will only further divide society along its fault lines. But in the postfeminist era, this is bound to happen. Nobody here gets to institutionalize feminism. Like a block chain,[61] different groups of ideological women will guard their knowledge and ways of seeing. Allyship now entails more than ideological equivalence.

At end of the day, there 'is nothing about being "female" that naturally binds women.' As socialist feminist Donna Haraway states, '[i]t has become difficult to name one's feminism by a single adjective. ...Identities seem contradictory, partial, and strategic. With the hard-won recognition of their social and historical constitution, gender, race, and class cannot provide the basis for belief in "essential" unity.'

---

[61]Where blocks of data are linked using cryptography, essentially maintaining each block's uniqueness.

This is all the more accurate in the Indian context. Coalitions between women here (feminist or undeclared) are only possible with regard to specific issues, not entire ideologies. As women increasingly begin to visualize themselves as inherently empowered change-makers, demanding gender equality and opportunity, they want allies who see them without pity or scorn. Perhaps, for starters, we need to decouple feminism from other totalizing ideologies and learn to respect female subjectivities.

What's So 'Post' About Postfeminism?
Postfeminist agency allows for a discursive construction of the self that does not negate feeling. It gives women the freedom to constantly transform themselves without the fear of feminist or societal judgement. Under its aegis, women can question who they are and how they've become so—redefining their idea of empowerment in individualist terms instead of collective. This effectively opens up the arena for women of all sorts to state their own truths. Strive for the liberation of mind, body, or soul, in their own particular ways.

Unlike feminism proper, which pursues a negative dialectic (being a derivative of Marxism's oppositional discourse[62]), postfeminism promotes positive psychology and self-empowerment. Its language is uplifting. Even while it questions the status quo on a collective plane, its emphasis is on tangible change on an individual level. This not only encompasses the fight for equal opportunity and rights, but also centres on every woman's emotional well-being. It urges

---

[62]Professor Sue Ruddick suggests that the West's negative dialectic stemmed from Hegel's profound misreading of Spinoza, and Marx's subsequent inversion of it. She argues that we should strive towards a positive dialectic that 'might enable us to think across our differences to a political ontology that embraces the posthuman, immanent, and affirmative qualities of struggle'. This manner of reasoning has always existed in India. While negation is central to Indian thought—everything is maya—affirmation promptly follows. Except the Lokayata and Carvaka schools of thought, the aim of other philosophies is to help us attain moksha or liberation, to reach the Absolute or understand the Truth. In Buddhism, it is to break the wheel of suffering.

women to take time to mend themselves, because the patriarchy is bad for women's brains.[63] It's not enough to be hypervigilant and rage against the patriarchy, it's equally important to heal our own selves individually once we identify what causes us emotional trauma. Otherwise, we're setting ourselves up to go into war with an elusive enemy, even though we aren't done battling the fiends in our own heads. (Of course, this goes against some radical feminists[64] who dismiss certain forms of therapy because it individualizes women's oppression.)

On the other hand, the postfeminist battle centres on the female body. Not only does having agency over one's body constitute demanding protection from sexual abuse and possessing reproductive choice, for most millennial and Gen Z women, it also involves the freedom to explore and embrace their sexualities. Of course, the anesthetized 'right to sexuality' is very much part of the mainstream feminist discourse, while allyship with the LGBTQIA+ community is seen as quintessential to the movement. However, for the most part, feminism is still averse to talking about illicit sex, desire, and love[65]. Queering feminism has meant mere inclusivity so far. But that isn't what postfeminism is about. Here, the subversion of patriarchal gender normativity is centred on queerness. This is about performing femininities and masculinities through a gender equal framework, inspiring every woman to open up the limits of her body and experience the pleasure (and power) that comes with it.

A sexual revolution is already brewing in India. Young women are

---

[63]According to the *Indian Journal of Psychiatry*, depressive disorders accounted for 41.9 per cent of the disability among women as compared to men (29.3 per cent) in 2015. Anxiety disorders and psychological distress were 2–3 times higher in females as compared to males. Suicide attempts and deliberate self-harm were also found to be more likely among women.

[64]Read 'Making the political personal: how psychology undermines feminist activism' by Swedish feminist Tove Happonen.

[65]As Professor G. Arunima notes, '[w]ith its intense reformist streak and puritanical zeal, mainstream feminism's own history and contemporary dilemmas align it far closer to middle class complacency and conservatism than any subversive position.'

redefining consent and are deciding for themselves what constitutes pleasure and what doesn't. However, this doesn't mean that all young women are advocates of theoretically feminist sex—where you'd have to deconstruct every sexual position and dirty phrase to figure out if it's gender equal. In fact, millennial women are a complex and quirky lot. Looking to bend their genders in bed, these women often get on top but also practise BDSM[66]—anything to experience the ultimate pleasure, get that amazing orgasm. This could even involve real life kink, as in this woman's case: '[t]o have a right-wing guy go down on me, a left-leaning activist and journalist, became my own version of dominatrix kink.'

Indian feminism has had a difficult relationship with sexuality. It would seem that it is only interested in talking about female sexuality when it's victimized, not when it's agentive or libertine. How we talk about porn and sex work, for instance, does a lot to show our hypocrisy on the matter of sexuality. Not only is porn banned in India (thanks to feminist and sanskari intervention), we still talk about sex work exclusively through the lens of trafficking and violence.[67] Sure, many women are forced into doing porn or sex work, but not all[68]. The real issue that alienates these women is the shame and guilt society (and some feminists) force them to feel for capitalizing on their sexuality, completely disregarding their choices

---

[66]BDSM is a trove of erotic sexual practices which entails roleplaying, bondage, submission, dominance, sadomasochism, and sadism. Basically, all the forbidden fetish.

[67]Few feminist academics, like Dr Geetanjali Gangoli, hold that 'prostitution is work, both in terms of organization, economic and social contribution to society.' Political theorist Nivedita Menon, meanwhile, argues that the '"choice" to do sex work is no more or less constrained than the choice of any other work is under capitalism. As for forced sex work, which is precisely bonded labour, as feminists, we should back policies and institutions that support women who want to leave the profession.'

[68]Kerala based sex-worker Nalini Jameela's books *Romantic Encounters of a Sex Worker* and *The Autobiography of a Sex Worker* are eye-openers on the subject. She breaks the taboo surrounding this topic: '[s]ex work and sexual exploitation are two different things.' She continues, '[i]t's not as if elite women don't know this; but it is convenient for them not to recognise this. They have much to gain if the divide between "dignified" them and "undignified" us stays intact.'

and bodily agency. Conversely, postfeminism liberates women's bodies from a false feminist morality.

Further, postfeminism does not criticize a woman's religiosity per se. After all, female empowerment is not only for atheists, agnostics, and woke lay Buddhists. Especially in a time of communal polarization, it's crucial to respect every woman's right to her own beliefs. While we may be opposed to it when it discriminates against other women on the basis of religious difference, it is none of our business what faith a woman practises or what rituals she performs in her personal space. If women are to be whole creatures, where we strive for the emancipation of our minds, bodies, and souls, we cannot insist that women give up on religion because patriarchy has embedded itself into it. Patriarchy is everywhere. Women are entitled to seek the ineffable through metaphysical means if they so please. Of course, this may involve following texts that were written by men. But what philosophical texts do we have that men haven't already appropriated?

Postfeminists will define their own agendas. They'd do feminist battles in every corner of the patriarchal world. While for some the goal may be to break superstructures entirely, for others their aim may be to build an equitable existence within an existing structure, by strengthening their position. But if you're still wondering whether the latter is feminist enough, I'd say open up your mind. As sociologist Shelley Budgeon observes, postfeminism is about 'understanding the multiple ways of being a feminist'.

1

ON BEAUTY

Fair skin. Sharp features. Silky straight hair. An hourglass figure: 36" 24" 36". These are the chosen attributes of a perfect Indian beauty according to cultural norms. Never mind that in a country with more than 656 million women of diverse ethnic groups, there are bound to be multifarious ideas of beauty. Yet our entertainment, media, and corporate nexus pay little heed to inclusion for the most part. Alongside the beauty and fashion industries, they consciously glamourize some physical attributes over others and uphold unreal standards, thanks to their implicit upper-caste, patriarchal bias. The result? Every Indian woman is expected to look flawless, fair, and lovely in order to marry, to star in a Bollywood movie, to get a job, and even to have sex.

Beauty then becomes a deeply personal matter that affects the majority of Indian women. Whether we scoff at the idea of linking self-confidence to physical appearance or empathize with the issues that tie women to their bodies, the reality is this: women invest a lot of money and time in looking and feeling gorgeous, because grooming oneself has become quintessential for social and professional success. According to data from 2015, the women's cosmetics industry in India is growing at 16 per cent CAGR. With millennials and Gen Z accumulating more purchasing power, the cosmetics market is expected to grow to US$ 20 billion by 2025. In a globalized time, all kinds of things can be bought: from a range of self-care, make-up, and hair products, to wax strips for body hair, patches and suction guns for blackheads, vaginal bleaching creams, and plastic surgery.

Traditionally, feminism has been suspicious of beauty routines, considering them a distraction from one of its main goals: ending female objectification. Critics of capitalism, meanwhile, assert that the beauty industry is manufacturing femininities for unsuspecting women to consume, thereby making profit and regulating women's bodies and lives. In her book *The Global Beauty Industry*, sociologist Meeta Jha writes, '[t]he concept of "beauty capitalism" best describes the importance of consumption to the different institutions using beauty, sexuality, and femininity as a marketing device.... The commodification of women's bodies constitutes the marketing and brand logic of capitalism.'

It would seem that these critics of beauty are not so much against the product[1] itself, as compared to what it represents. After all, chemically-speaking, an under-eye cream can only fix dark circles. But what it stands for is the idea that women are not supposed to look tired even if they have not slept for months as they try to balance work and family and existential anxiety, and that is the problem. And this idea of the glamorous superwoman, who does it all and still looks phenomenal at the end of the day, is by and large a result of marketing campaigns and mainstream Indian cinema. But let me double back here for a minute to separate the ideas of beauty and glamour.

Anyone can put on red lipstick, a sparkly skirt, and the latest pair of Jimmy Choo[2] stilettos and feel glamorous. Except, because of the unreal standards of beauty that have become ingrained in our collective consciousness, we'll never all feel truly beautiful. Women are not only dealing with their own personal insecurities about beauty, but also with those of their chauvinistic culture.

Because beauty, my sisters, has never been skin-deep.

---

[1]In India and around the world, independent organic beauty products are increasingly preferred by consumers—even though they cost much more than big brands. Many millennials and Gen Z are environmentally conscious and do not mind spending those extra bucks to save the planet, and their skin!

[2]Okay, not everyone can afford that. What I mean is that with money, high glamour can be bought.

For too long now, across the world, beauty has been tacitly linked to every woman's character. All the witches and demonesses of lore are dark and asymmetrical, with hooked noses and bad teeth, while goddesses and concubines are fair and have proportionally chiselled bodies. This misogyny is all-pervasive, dripping down from generation to generation, preserved by men in power, and has seeped into our languages and reality. And misogyny owes a large part of its prejudices to racism. Beginning with the Vedas[3] that talks of dark-skinned, flat-nosed dasas and dasyus with disdain, to Babur, the first ruler of the Mughal Empire, who complained that the people of Hindustan were not much to look at, to, finally, the British, who came to tell everyone in the subcontinent that theirs was, in fact, the fairest skin of all, and most suited to rule over other grades of melanin. Only when the Harappan script is deciphered will we know what racial prejudices the Indus Valley Civilization held. In any case, we know that India's obsession with fair skin and mythical Aryan/Persian features began fairly early.

And today, we're being brainwashed by PR and advertising machines to marvel at the same kind of beauty over and over, stifling our capability to admire the splendour of diversity. Most image-aggregating websites promote fixed beauty standards through the length of its channels, effectively turning digital reality into a multi-mimetic machine that references itself. Consider the Times of India's yearly polls that test which Bollywood actress is the hottest. The majority of Indians mechanically agree on the top fifty every year since 2009. The amusing thing is that, to someone who isn't up-to-date with Bollywood, most of the top fifty actresses will look exactly the same at first glance. Generally fair, a few dusky (if they managed to star in critically-acclaimed films), with big boobs, sharp features, and of slender build, some with curvy waists but no flab.

---

[3]Sure, the Vedas also speak of some dark-skinned heroes. As Neha Mishra specifies, there's Trasadasyu, son of Purukutsa; Angiras, the author of the Rig Veda, who himself is dark-skinned; then there's Krishna which translates as black in Sanskrit. Pray, where are the brown and black heroines?

Times Most Desirable Women 2019 serves as a case in point[4]. As a result, across the country, dark-skinned, flat-chested, plus-size, or too-skinny women, and those with Sino-Tibetan or Austro-Asiatic features face harassment and abuse in their personal and professional lives. There are several reported instances where women have been denied jobs because they're dark or 'ugly' or too foreign looking: in aviation[5], media, and film. And we all know that the Indian marriage market is strictly for gori women with skin like butter.

So, we're up against a misogynist society that has historically nurtured antipodal sentiments towards the female form: simultaneously lauding it as the mother goddess and the sacred giver of life, and also scrutinizing it as a sex object and violating it at will. A racist and casteist society that constantly tells us we aren't beautiful because we don't look like the 'fifty hottest' or fit puranic/medieval descriptions of timid beauty or have the right genes. And as if this isn't enough of an intrusion into our thoughts; religious, cultural, and, now, nationalist groups make it their business to tell all women how to perform femaleness with integrity. Insecure about their own identity in a globalized world, Hindu nationalist groups constantly redefine sanskar and endorse antiquated ideals of womanhood in a bid to restore the honour of Hindu women. The length of a woman's hair, the cut of her blouse, and the colour of her lipstick have come to determine whether she's to be put on a pedestal and celebrated as a reincarnation of pure Sita, or, physically assaulted for non-conformity, for channelling promiscuous Surpanaka (or worse). Radical Muslim groups, on the other hand, enforce the burqa on unwilling women to protect their izzat; they also demonize Western influence and consider a woman's sartorial choices markers of morality.

---

[4]Among the top ten in this list are Disha Patani, Deepika Padukone, Vartika Singh, Kiara Advani, Yami Gautam, Jacqueline Fernandez, and Katrina Kaif.

[5]100 tribal girls were trained to be airhostesses and cabin crew under a government scholarship program in Maharashtra (in 2008), but only eight of them got a job, that too as land personnel. They were refused admission into India's elite aviation industry because of the colour of their skin.

Let's not forget that everyday feminists also freak out about women's sartorial choices. Remember the outrage when actor Priyanka Chopra put sindoor[6] on her forehead after marrying Nick Jonas? Or when A. R. Rahman's daughter Khatija was trolled[7] for wearing a full niqab? It would seem that to be a truly liberated Indian woman, one has to delink herself completely from her religion (and if possible, all markers of gender)—especially renounce every symbol that apparently reeks of patriarchal bondage. Just as fanatic protectors of religion consider the minutest of non-conformities to tradition as heresy, *proper* feminists denounce every woman who conforms, even if she does it on her own terms.

In such a problematic cultural and social space, women are not only objectified but also subjectify their own selves. They are constantly vigilant about every act they perform and recognize that their bodies are seen as symbols of socio-political agenda. They know that their sartorial choices matter because society judges them based on their choices. Have you wondered what really goes on in the mind of a woman as she puts make-up on her face or sindoor on her forehead, or wears a bikini or drapes a six-yard sari or slips into her pants? Is she a naïve, unthinking creature that simply conforms to the norm (of pop culture or organized religion), or does she deliberately make her choice?

A Matter of Style

'When I moved from the United States to India to start my own capital management firm, I instantly started wearing a sari to work every day. My job involves raising capital, and it's important to

---

[6]The vermillion mark on a married Hindu woman's forehead is a problematic symbol for traditional feminism—to which it represents female subjugation. It is seen as a mark of accepting one's possession by a man: the husband. Moreover, a Hindu widow is denied the right to wear sindoor—making its absence a sign of inauspiciousness.

[7]Feminist author Taslima Nasreen wrote on Twitter that she felt suffocated when she saw Khatija in a burqa. Khatija replied: 'Dear Taslima Nasreen, I'm sorry you feel suffocated by my attire. Please get some fresh air, cause I don't feel suffocated…I suggest you google up what true feminism means because it isn't bashing other women.'

look responsible and formal, and to create a sense of trust,' says Radhika Gupta, the CEO of the financial services conglomerate, Edelweiss Asset Management Ltd. She's the only female head of a major asset manager in the country. 'Indian wardrobe is more powerful in India,' she tells me, 'as it's an established idea rooted to the land, it makes the right impression.' Since helming Edelweiss, Gupta has redefined the strategic direction of the US$ 7.5 billion company. And with the sari, she's setting a precedent that reinforces native culture and femininity while seizing power in the corporate workplace. 'My mother used to say that one doesn't buy, but collects saris. I understand why now,' she discloses. 'Colleagues bring saris for me from all around India. Recently, a sixty-eight-year-old colleague's wife passed away and he gave me all her old saris because he knows I value them. Events like this stem from a truly Indian sentiment and create bonds with peers.'

Indian women from several cultures are rediscovering the power of traditional attire. Online, many femsplain the perks of everyday sari-wearing using hashtags like #sareeswag and #livinginmysari. But the sari is not the traditional outfit of all cultures from the subcontinent. Women from the Northeast[8] wear sarongs and exquisite silk blouses; many Muslim women across the country wear burqas. Now, whether a woman chooses to wear her native garb for the purposes of fashion, strategy, or custom is her own business. However, several feminists have criticisms to make in this regard. Political theorist Nivedita Menon writes: 'the burqa offering a refuge from sexual harassment …and the beauty parlour standing in for the realm of self-expression [is a] painful seesaw for a feminist to be trapped on! Is cultural policing any less effective when not backed by a gun but by societal consensus?' In the same essay, Menon cites the example of J&K's ex-chief minister Mehbooba Mufti who wears a headscarf, to illustrate how powerful political women conform to tradition once they enter

---

[8]Instagram accounts like @nagastreetstyle and @manipuri_fashion_portraits bring Northeastern women into mainstream imagination through their trendy and hipster fashion which brings native attire into the twenty-first century.

the public arena. But is it a crime to perform one's femininity the way one wants?

An eclectic dresser and collector of posh footwear, Mumbai-based architect Devanshi Shah tells me that 'fashion and make-up are a method of self-expression for me.' Fond of pink-coloured eyelashes and loud jewellery, she notes: 'make-up is about putting on a mask, one that is carefully crafted by you. It's not so much about hiding, but about drawing attention towards something.' Shah conducts panels on the future of urban spaces, writes for magazines, curates exhibitions at reputed museums, and has been a resident at international academies. 'I am very feminine in my attire and appearance,' she says. 'All too often, I have seen people shocked after I say something well informed. [Surprised] that I was capable of forming such an argument.'

It is bizarre to imagine that the intelligentsia can be judgemental about a person's attire. But it seems so is the case in India. It is not an accident that when we imagine a female professor or intellectual, we mostly think of handloom outfits and handcrafted jewellery. A uniform of sorts. When women flout this norm and dress flamboyantly, their intelligence is questioned. Now, if this is the case among India's intellectual elite, imagine how much more women are likely to be judged by those who don't care for political correctness.

'I worked in ICICI Bank for three years,' Charunya Kalidoss tells me, and they 'had a dress code. No casuals. Churidar with dupatta in place. No haircolouring. No danglers. Just button type earrings. Hair tied. Nothing too attractive. You're supposed to dress like a nun.'[9] An AML analyst based in Chennai, Kalidoss says that women who dress up (read: wear red lipstick) are judged negatively in the banking and corporate world. 'I wear ethnic kurtis to work. [They suit] me and I feel comfortable in them,' she explains. On the other hand, in other cities and workspaces, women's styles correlate to the opportunities they get. 'I never used to pay attention to fashion

---

[9]Kalidoss adds 'I do not know if they have dress codes now. I currently work at TCS and women here can wear anything except sleeveless and shorts.'

back in my college days, but now I am very cautious with the way I dress because it talks a lot about the personality of a person,' says Sanjana Sambandam, an engineer working in Bengaluru's tech industry. 'Stylish people gain a lot of attention from others. It does determine the power structure.'

In *Aesthetic Labour: Rethinking Beauty Politics in Neo-liberalism*, the authors explore how in today's world all women are required to be 'aesthetic entrepreneurs'. They shed light on why beauty blogs and how-to YouTube videos have millions reading and watching. Not just a skin-deep phenomenon, the authors hold that as women self-regulate and make personal choices about glamour and aesthetics, they're transforming their own subjectivity. Simply put, women aren't putting on make-up any more only to please the male gaze or in pursuit of some mythical beauty ideal, but to appear their best in a neoliberal economy where aesthetic labour[10] is a focal point. With the rapid expansion of the service industry around the world, and especially in India, where client-facing positions entail that the employee is presentable, it is only natural that women pursue beauty and fashion to keep up with the trend.

'In the beginning of my career, I was a typical Kerala girl wearing only salwar kameez, with hair tied neatly and with chandan on my face,' avers Seema Menon, a soft-spoken HR manager living in Thane. 'I realized people were selective in dealing with me or approaching me as they assumed I was handling backend jobs. As I moved up [in] my career, I transformed myself to more corporate looks but ensuring I carry my basics strongly. Irrespective of what I wear, western attire or Indian, my signature style includes sindoor, two sleek gold bangles, and my thali.'

In more traditional industries, the trend is entirely the opposite. 'I have noticed a higher sense of respect and gratitude in a sari when compared to any other form of formal wear, including salwar

---

[10]Aesthetic labour refers to the practice of screening, hiring, and controlling workers on the basis of their physical appearance. The concept primarily focuses on the service economy, where worker corporeality matters.

suits, kurtis, and western formals,' says Dr Kirti Katherine Kabeer, an oncoplastic breast surgeon who has worked across South India before moving to the UK. 'Loud make-up (including bright lipstick) in my profession is disliked.' However, the Indian medical industry isn't as patriarchal as in the past, Dr Kabeer notes, 'In my opinion, being in the surgical field, I feel that it has changed over the years.'

The idea of female respectability keeps shifting in patriarchal India. While in overtly liberal urban spaces like Mumbai, Delhi, or Bengaluru, women who dress traditionally are assumed to be uneducated or underprivileged, in seemingly conservative cities like Chennai, Trivandrum, or Indore, those who dress a bit risqué are looked down upon as loose women.[11] In fact, some corporates discourage female workers with client servicing roles from dressing in all-out traditional Indian attire so that they look professional. On the other hand, Indian courts consider knee-length skirts inappropriate for female advocates; and government offices expect women to wear dignified clothes: sari or salwar kameez. Everyone has an opinion on what constitutes respectable apparel and what doesn't. Indian women are then forced to reckon with what they wear to work every day.

Millennia-long sexist biases persist, it seems, subtly in some pockets and overtly in others. But there's more to judging women's attire than meets the eye. The matter of female respectability extends well beyond the dichotomy of modern and traditional. Ancient caste, linguistic, and medieval religious prejudice plays out with all its misogynistic fervour even in the twenty-first century. Online, we constantly see samplings of this bigotry, where women from marginalized communities (DBA, Muslim, Christian) are harassed relentlessly no matter what they wear. Microaggressions are everywhere. People still say things like 'why are you dressed like a parachi' and proclaim that wearing a burqa is 'sinister and against

---

[11]'Respectability is one of the most ubiquitous signifiers of class,' writes Beverly Skeggs in *Formation of Class and Gender: Becoming Respectable.* 'It informs how we speak, who we speak to, how we classify others, what we study and how we know who we are (or are not).'

"modern" society.' Meanwhile, in social spaces, style is also a marker of class (and caste). In her book *Coming Out As Dalit*, author Yashica Dutt writes about how she had to learn to dress like her upper-caste peers to fit in at school and college. Kiruba Munusamy, an anti-caste activist and advocate writes: 'When I posted a picture in [a] western outfit, I faced moral policing on my choice of dress and the troll said that instead of wearing such modern dresses, I should be nude. …This moral policing of dress code happens much more to dark, fat women rather than those who are fair and thin. This is only a simple demonstration and there is a flood of casteist, racist, sexist, extremist, hateful, and chilling content on social media.' If educated upper/middle-class women face harassment along these lines, for women from the working-class, the sting of judgement is ever sharper and the repercussions of the same ever more real.

'When I am working, I don't dress up well,' says Lakshmi Arumugam, a fruit and flower seller from Ambattur, 'because men assume I'm available if I look attractive, and try to misbehave with me, even the police. So, I want to look simple. But I am fond of dressing up and beautifying myself for other occasions. At family gatherings people don't respect you if you are not dressed up well.' Known to bring every harasser to book, Arumugam tells me that men and women are essentially the same. 'Both are human. It's unfair that society lets men dress however they want, but judges women. Even when men commit crimes, they're pardoned easily. When a woman does something wrong it is blown out of proportion.'

In a country where sexual harassment is routinely blamed on women for dressing inappropriately and attracting unwanted attention, many of us often end up self-regulating our attire. We always think about the male gaze and the nature of the space we're in, as embracing the seemingly feminine pleasures of bright lipstick or mascara, or wearing sexy[12] clothes is perceived as coquettish across

---

[12]What constitutes sexy? Indian men sometimes find tight T-shirts or sleeveless blouses irresistible, the desperados!

social classes. 'I would always make sure that I carry an extra shrug or shawl when I knew I would be wearing something slightly risqué,' reveals editor Shreya Punj. 'During college days, if we had plans post study hours, I always made sure I carried the clothes instead of wearing them to avoid any awkward interaction[s].' Clearly, the patriarchy doesn't like it when women perform femininity on their own terms, but what about female masculinity?

'They think all short-haired people are lesbians. My principal suspends every tomboy who has got a short haircut,' writes a student. Social judgement is relentless for girls and ladies who primarily perform masculinities. Indian society may even begrudgingly tolerate female masculinity in women who are cis-het or bisexual (with the potential to be feminine), but when a person is trans or a butch lesbian, the stigma is all-encompassing. As queer and trans theorist Jack Halberstam[13] notes: society 'locates masculinity in females as abhorrent, repulsive, and unsustainable.... Lesbianism has long been associated with female masculinity and female masculinity in turn has been figured as undesirable.' In today's India, this is a reality[14]. Even though it's not illegal to be homosexual now, prejudice against those who perform queerness in their everyday lives is still widespread. However, several bold young womxn[15] are taking the intolerance

---

[13]Article published under the name Judith Halberstam.

[14]In pre-modern India, men wore kajal, pierced their ears, wore silk saris, and performed as women in dance and theatre. Crossdressing was not entirely scandalous (even today, Indians celebrate some pre-modern temple festivals, like the Chamayavillaku festival in Kerala, where men dress as women to offer prayers to the female deity, complete with turmeric on their faces, jewellery, and designer blouses. There's absolutely no taboo attached to it.) But gender fluidity seems to have been a one-way street in the past. Women who humoured their masculinity could not perform it with the same ease as men indulging in their feminine sides (read the mythical Manipuri princess Chitrangada's story in the Mahabharata). Today, however, both men and women are judged equally for performing queerness.

[15]An intersectional term, womxn was originally used to include those left out of the white feminist discourse, like women of colour and transwomen. Today, womxn is largely used as an inclusive term that denotes women of all sexualities and from marginalized communities.

head-on. They use personal style as a creative tool of resistance against gender stereotyping.

'Fashion is important to express one's identity, but often, people don't give it much thought—like I have to wear a sari because I am a woman. [As a gender-fluid person] I wake up feeling different every day. I spend some time in front of the mirror to see what traits of my face are popping out. It's almost like a ritual to cope with the discomfort that I feel with my dysphoria,' says Durga Gawde, a sculptor, activist, and drag performer from Mumbai. 'Some days I see more masculine features jump out, other days it's more feminine. I try and make it fun, by playing around with my make-up and clothes. I shop in both [men's and women's] sections.' When Gawde was invited to meet Canadian president Justin Trudeau during his visit to India, they wore a crop top, a rainbow tie, a green mohawk, and a green sari.

Psychoanalyst Joan Riviere asserted that womanliness is a masquerade. I believe this applies to all women. Whether we are cis-het or queer, we are all capable of alternately playing up our masculinity or femininity in our own ways. When straight women strut around urban spaces in jeans or salwar kameez (both genderneutral outfits), I often imagine that they are performing their masculinity or androgyny (sometimes unconsciously). Wearing a sari or a skirt is effectively an overtly femme performance of femininity that most are averse to doing all the time, not only for reasons of comfort, but also because gender boundaries have blurred. Being perceptive creatures, women are deeply aware of what society expects of them in social situations, and know what constitutes acceptable gender performativity and what doesn't. Today's women shrewdly comply or rebel against those standards according to the need of the hour.

In the hyper-visible landscape of today, where a woman's image is very often her brand, every woman puts thought into how she represents herself and creates a little caricature of herself. 'As a good millennial feminist, I recognise that the quest for perfect hair is a distraction,' writes Kahini Iyer in 'Goodbye 2010s: The Decade

We Embraced Fleabag Feminism',[16] 'but that doesn't change my belief that hair is everything. From break-ups to new jobs, my milestones are usually marked by a hairstyle change that will, I am convinced, better represent my newest avatar.' A generation that grew up watching glamorously empowered women[17] on HBO, Star World, and MTV, while being simultaneously confounded by all the contradictory feminist lit online, Indian millennials, now in their adulthood, define their own (post)feminisms, inspired by self-critical and sarcastic Netflix and Amazon heroines.

Personal style then, is about much more than fitting into trends. It reflects a woman's subjectivity—her heritage, self-image, politics, aspirations, sexuality, aesthetics, and wit. But if you think that you do not subscribe to fashion entirely and are above it, think again. 'Whilst individuals may be invested in seeing their own look as entirely personal and idiosyncratic, appearance is, we suggest, thoroughly social and cultural, and however quirkily they self-style, few people live outside the fashion-beauty complex entirely,' write the authors of *Aesthetic Labour*. 'Even rejections of it are patterned.'

The Saga of Self-Love

'There is plenty of research indicating a strong correlation between the display of unrealistic body images on the internet and eating disorders,' says Neda Ansaari, a senior therapist at Mind Fit in Bengaluru. 'Girls and women tend to evaluate themselves against what is often presented in the media. This idea is reinforced by films and advertisements. This is further perpetrated by body shaming and lack of conversation about the same in families and societies.' Trained

---

[16]Fleabag is the flawed heroine of the eponymous British show. 'In an absurdist take on a classic feminine trope,' notes Iyer, 'Fleabag worries that she looks too good at her mother's funeral and tries unsuccessfully to rumple her hair to appear appropriately grief-stricken. It's a dig at the expectation on women to perform their emotions in a narrowly prescribed way.'

[17]Feminist media critics say those characters/personalities aren't really empowered, as the studios that produced them were run by the capitalist-patriarchal nexus, with the intent to peddle a narrow version of feminism to make money.

at the Chicago School of Professional Psychology, Ansaari has worked with scores of women to build resilience and cope with mood and anxiety disorders. 'While it is more socially acceptable for men to display their emotions through aggression or anxiety, the social norm for women is to internalize behaviour such as somatic complaints, self-criticism, withdrawal, and fearfulness. That is why depression presents itself more in women.' However, women are becoming more aware of this. Ansaari adds, 'I have noticed that more women tend to seek help through therapy. It definitely seems more acceptable for them to talk about their issues, concerns, thoughts, and emotions.'

Millennials and Gen Z are known to be their own most vicious critics. After all, we live in the age of hyper-imagery, where our phones, desktops, televisions, magazines, offices, and public spaces are filled with images of flawless/air-brushed models. Hard not to draw comparisons. Further, our society is one that has for ages defined sexy from a man's point of view—from voluptuous nymphs on the walls of Khajuraho's temples to skinny models on Mumbai's billboards. Beauty is idealized and monolithic. Even as feminism has popped the bubble of perfection, for most urban, educated women beauty still remains a site of vulnerability. In fact, a survey[18] conducted in 2016 found that 74 per cent of Indian women believe that beauty equals success. But why do smart (and well-informed) women feel pressured to confine themselves to patriarchal beauty standards? Author Gitte Marianne Hansen proposes the idea of 'contradictive femininity', and posits that when women's identities feel fragmented, they resort to self-harm as a coping strategy. India's outspoken and fearless young women who constantly battle patriarchal norms and rise above them have another side to their personalities, where the dark phantom of insecurity resides. A lonely space inside their heads where contradictive thoughts oscillate between self-love and self-loathing.

'I am five feet nothing and have modelled for brands like

---

[18]Conducted for the personal care brand Dove, 4,000 women between the ages of eighteen and sixty-four, and 2,800 girls aged ten to seventeen, in seven countries (India, the US, Britain, Brazil, China, Japan, and Turkey) were interviewed on their opinions on beauty.

Swarovski, Pankaj and Nidhi, Indigo, and Fendi, to name some,'
says Delhi-based influencer Devyani Kapoor.[19] 'The main reason for
me being where I am today is to break the idea of [negative] body
image that we all have.' Constantly dismissed for her height during
college and stereotyped as the short girl, Kapoor asserts that 'body
image is a big factor in any person's life. Younger and older women
write to me asking how to deal with people making comments [about
their bodies] that make them feel uncomfortable. The only thing I tell
them is to be the best version of themselves. ...The day you decide
that this is how you are and you accept yourself, nobody can make
you feel otherwise.' When I ask her whether beauty can empower a
woman, she replies: 'Anything that empowers you is worth taking a
risk for. Beauty has empowered me and made me who I am. It has
taught me the basic lesson of respect, gratitude, and confidence. I
am what I am and I will have it no other way.'

Millions of Indian women are adopting rituals of everyday
positivity—embracing their bodies and learning to be comfortable
in their own skin. They perform femininity (and masculinity) on their
own terms and have reappropriated the simple pleasures of admiring
oneself. They understand that each is entitled to one's own idea of
beauty, an idea that can empower one's everyday life and increase
one's self-esteem. Queer artist and poet Priyanka Paul tells it like it
is in an Instagram caption, alongside a sassy photo of herself in a
bikini: 'if u r a fat person and u feel the need to write a body positive
caption every time u put a nangu pic of urself, i want to tell u that
u don't have to, that u can post it like all the other conventional
pale vampires who do it without serving an apology for not hiding
your body.' Go through Instagram and you'll find a million images
of women flaunting their sexy bodies, even while telling you about
their insecurities. They speak about the taunts, the shaming, how
their self-esteem was affected by other people's prejudices before, and,

---

[19]Kapoor is also the founder of Shuffling Suitcases, a travelling pop-up that promotes
eco-friendly fashion throughout India.

most importantly, why they don't care any more.

In the 1990s, sociologist Meenakshi Thapan wrote that the 'female body could be experienced as both celebratory as well as oppressive. ...Experiencing the body as celebratory implies that desire attains fulfilment in our perceptions of our bodies as well as in the gaze of the other. Film stars, fashion models, professional dancers, theatre professionals probably experience the celebratory aspect of their embodiment. We however experience our bodies as oppressive when our desires remain unfulfilled.' Now, women who aren't in film, the performing arts, and fashion also celebrate their bodies. These women include homemakers, corporate executives, pilots, doctors, engineers, lawyers, sportswomen, and even politicians. As Thapan rightly notes later, it is 'important for a woman to see her body on what *she considers* her own terms and not as defined by the other. It is also important for a woman to experience her body, and her manipulation of it, in terms which are seen as being profitable to her physical and emotional well-being.'

Most feminists, however, are wary of women's potential to consciously perform their sexuality to their own benefit. 'It is true that make-up can be empowering for trans women to really come into their own and express their femininity. But cis women who claim to "do makeup for themselves" are deluding themselves,' writes Manasi Pant, a digital editor at *Feminism in India* (*FII*). 'Unless makeup is being used for some other artistic purpose, the only reason it would make someone feel better about themselves is because they feel more "beautiful".' Globally, the feminist argument seems to be that by (un) consciously subjecting ourselves to all the poking, prodding, waxing, and threading, we are submitting to the patriarchy and commodifying ourselves. Setting ourselves up to be exploited. The pursuit of beauty is seen as painful, harmful, and constitutive of female suffering and oppression.

'Women come to the beauty parlour to feel good about themselves,' says Sarita Ganesh Ram, a beautician from Darjeeling. 'Many of my customers are housewives. They spend all day working for their families. When they're at the parlour, they get time to think about themselves and relax. Some come with friends and chat all through. It's very important for women to do self-care. Beauticians need it for themselves too.' When I ask Sarita about beauty standards, she replies: 'Our beauty is different from the rest of India anyway. Women want to look their best nowadays. I don't think they all do it to look like movie stars. Of course, they get inspired by them, but each woman has her own beauty. Some quality in her face that's beautiful. I try and highlight that.'

Philosophers have debated the nature of beauty since antiquity. They've wondered whether beauty is an objective ideal or a subjective impression. Despite the fact that the aesthetic sensibility of classical civilizations found joy in balance and physical symmetry, alternative forms of beauty weren't completely rejected.[20] However, most people believe that beauty is an unchanging, timeless phenomenon. That one is either born beautiful or is ugly. Science tells us that this isn't the case. It's all about propaganda and perception. A few years ago, researchers conducted an experiment in a remote village in Nicaragua to see how a person's idea of beauty develops. The village had no electricity, no televisions, and had not been exposed to mass culture. Each villager in the focus group of eighty was first asked to create their ideal woman using computer software, post which the group was split into two. To one group, the researchers showed images of conventionally attractive skinny women, and to the second they showed images of attractive plus-size women. When finally asked to recreate their ideal woman, the first group drew thin body types while the second group drew rounder women.

Today's beauty ideal extends much beyond body type and skin tone: it takes into account every minute detail of the human form.

---

[20] In Sanskrit works of aesthetics too exist this seed of subjectivity. For example, the rasa theory (formulated between 500 BCE and 500 CE), which is a compendium of rhetorical sentiments that shape aesthetic relish, deals with varied subjective responses of the self-conscious Self to the Object, which results in the experience of beauty. Plurality, therefore, seems to be key in understanding beauty.

We are now obsessed with our flaws: freckles, pimples, scars, locks of frizzy hair, sideburns, gaps in teeth, ad infinitum. Before posting an image of ourselves online, we ensure all our flaws are hidden. Thanks to Instagram filters and phone cameras that come with 'photo beauty' and 'HD ready' applications that automatically correct our flaws, we look the perfect version of ourselves in every image. While we may get instant gratification from seeing our flawless selves, are we slowly forgetting how to admire our raw human form? Is there beauty in our imperfections?

Roshini Kumar thinks so. 'Beauty is everywhere,' proclaims the Mumbai-based photographer and advocate of body positivity. Through raw and uncensored images in a lauded photo series titled 'Fearless', she has tried to break the stigma that surrounds nudity and perceived flaws: stretch marks, discolouration, flabby skin. Created in a stark nude colour palette, her photo series portrays the human form in all its natural glory. 'I was a victim of societal pressure that led me to hate my body,' she boldly reveals, 'After surviving stage-4 bone cancer, I had a new perspective of life. I saw how important it is to be loving and respectful of our bodies. Our bodies are a reflection of our battles. We must embrace it. Not fall for beauty standards or societal judgements.'

Even as millions of Indian women reject beauty standards to find their own idea of physical beauty, a million more have relinquished its pursuit altogether. For this lot, body neutrality is the new body positivity. 'According to me, inner beauty is more important than outer beauty,' Ahmedabad-based Sujani Thakore tells me. 'A peaceful mind and pure heart are the main aspects of any person.' Self-love, it would seem, can take many forms and can be achieved through many routes. These days, many Indian youngsters are metamodern. They think of their bodies as temples of the spirit.[21] They go to yoga

---

[21]Indian women today are choosing very consciously to see their bodies as vessels of divine liberation. Artists like Sakshi Yadav, Shilo Shiv Suleman, Sarah Naqvi, Lyla FreeChild, and Aditi Gupta depict the pains and pleasures of the female body in a positive light through art. In the #HappyToBleed campaign, women and girls put up photos online

retreats to strip themselves of the ersatz and bond with their bodies again. Some look to Buddhism, Sufism, and Vedanta, to moksha, tanzih, and maya, in an effort to transcend their bodies. Although these ideas were created for the philosophical benefit of upper-caste/ class men, women today have reassessed and reappropriated them. For if the Self is the Absolute, then liberation is not some other-worldly notion, but the realization that you are *it*. You are the divine, or the divine is within you. So, love yourself. Despite your contradictions.

'Beauty to me is having a seamless connection between who you are as a person and the way the world sees you. The more synchronized that is, the more beautiful you are,' says Samara Mahindra, founder of the CARER program, an Indian healthcare start-up that guides cancer patients during their treatment journey and helps with post-cancer care. Mahindra lost her mother to cancer and has personally witnessed the apprehensions of cancer patients. When I ask her how she helps women deal with the taboo of baldness, she replies: 'Being a woman, I can comprehend the fear, embarrassment, and anxiety that would bring. At the same time, I also think of my mother who very openly and unapologetically accepted the change and did something about it. In fact, she was excited about getting new hairpieces and trying out various turbans.' Her start-up, she says, 'focuses first on helping patients accept the illness before anything else. Once acceptance happens, a lot of the apprehension and anxieties are released and patients are able to cope much better with the situation.'

Feminist existentialists have written extensively about the importance of talking about our bodies and bodily processes in a positive space. In today's time, this must include a third, that of our bodies when they are ill. Indian society does not encourage women to talk about their illnesses. And when women do, they're either looked upon with pity or revulsion[22]. 'To lose confidence in one's

---

holding up sanitary napkins, normalizing menstruation. Kiran Gandhi ran the London marathon during her period, freely bleeding for all the world to see.
[22]My mother is a breast cancer survivor, and I have witnessed first-hand the sort of insensitive comments people make.

body is to lose confidence in oneself,' writes Simone de Beauvoir. Patriarchal societies, she argues, have implanted in the minds of women the idea that our bodies are a burden and disadvantage to start with. When a woman's body becomes afflicted with any form of illness that affects her physical appearance, society isolates her altogether. It seems to me that self-love, both inner and outer, is essential to thrive as a woman.

Breaking the Stereotype

'Film heroines in Bollywood and Kollywood don't reflect the diversity of Indian beauty. Fair skin dominates still,' says Kochi-based journalist Dhanya Sijo Chiramel. 'In my observation, Malayalam cinema has always been more realistic than other industries. P. K. Rosy, a Dalit woman, was the heroine of the first Malayalam language movie: *Vigathakumaran*. She was dark-skinned.' For an average Malayalee, fair skin equals beauty, notes Chiramel, but a new generation of films are changing this narrative. 'This trend started in the early 2010s,' she says. 'Movies like *Maheshinte Prathikaram*, *Kumbalangi Nights*, and *Thanneer Mathan Dinangal* became super hits. Such movies show different kinds of heroines in their natural skin colour even without any make-up.'

India's commercial film industry[23] isn't exactly known for its commitment to racial diversity. All our top-paid actresses are fair-skinned. Even if there happens to be a dark-skinned female character, it inevitably devolves to brownface[24] (where fair actors are made to look dark). But why? 'Upper caste equals fair skin equals touchable. Lower caste equals dark skin equals untouchable,' wrote Indian actor Tannishtha Chatterjee on Facebook[25]. 'Yes, I have pronounced it.

---

[23]Across Bollywood (Hindi), Kollywood (Tamil), and Tollywood (Telugu).

[24]A recent example is the 2019 film *Bala*, which has Bhumi Pednekar portraying a dark-skinned character.

[25]To record her frustration over how her skin tone was made the central theme in a comedy roast, where the hosts jibed incessantly about her colour. Chatterjee had agreed to participate in the show as part of promotions for her film *Parched*.

Probably most of us will not admit that our hatred for dark skin also comes from caste bias.' It is telling that there are no DBA female actors in the realms of stardom. Even the few who have managed to rise up the film ladder are those with lighter skin tones. Across the film, beauty, and fashion industries, the fancy for fair skin remains. It comes as no surprise then that fairness creams are ubiquitous in India. The fairness cream market is projected to make revenues worth US$ 682 million by 2023. As celebrities endorse fairness creams with no qualms about the regressive messages their commercials send out, millions of women try every day to lighten their skin tone—egged on by screen goddesses and social pressure. Only recently has the Health Ministry proposed five years of imprisonment and a fine of ₹50 lakh for 'misleading advertisements' of products that guarantee fair skin.

'For the longest time, I was not confident about my skin tone being brown. In India, where I was born and raised, there's a stigma attached to being brown,' says Houston-based instablogger Aishwaryaa Raja.[26] 'Oh, men can be brown, that's ok, but women, nope, they have to be fair to be considered beautiful. To put things in perspective, here's an anecdote of how Indian aunties insult you in a very nice way. "I knew a girl who was your colour, but just before she got married, she drank lots of orange juice and then she became fair, maybe you should try it." Thank you but no thank you.'

Increasingly, young women are calling out bias instead of ignoring it—because they now want to have a real conversation about beauty. And as digital natives they know that the internet is the space where hashtag revolutions begin.[27] From slam poet Aranya Johar's *A Brown Girl's Guide to Beauty* to #unfairandlovely, #changetherhyme, and 'Dark is Beautiful' campaigns, various online trends have pushed companies to rebrand their products and make progressive ads like Dove's 'Let's Break the Rules of Beauty', Tanishq's 'A Wedding to Remember' featuring a

---

[26]She can be found at @aishwaryaaraja on Instagram.

[27]In the same breath, it is also pertinent to note that most women in India still do not have access to the internet, and hence no alternate conception of beauty other than what they're told by the patriarchy.

dark-skinned model, and Joy Cosmetics' ad with plus-size comedian Bharti Singh. These videos and hashtags became trends because millions of women across India shared or liked them. In today's India, women possess 85 per cent influence over whether a particular service or product is bought, according to Fortune India. If brands don't give women what they want, they'll simply move on to other brands that reflect their aspirations and ideologies. Everyone knows millennials and Gen Z have zero brand loyalty.

'The greatest currency that we have now is our consumption power,' declares firebrand rapper and activist Sofia Ashraf, a.k.a. Sista from the South who brought Unilever to its knees with her viral song 'Kodaikanal Won't'[28]. 'The moment brands or corporates or governments realize that women have consumption power, that's when they'll start looking at women's issues. Especially with brands, that's when they'll stop objectifying and start femvertising.'[29] Over the years, Ashraf has smashed several conventions to create a unique identity for herself. In an industry that often sells normative ideas of femininity, she has made several viral videos about acne, periods, and in the song 'I Can't Do Sexy', she tackles the social pressure of sexiness. 'Digital content is a man's domain right now,' she says. 'Just being seen as a woman [on] the internet is a statement in itself, and it's crucial to bring a female audience to that space.'

Digital ad culture is a crucial tool through which we can analyse how women like to see themselves. After all, ads are like mirrors. We recognize ourselves in the product ads that reflect our identities or aspirations. Viral adverts that promote gender equality and female self-empowerment are suggestive of the postfeminist trend that's catching on in India. The ambivalent neoliberal young woman is interpellated by the diamond ad that reads: 'A little modern. A little traditional. A

---

[28]The dissent song highlighted how Unilever poisoned Kodaikanal's lakes with mercury through one of its factories; it sought reparations for the damage caused to the environment and the locals. After the song went viral, Unilever was forced to confront its past wrongs in the public domain, under the watchful eyes of social media.
[29]Advertising that sells female empowerment.

lot like you.' The strong independent woman likes to buy expensive shampoo that proves she's 'worth it'. All in all, young women aren't interested in buying products that don't make them feel good about themselves any more.

'India is diverse, deep, rich, and all kinds of beautiful. No matter what the age, race, socio-economic background, or skin type—all women like to look pretty and make the effort to do so in some form,' says Anvi Mody, a global assistant brand manager at Dove and marketing mentor at Miami Ad School. 'The most exciting challenge is to understand these women and speak to them in a language best for each.' Mody tells me that companies these days conduct research on extremely detailed and categorized levels to understand their market. 'The Indian beauty industry has evolved tremendously over the past few years. Brands are celebrating and empowering women of all skin tones and body types, hence spearheading the revolution and paving the way to a future of equality and embracing each other. Initially the only definition of beauty was a fair, thin girl but [that] does not hold true any more.'

As women rise through the ranks of Indian advertising and media[30], things are changing. In fact, it's considered good for brand PR to make ads that #breakthestereotype. Even ads for furniture and washing detergent are often about female self-empowerment these days. Corporate brands that don't keep with the trend are called out on social media and pushed to reform their marketing material to stay relevant. From a purely economic point of view, if big companies do not change their 'standardizing' attitude, they will lose their ground to smaller companies that take age, race, gender, and culture into account. And, make no mistake, this is already happening around India, especially in the beauty and fashion industries, where upcoming homegrown brands design and market their products with native bodies in mind.

---

[30]Tista Sen is the regional creative director at JWT, Kainaz Karmakar is chief creative officer at Oglivy West, Deepa Geethakrishnan is the national creative director at Lowe Lintas, and Lulu Raghavan is the MD at Landor, to name a few.

However, Foucauldian feminism points out that beauty is disciplinary technology in any case: 'some form of aesthetic labour is increasingly demanded of all women...as we live in societies that become ever more dominated by new forms of visibility, appearance, and looking, and in which more and more of us partake in the endless labour of "curating a visible self" on and offline.' Cultural theorist Angela McRobbie argues that this trend encourages them to work endlessly on a perfectible self, and there's no space for a renewed feminist politics in this 'new sexual contract'. I find this approach rather restrictive and self-defeating. I prefer gender and media theorist Sofie Van Bauwel's line of thinking in a book about continuity and transformation in culture: '"Flexibility" has been stressed as the keystone of the current neoliberal agenda,' she writes, and this is 'embodied in the fluid movements and restructuring of labour, capital, and information, at the individual level, in a flexible competence for creative self-invention and self-mastery.' This is true of all forms of labour that women indulge in, including aesthetic labour. It is also crucial to note that in twenty-first-century India, many men are just as interested in buying beauty products and doing body work—they even get Brazilian waxes for smooth shiny skin. Badass ladies like Harnaam Kaur keep all their body hair[31] and groom it with love. Even as you read this, beauty routines are fast becoming gender nonconforming.

Perhaps our colonial inheritance of puritanical antipathy has made us forget the simple pleasures of indulging our bodies.[32] Beauty and

---

[31]If I can claim any collective consciousness with women around the world, I'd say most of them like their body hair. If they hadn't been told by society that body hair wasn't attractive, they'd roam around town with hairy legs and unibrows. In the Indian context, it seems society only recently decided that body hair is chhee-chhee. Glimpses of smooth hairless memsahibs of the Raj and ancient sculptures that didn't go into the fine detail of body hair must've inspired men and women to pursue new standards of beauty. In any case, it's time we spoke more about the virtues of body hair and why we should keep all of it.

[32]'[M]ajor aspects in the culture of Victorianism influenced the emergent model of the Indian reformed woman' notes Professor Maitrayee Chaudhuri in *Feminism in India: The Tale and its Telling*. 'Some of these can be identified as domesticity and family,

fashion were always part of performing gender in India, but we've suddenly decided that the thinking woman cannot want these things. Must the ideal (feminist) woman wear only hand spun khadi and restrain herself from self-indulgent vanity? Should we all mould ourselves in the framework that Mahatma Gandhi laid out for perfect femininity?[33] Many Indian feminists seem to think so. Some of the more puritanical among us, even go further and say that women who trade in glamour and beauty are agreeing to also become objects of trade. '[W]e really need to start worrying when one of the most talked about actresses representing the country internationally chooses to self-objectify,' writes Suchetana Sinha about the lead female actor of the film *Raaz*. Well, theoretically it is true that women in glamour and beauty are objectifying themselves. But is it wrong? In a market economy, we're all commodifying and trading something or the other for profit. Our technical expertise, our identities, our ideas. Why not our bodies?

'Madhuri Dixit's bosom heaving sensuously in the song "Choli ke peeche kya hai"…divided feminists nationally,' writes sociologist Manjima Bhattacharjya[34], 'into those who thought this constituted vulgarity and objectification of the body, and those who thought this was an expression of female sexuality, even erotic in its delivery.' More than twenty-five years later, feminists remain divided. Bollywood's ladies, meanwhile, have not only empowered themselves to become screen goddesses,[35] but have also embraced their sexuality and gone

---

respectability, improvement, and conventional Christian morality.'

[33]The Mahatma married Hindu asceticism with Christian puritanism and created an ideal woman who was halfway between a nun and an asexual Sita—always dressed in homespun clothes and with her head covered, thinking only the purest of thoughts.

[34]In the book, Bhattacharjya reframes the conversation by viewing women who commodify their bodies not as victims but as women with agency.

[35]If you have fundamental issues with the manner in which screen goddesses are represented in cinema, read *Celluloid Deities* for a different take. In it, art historian Preminda Jacob argues in that 'the fetishistic fragmentation of the figure via the close-up shot is most evident during the performative interludes of the film—timeless dream sequences, choreographed fights, musical elements, or melodramatic soliloquies—during which actors and actresses are equally subject to the fixing and iconization that Mulvey describes. I would argue that

on to break taboos on screen—which we must agree influences Indian society's morality much more than critical theory, acclaimed art, policy, or activism. Stars like Deepika Padukone and Kareena Kapoor take on meaningful roles but also willingly dance in item numbers, breaking the false dichotomy between good sexy and bad sexy. Then there's Sunny Leone, actor provocateur and porn star, rising up the ranks in Bollywood right now. Her movies are almost always blockbusters. And her entry into the mainstream has made modern India finally grapple with its morally ambiguous opposition to nudity, porn, and sexually explicit entertainment (which it secretly relishes: just look at our ancient temple walls or watch TV).

'I embrace nudity as I have nothing to hide,' Bengali actor Swastika Mukherjee states. 'Actors like me have made a conscious decision to make movies that explore different aspects of life, including sexuality.' In Tollywood and Kollywood too we find an increasing number of actors who gladly star in adult films. But when women break stereotypes in the public eye, they're not only likely to be labelled as feminist fails, but are also harassed relentlessly by India's cocky hate brigade. Actor Yaashika Anand, a former Bigg Boss contestant with a large fan following, describes the perils of starring in adult films: 'Instagram is a part of my life and there is a lot of negativity on social media, especially with people commenting under your pictures not knowing the difference between adult films and pornography.'

For those from minority communities, the surveillance is ever more personal. Actors like Fatima Sana Sheikh of *Dangal*-fame are routinely trolled for owning their bodies—in her case, she was abused online for posing in a swimsuit during Ramadan and for wearing a sari with a bindi on her forehead. Model Andleeb Zaidi has spoken out about the judgement she's had to face for doing bikini photoshoots. The social ire that actress Gilu Joseph received

---

the primary intent of the close-up device in Indian cinema is not so much to produce a subjugated identity of the female but to aid in the construction of a cultism around the characters of both the hero and heroine.'

for her open breastfeeding magazine cover[36] exposed (once again) India's misogynistic unease with women: Joseph was not only called out for partly showing her breasts, but also for applying sindoor on her forehead as she is a Christian.

Haters can hate, but daring women aren't about to stop. Across the country, they are twisting the beauty narrative and participating in body politics to make a point. Roshmita Harimurthy became the first woman with Dalit roots to represent India at the Miss Universe pageant, breaking the centuries-long misconception about Dalit beauty[37]. Anjali Lama made history when she walked the ramp at Lakmé Fashion Week, being the first transgender model to ever do so, paving the way for other women from her community[38] to enter the glamour and fashion industries. Acid attack survivors like Laxmi Agarwal and Reshma Qureshi have taken the world by storm—hosting shows and modelling, foregrounding their stories and experiences, breaking the silence about acid attacks.

Seeing Through the Illusion
'Working in the online beauty industry, I used to be a hoarder. Latest fashion, make-up products, personal care, everything was just one click away and the temptation to be trendy and cool very hard to resist,' digital artist Kaviya Ilango tells me. 'The tipping point for me was the Dove "Real beauty, Real you" ad campaign. Watching it, I realized that Dove is owned by Unilever, which also owns Fair & Lovely[39], Axe, Lakmé, and Ponds, where the brand message portrayed is often frivolous and quite the opposite to celebrating the

---

[36]The cover for Malayalam magazine *Grihalakshmi* triggered sexism, with a petition to the high court claiming that the cover affected 'society's moral fabric'. However, the courts dismissed the petition, saying 'obscenity lies in the eye of the beholder'.
[37]There's an actual Quora thread titled: 'If there's nothing such as race, why do the Brahmins look more attractive than the Dalits?'
[38]Nitasha Biswas was crowned the first Miss Transqueen India; Anjali Ameer starred as the lead actress in a Malayalam film; Rose Venkatesan hosted her own Tamil talk show. These women have gone against all odds to make their dreams come true.
[39]Now Glow & Lovely.

real you. The deplorable irony makes one sit up and take any beauty ad campaign with a pinch of salt. The last straw in my personal beauty journey, however, was this product ad that popped up—a vaginal bleach & private skin lightening cream.' An intrepid artist who takes on the hypocrisy of society regarding female sexuality through satirical sketches, Ilango did #100daysofdirtylaundry on her Instagram feed @wallflowergirlsays—an honest account of millennial female anxiety. 'To say that I am entirely off the farce temptation would be a lie,' she says candidly. 'The CC cream to cover up the acne-battlefield, a breezy summer dress, and winged liner to lift up your mood when you are PMSing, fashion/beauty does boost one's confidence, especially when you feel down or vulnerable. But I try. To get as far away from the superficiality of all this.'

There's no denying the fact that the entertainment, beauty, glamour, and media nexus are morally relativist: willing to cater to whatever demographic has the power to consume. This means the same brand can sell products or ideas that are entirely contradictory. Naomi Wolf wasn't exaggerating when she wrote that 'powerful industries…have arisen from the capital made out of unconscious anxieties, and are in turn able, through their influence on mass culture, to use, stimulate, and reinforce the hallucination in a rising economic spiral.' This holds true to a large extent even today.

'Women since the late nineteenth century have been perceived as consumers with commercial value,' points out Dr S. P. Srimathi, director for women's studies at NMKRV College in Bengaluru. 'In [the] early twentieth century the developing arts of retailing and advertising attracted a predominantly female clientele. Marketers and advertisers became significant definers of women's desires and aspirations. Women being among the more vulnerable sections of society got exposed to this.' Today, intelligent and aware women still consume products that propagate negative biases, carefully utilizing the product's benefits and ignoring the rest, notes Dr Srimathi, 'but the same cannot be said about teenagers who blindly adhere and are influenced by these advertisements, developing low self-esteem in the long run.'

Both body positive and negative promotions of products are capable of affecting our thoughts—the former pushes us to consciously feel better about ourselves despite our flaws, the latter shames us and then shows us how to improve. Either way, we may superficially change our perception of ourselves by using various products, but our inner self-image remains the same. This is also compounded by the fact that the Indian beauty industry primarily peddles products made for young Caucasian women of slender build, in a country largely populated by dark-skinned women of varying body and skin types. Even while it is slow to tweak the products to suit native women's bodies, it is quick to tap into local (racist) beauty prejudices to sell its wares. So, how do women break out of the illusion?

'I look after my skin with homemade remedies and use only natural products where I can. My make-up is minimal. I do not frequent parlours for facials but keep it restricted to maybe twice a year,' says Deena Pinto, an investment banker turned lifestyle blogger.[40] 'The modern-day woman is so keen to try out all the fancy brands that are out there, without first eating right or healthy. The focus should be to heal from the inside so it reflects on the outside,' notes Dubai-born Pinto. 'I am yet to use anti-ageing products as [they're] loaded with chemicals and not exactly something my delicate face needs. Our ancestors knew what they were doing and aged gracefully.' When I ask her about her body image, she replies: 'I grew up with an inferiority complex, but over time I learnt to appreciate myself more. I discovered the art of self-love and confidence. I studied about how eating right helps balance us from the inside and shows on the outside. At forty, I feel great and proud of how I look without ever having been to the gym.'

To escape the web of beauty prejudice constructed by big media, most millennials and Gen Z prefer to take their beauty (and fashion) advice from influencers instead of corporate media portals. Born and bred in consumer culture, influencers know how to seamlessly blend

---

[40]Pinto blogs @skinnygirldiariez.

the message of self-love with self-improvement, giving a personal touch to their approach[41]—earnestly pedalling brands. Their relatable aesthetic sensibilities and lifestyle philosophies inspire millions. Amidst all the (feminist) outrage against mass manufactured beauty and fitness culture, most young women (be they influencers or passive consumers who post selfies as cathexis) are not opting out of pursuing them altogether. Instead, they are diversifying the methodologies they practise and the merchandise they buy. From following holistic (desi) fitness regimes formulated by dieticians like Rujuta Diwekar, to reaching back to ancient cosmetology in search of natural unguents for self-care, women are reimagining self-improvement.

On the other end of this formulation are female entrepreneurs who are making (organic) beauty products and selling services.[42] There's a lot of money in beauty. The Indian cosmetics industry is growing exponentially and has one of the largest female workforces in India. It is expected to generate 1.42 crore jobs by 2022. Instead of arguing against its very existence, perhaps it makes more sense to cheer on more women to enter this field and revolutionize it from within. The same is true of the fashion industry too. But again, we'd have to ask: do women in these industries *feel* beautiful?

'Insecurity is the reality of our times,' says model and entrepreneur Surya Ganapathy, 'so loving who you are, with all your flaws, being your first admirer is the need of the hour. I think when you feel good you look good anyway.' Petite, often seen dressed in silk saris, and trained as an engineer, Ganapathy isn't the conventional model. She rose through the ranks in the industry through a sheer sense of

---

[41]Now, we may very well bicker over whether influencer posts are real. You may point out that their poses are contrived and strategic. But that's Instagram for you—an endless fashion parade. On Tik Tok, meanwhile, influencers pursue the grunge real aesthetic—but that's a masquerade too. What did you expect in the hyperreal world? Everything is manufactured, even truth.

[42]Zahara Nedou created Zahara Skincare, Rubeina Karachiwalla set up Ruby's Organics, Malika Sadani started The Moms Co., and Shubhika Jain began RAS Luxury Oils, Parinitha Manohar launched Spalontime, a sort of Zomato for salons, and Simrita Singh opened Just B Au Naturel (to name a few).

self-worth: 'I don't seek validation outside of myself,' she tells me, 'I pursue beauty and fashion to empower the self.' With 73,000 followers on Instagram and her own deli business in Chennai, she doesn't have time for what others have to say.

One's perception of the physical self has far-reaching ramifications that affect personality development and life choices. To rise above society's bias against her body, the self-confident woman builds a wall around herself to keep out the haters. In this safe space, she defines herself and thrives. But as anthropologist Veena Das writes: the 'sense of being a woman is internalized' through the double perspective of 'the body as object and body as subject'. So, at some point, we do have to reckon with how the world outside the wall perceives us. While some women are strong enough to ward off all forms of negativity, for many of us, the negativity is distressing. It messes with our heads and affects our self-esteem. And a distorted view of the self makes one vulnerable to feelings of inadequacy. This also has psychosomatic repercussions. Anxiety and self-loathing centred on body image drive several women to rapidly gain and lose weight. Women with eating disorders alternate between giving the body what it wants and denying it. This can lead to several physical ailments including cardiovascular disease, diabetes, and hypertension. Alas, beauty does come at a high cost.

'I'm happy to say this is my life, my face, and yes I've had plastic surgery which I'm not ashamed to admit. Do I promote it? No. Am I against it? No—it's just how I choose to live,' writes actress Shruti Haasan on her Instagram. 'The pain isn't easy, the physical changes aren't easy but, what's become easier [for] me is to share my journey. No one famous or not is in a position to judge another person. Ever. That's just not cool.' With actresses and models openly discussing their beauty regimes and experiments with surgery, girls and women do not consider plastic surgery taboo any longer.[43] The number of Indian women getting cosmetic surgeries

---

[43]The worrying development though is in the low-quality procedures provided to women

has, in fact, gone up. Most common among the procedures done are lip enlargements (lip-filler augmentations), nose jobs (rhinoplasty), and fat removal (liposuction). And these procedures shouldn't be considered sinful in an open society per se: in Brazil, cosmetic surgeries are free or low-cost in public hospitals (every woman has the 'right to beauty')! While it is unfair to label everyone who gets a facelift or tummy tuck as suffering from beauty obsession or being 'beauty sick', the unending quest for perfection can lead some women into disaster. Plastic surgeries can go terribly wrong. Botox isn't exactly a health supplement and breast implants may backfire (as can any surgery). By obsessing over their images online and offline, are women tipping over the cliff from self-esteem to narcissism?

(Some) psychologists will have us know that narcissism is actually related to our greater well-being. It doesn't always have a negative connotation. Yet, because narcissism in women is often located in a libidinal space[44] (while male narcissism is located in power/control), women who are obsessed with their physicality are assumed to be sexually libertine or prone to philandering. So, for millennia we have been told that narcissism is a woman's fatal flaw. Sure, a woman's tendency to over-correct herself to look perfect will have emotional and physical side-effects. We can talk about that with concern, but to altogether question a woman's pursuit of narcissistic beauty on the basis of its immorality is akin to reiterating ancient patriarchal bias. Is the pursuit of beauty solipsistic? Perhaps. Does it involve spending money? Yes. Do all women roil in guilt at the end of such an undertaking? No.

'Right after I got a makeover, I was shaken by my own image,' confesses Annie Rashmi Tensingh, a biotechnologist, who serendipitously tried out a makeover at an airport as her flight got delayed. 'I was just one among thousands of passengers, lost in the crowd,' she says, 'but after the makeover I was noticed as I

from the lower strata of society, especially aspiring models and actors from small towns and villages who come to megacities like Mumbai in search of work.
[44]More on narcissism in the chapter 'Demystifying the Feminine'.

walked to my gate and it was surreal, because I wasn't used to that kind of attention.' After this experience, Tensingh consciously started exploring make-up techniques, bought products that suited her skin tone, and began pursuing everyday beauty. It helps boost her confidence, she says.

Like it or not, many women feel empowered after they spend a couple of thousand bucks on a new haircut or carmen red lipstick.[45] Given all the pressures in one's life, if the pursuit of beauty gives a woman a dose of self-esteem and lifts her mood, there's no reason to deride it. On the other hand, it must be noted that millions of Indian women do not like make-up. Most brides-to-be reluctantly undergo beauty makeovers relenting to societal pressure. Women in service industries are compelled to dress up for work every day. For these women, defying the beauty norm is the goal. Every woman, it seems, has her own set of challenges to face. Her pursuit or rejection of beauty in such a scenario, is a subjective phenomenon. To each her own then. Peace out, ladies.

[45]Lena Dunham's piece for *Vogue*, 'Why Red Lipstick is Feminism's New Calling Card', argues that the revolution will wear red lipstick. She writes that while second-wave feminists denied their femininity, the women of today are reappropriating the simple pleasures of make-up and reminding the powers that be that femininity is an asset and not an albatross.

2

ISHQ IN THE TIMES OF TINDER

Everyone is a little cynical about love these days. Of course, we've all done backflips to please our partners at some point or another—burying deeply ingrained feminist ideals under the sheets to cuddle with the main man while he protectively embraces; or putting up with *his/her/their* emotional abuse so we can stay in love; or the most senseless of them all, falling in love with someone who doesn't reciprocate, because we are all happiest when we're deluding ourselves. But, eventually, we realize how stupid we are when in love. But such is its nature, isn't it? That ineffable emotion, call it kadhal, premam, mohabbat, whatever. It's meta, divine. After being bitten by the love bug once or twice, many become immune to it. They navigate intimate relationships using their heads going forward. Some others, however, are addicted to passionate love, and yearn to experience its pain over and over again, breaking their hearts in the process.

With a trove of dating and matrimony apps/sites[1], finding partners for companionship or marriage (of both the sedate and fervid varieties) has never been easier, or so it seems. Except, it really is harder. The sheer number of options has women swiping, left mostly, with endless disappointment that an interesting face has a crap bio or unreal expectations. And, even after making an online connection, there's no guarantee they won't ghost you. Or stand you up. Also, and I hate to break it to you, but 'all romantic experiences are essentially

---

[1]Love and lovers are commodities in the world of Big Data. Computer algorithms decide who we are matched with. On the upside, many dating platforms filter potential partners based on one's preferences.

caste experiences' in India, online just as offline. Most desi people bring with them a sceptical approach to love, dappled with mild religious/racist/casteist/classist bias—effectively narrowing down their prospects. It is no surprise then that even in a country with more than a billion people, it is difficult to find a mate you experience a real connection with.

Sex, however, is a different matter. Even though millennials and Gen Z grew up in an India where they weren't exactly encouraged to seek sexual pleasure in their lives, they had the internet. A little portal through which they glimpsed sexual freedom. Even as society considered female pleasure a secret shame that needs to be stifled, they indulged in the forbidden. Located their own gender identities and sexual proclivities within global communities online. They let their transgressive desiring bodies explore themselves offline. Naturally, today, as a generation that has come of age (post puberty, post chaste, post marriage, post #MeToo), they want to talk about sex and expectations. Because each of them has a hyper-individual sexuality. Be they hetero-, bi-, homo-, trans-, asexual or queer, their individual experiences are unique.

Since the time of the *Kama Sutra*, women's sexuality has been discussed only with respect to male pleasure. In the mainstream Indian imagination, feminine pleasure is often characterized by muffled moans of assorted heroines in films, or by the loud laments of orgasmic porn stars. There's no nuance. What better can we expect from a society that has regulated women's sexuality as a sort of pet project for centuries? The idea of the contemporary woman openly talking about sex for her own sake is outright sacrilegious for most folks. Because not only will this further open up the space for women to pursue unconventional sex (outside marriage or with other women), but it will also empower women to say no to sex. Patriarchs go livid just thinking about it. Let's not kid ourselves, even woke men don't really get the idea of consent. Yes doesn't always mean yes. And when a woman says no, men somehow think that she's saying it to turn them on or to play hard to get. It's like even the most progressive of men are too daft to understand subtle boundaries. No wonder then that marital rape is not even a thing in India.

'The time has come to think about sex,' writes anthropologist Gayle Rubin. 'To some, sexuality may seem to be an unimportant topic, a frivolous diversion from the more critical problems of poverty, war, disease, racism, famine, or nuclear annihilation. But it is precisely at times such as these, when we live with the possibility of unthinkable destruction, that people are likely to become dangerously crazy about sexuality.' Sexual abuse is rampant across the world because most men are conditioned to be hyper-masculine—men in democracies, theocracies, and autocracies, all feel entitled to women's bodies. When they are denied access, however, their insecurities play up and they rage violently against women. 'Incels aren't looking for sex,' writes Jia Tolentino about the subculture of involuntarily celibate men who hate women, '[t]hey're looking for absolute male supremacy.' In India, where class, caste, and creed add further impediments to a man's access to women, one can only speculate about the damage and rot that must exist in morbid male minds. Cyber violence[2] is on the rise in India, where men increasingly harass women—threatening to/or publishing original and doctored photos/videos with the intention of insulting women's bodies and characters. Not to mention the spate of acid attacks, sexual and violent crimes that spurned men perpetrate on the women who (they feel) have maligned their masculinity.

Of course, not all men are dicks. Women want to have sex with partners who give them the profound pleasures their bodies deserve. It's crucial to undo 'the false impression that since women don't want to be sexually exploited, they don't want to be sexual'. Many millennials and Gen Z have experimented with their sexualities, and most have read/watched quite a lot, only to realize that sexual positions that are touted as kinky are ones that give men more pleasure than women. How many men learn the different ways to

---

[2]This includes cyber stalking, bullying, harassment, identity theft, breach and violation of privacy/confidentiality, voyeurism, and revenge porn.

go down on a woman, even as women spend time practising blow job techniques? Luckily for lesbians and bisexual women, sex can be ever more liberating—because women know how to give another woman pleasure.[3]

In any case, it isn't only for the sake of amazing orgasms that women must talk about sex. It's also to do with power. If women don't embrace their sexuality in the bedroom (where they may choose to either not have sex when they don't want to, or, guide their partners to give them more pleasure), then how can they be fully empowered? 'Sexuality is integral to women's political and economic empowerment,' notes a policy paper[4] by Pathways of Women's Empowerment Research Programme Consortium. 'Women need control over their bodies, be able to assert their right to physical autonomy and protection from abuse, and realise sexual rights such as the right to a safe and satisfying sex life. If they do not have this, women have limited scope for making claims in other areas of their lives.'

Owning their sexuality and bodies enables women to challenge cultural expectations. Even while gender and development theorists have framed female sexual pleasure as a human rights issue and as a necessity for health and well-being, the theory that appeals to me most is the one concerning political power. In *Women, Sexuality and the Political Power of Pleasure,* the authors explore how claiming the right to sexual gratification empowers women to subvert gender norms and oppressive power relations. They argue that promoting pleasure among women can make them more effective politically. In a world where women can't be shamed for being sexual, gender dynamics shift. Power shifts.

It would seem Indian women are rediscovering this power. They've come to see that they don't have to depend on a partner to give them sexual pleasure. Because most women can turn themselves on.

---

[3]This is not to suggest that all Indian men are bad in bed.
[4]The paper states that international development has dealt poorly with regard to sexuality issues (by primarily framing it through the lens of sexual violence).

According to a survey conducted by an Indian sex products seller That's Personal, their highest-selling product among women were intimate massagers: a sex toy that guarantees orgasms and does not require a partner. Self-pleasure is the new telos to aspire to. Look at viral articles like Nishtha Relan's 'I Am A Woman, And I Masturbate' for *Youth Ki Awaaz*, or videos like Nisheeth TV's 'Girls Openly Talk About Masturbation'. One can tell that a lot of women in India are doing it or at least thinking about doing *it*. The lusty and curious are voyaging into their own bodies to find those secret alcoves of pleasure. Yes, they're touching themselves, getting horny. Indulging in fetish fiestas and talking about it all.

Circling back to partnership (irrespective of whether the match was made in heaven, a dingy bar, or auntyji's living room), it's imperative to note that not all long-term relationships revolve around sex alone. In fact, millennial couples have far less sex compared to previous generations. It's not for nothing that many literally send out Google invites to their partners to make time and prepare for sex, or take vacations for lovemaking. Nobody likes to be caught off-guard these days. Always *sext* first. What with a trove of #couplegoals and individual milestones to achieve, people are more inclined to spend their time renegotiating love and upgrading their relationship protocols—having ABC sex[5] during dry spells. Marriage and partnership entail much more than coitus in today's time: it is 'an egalitarian understanding of relationship-maintenance responsibilities, and a sense that partners should help each other grow'. All in all, being in a real relationship with a contemporary woman demands outright adulting.

Modern Love
'Polyamory was a journey of self-discovery for me. It helped me with a lot of issues that I myself have when I'm in an exclusive relationship (my self-worth and sense of identity being very heavily defined by my

---

[5]Planned sex to observe anniversaries, birthdays, and other celebrations.

partner). It was a journey I wanted to share with the world, one that I honestly hoped would help and benefit a lot of people,' Mumbai-based Arnaz Irani tells me, when I ask her what prompted her to write a candid article[6] about her polyamorous experiences, a topic seldom discussed in India. 'In the liberal bubble I live in, and among the sort of people I choose to surround myself with, this stuff isn't really taboo,' she exclaims. Talking about the inherent contradictions in millennial feminism, where women often compromise on feminist ideology for love, Irani says: 'I wrote another piece for *Arré* about being an old-fashioned romantic while also being a feminist, where the thought was essentially about the struggle—between what we're taught to be and what we want to be. The way millennials are broadening the definition of feminism is good. Choices (in whatever form) should always be above/about more than just sexual politics.'

Young women have recast ideas of love and compatibility in India today. While many still believe in the fairy-tale ending (or beginning), others have self-partnered[7] and refuse to let romantic love define their lives (which isn't to say they don't want it). The epiphany that my generation seems to have had about love is that it isn't as selfless as we were told. As pop poet Rupi Kaur writes: 'I am learning how to love him by loving myself.' Because, at the end of the day, love has everything to do with the selfish *self*. Without that, there is nothing. So, millennial women's choices with regards to love, dating, and marriage often traverse a path of self-knowledge.

'I am not against the idea of marriage; it works for some and not for all. But I prefer to stay single,' says Sana Kazeem, who works with an airline company in Chennai. 'Despite the fact that I'm not interested in getting married, relatives of mine have brought proposals from other cities. When I simply tell them about my job (which I like very much), my pets, my family, my friends and my freedom, they tell me I don't have to work because the guy has money,

---

[6]Titled 'What My Experiments with Polyamory Taught Me About Love' for *Arré*.
[7]To borrow Emma Watson's terminology. She prefers to use the term 'self-partnered' rather than single.

it's okay to leave my pets (not realizing they're like my children) because he has pets too. They still think that it's a woman's role to sacrifice. And all for what? To have a companion when you're old. A companion could be a friend or a pet or just anyone, whoever said it has to be a spouse?' An avid traveller, yoga practitioner, animal welfare enthusiast, needle worker, and maker of crafts, Kazeem says there's no space for loneliness in her life as she's busy passionately pursuing her work and hobbies. However, the social pressure to marry is unending. 'Honestly, Indians will never stop asking questions or judging one's personal life. People ask me "wouldn't you like to see your parents happy?" for which I mostly reply that *my* happiness is of utmost importance and my definition of happiness is different from theirs.' Kazeem tells me that she has stopped attending family events to avoid being drawn into conversations about her relationship status. 'People don't want to know if you're happy the way you are or if you are peaceful in life, they measure a woman's achievement merely based on her marital status.'

The patriarchy expects all women to be selfless and nurturing wives and, later, mothers. A woman with ambition outside the ambit of family is seen as an anomaly. Every concerned uncle and aunty take it upon themselves to find her a suitable partner (within their own communities). Love doesn't feature as a priority in the Indian marriage scene anyhow. Neither does choice. As a society, we believe that a woman isn't settled down unless she is living with a (male) spouse. This is not surprising. All through history, women have been asked to marry not for love, but to solidify social alliances. 'Certainly, people fell in love during those thousands of years, sometimes even with their own spouses,' writes historian Stephanie Coontz, '[b]ut marriage was not fundamentally about love. It was too vital an economic and political institution to be entered into solely on the basis of something as irrational as love.' Fast forward to today, and not much has changed in India. Ninety-two per cent of marriages in India are intra-caste and arranged (which means most pre-marital romantic relationships fizzle away). This is not to say that all such marriages are bound to be exploitative or that the men in them are sexist. Some Indian women consciously choose to have arranged marriages, for various reasons. They may even look at the institution of marriage as an economic proposition.

'I don't want to sound like a snoot or anything, but I am used to living a certain way. I believe if I am comfortable financially, love would be easier,' points out Naina, a psychology graduate from Delhi. 'I know for a fact that if there is financial strain, even if you love the guy, it will be hard to make the marriage work.' This sentiment echoes across the country, among women from every community in the middle- and upper-classes. But before you put on your judgemental glasses, let me ask you, why is it wrong to want to marry someone with a good education and money, with the same socio-cultural background? It's an equally valid expectation as is wanting to be with someone who is from your own city or likes R&B. To each their own, right?

On the other hand, it's not like all Indian love stories are exemplars of gender equality. Modern love is sometimes not so modern in India. Have you read the women defending Kabir Singh's[8] anger as a legitimate expression of love on social media? You'd think that by now all women should be calling out every misogynistic nerve in a man. But in a time when men fall out of love easily and often, maybe it's sort of sexy to watch a man passionately stay in love even after his lover has married someone else? Or does his toxic masculinity cancel everything else out? Honestly, when it comes to matters of the heart, things get a little hazy. Violence has no place in romantic relationships, sure. But that's a decision many women make with the benefit of hindsight. For when we are in love, we often try to forgive our partner's transgressions. In a society where anger is a male privilege, and potential lovers can range anywhere from outright aggressive to passive aggressive, caution is advised.

---

[8] A Bollywood movie about an angry young man who almost rapes his love interest and harasses her after she leaves him.

'The idea that strong women cannot be abused within their marriages is a big myth,' fiery author Meena Kandasamy once said.[9] 'I believed that no man, no husband could lay a hand on me. I was fierce and feminist and no-nonsense. Then, within an abusive marriage, I actually realized that your strength is also what makes you a perfect target for an abuser.' More than 30 per cent of Indian women have experienced sexual, emotional, or physical violence perpetrated by their spouses. Since marriage is considered sacrosanct in all religions (and even by some judges in our courts), many women are compelled to 'adjust' with their men. As speaking out against their husband's abusive tendencies will put them at the centre of negative social scrutiny, most wives put up with everyday trauma, hoping they can change their abusers one way or another. But this takes a severe toll on their well-being. They are likely to experience depression, anxiety, and post-traumatic stress, apart from a range of psychosomatic complaints. With no support or an exit strategy, some even try to end their lives altogether.

Then again, #notallmen are violent. Feminine excess and aggression in intimate relationships aren't unknown either. But for a gender that has stereotypically been associated with toxic insecurity or obsession, performing arrogance is probably for the best. While this attitude may stir up the marriage scene and position women as shrews, as long as they get what they want, it doesn't matter what labels society thrusts on them. Look at it this way: in a country where divorce is considered the absolutely final option (India has the lowest divorce rate in the world, of less than 1 per cent), where couples are expected to compromise with each other to make things work, postfeminist women are taking full advantage of the situation. Being assertive and 'scheming' by nature, most of them are taking control of their relationships. They are increasingly figuring out stellar ways to sway their partners according to their whims and fancies.

---

[9]Kandasamy's celebrated book *When I Hit You: Or, A Portrait of the Writer as a Young Wife* is loosely based on her own marriage.

Sample this article: 10 awesome tricks you must try to make your husband obey you always: 'shut the nagging switch; compliment him; roll the ball when he's attractive; praise him in front of his parents; know when he is vulnerable; be compassionate; don't overburden him with a list of things to do; don't take things too seriously; don't be dominating;' (and my personal favourite) 'ignore at least some of his mistakes.' Most hetero and bisexual ladies spend much time pondering Menology. After all that talk about gender equality, men can still seem like they're from Mars sometimes. So irascible. Yet, it's that difference that attracts some women to such men. But after the mystery is gone, and he becomes more like a room-mate, the same male irascibility makes women despise their men, turning love into livid fury.

'Young married women go to extremes,' Dr S. Thenmozhi tells me, 'they are either submissive and don't question, or they become very aggressive and don't take on any responsibilities or respect family values. Because they are empowered, they believe they can do whatever they want. They don't like to be questioned.' Based on her experience with millennial clients, Dr Thenmozhi, who is the head of the counselling psychology department at the University of Madras reveals: 'These days women are more emotionally independent and more expressive than men. The trend is changing. Women are ruling over men.' According to her, independence is not the solution to relationship problems—there must be interdependence.

Even while the actual divorce rate may be low in India, the number of young women thinking about separation is rising. According to a report by Sulekha, a digital platform for expert services, there has been a spike in searches for family and divorce lawyers recently. Chennai, Mumbai, and Bengaluru top the list. Increasingly, young women are losing patience with their spouses. Many of the men these women want to separate from may seem like sensitive blokes. However, within a marriage, gendered social expectations inevitably put women in the corner. Whether career-oriented or not, a large section of Indian women wants equal companionship. They aren't willing to put up with insecure men or those who don't support their passions. Finally, there's also the inescapable saas-bahu angle to consider (and husbands who are mama's boys).

'My husband always took his mother's side when she and I had arguments,' says Prachi Jain[10], a commerce graduate from Hyderabad. 'I had to take permission from my mother-in-law to stay out late, buy something expensive, or even to meet my friends.' Jain married into a joint family, where three generations lived together. When she married, she quit her job as the family didn't approve of women working. She says that it was considered disrespectful to say or do anything that the older women in the family didn't favour. 'I couldn't continue living in that situation. It got to a point where I decided to leave my husband and asked him for a divorce. That's when he realized that he didn't want to lose me.' Prachi and her husband eventually decided to move out of the family home to try and save their marriage.

Even as a growing number of Indian women choose to live in nuclear families, much to the chagrin of their elders, several others live within the confines of joint families to keep with tradition. It is imperative to note that every joint family is different. While the conservative among them ban their daughters-in-law from working outside the home and minutely monitor their mothering techniques, some others are more open, even willing to help out with childcare while daughters-in-law work (this, however, is not the norm, but the exception). Be what may, men, in general, don't seem to fancy the idea of their wives working all the time at the expense of family duties—be they a part of a nuclear or joint family.

'I earn more than my husband,' says Reshma T., a domestic helper in Vashi. 'When wives don't work, men consider them their slaves.' A mother of two, she leaves her children with her sisters while working. 'Although both of us work, it is my responsibility to find money for gifts on occasions and loans during crisis to relatives because I

---

[10]Name changed to hide identity.

earn more.' However, she points out, 'when we have a quarrel, my husband is allowed to shout at me, but when I raise my voice, I'm labelled as rude.' Reshma tells me that her husband doesn't like it when she comes home late or when she talks to other men. 'When I was working at a factory, a man used to give me extra attention, so I told my husband about it. He said that I must have encouraged him. It made me so angry.'

Ever had a boyfriend or husband who was the embodiment of male insecurity? I'm sure many of us have had one or two of those in our lives. Slouching men who expect their ambitious girlfriends/ wives to emotionally (if not physically) prostrate at their feet. Several studies around the world have confirmed that men are stressed out when their wives earn more than them.[11] And it's common knowledge what happens to the male ego when a woman gets ahead of him. It's not for nothing that mothers tell their daughters not to compete with the men they're with. Heard the Tamil adage, 'kallanalum kanavan, pullanalum purushan'?[12] Even in the twenty-first century, not much seems to have changed—55 per cent of married millennial men believe that wives should always listen to their husbands, while 46 per cent married women disagree. Clearly, connubial bliss is bound to be elusive. Marriages, be they arranged or a love-match, are poised to be filled with contradictions. Because heteronormative coupling in India poses the threat of gendered social expectations and intra-relationship conundrums verging on sexism. So, for queer women, who are often not defined by their romantic relationships with men, is love ever more worthy?

'The merest expression of same-sex desire or want is often met

---

[11]'With stress levels high when they are sole breadwinners, men appear to be more relaxed when their wives or partners earn anything up to 40 per cent of the household income,' writes Joanna Sydra, a lecturer in business economics. 'But their distress levels increase sharply as their spouse's wages rise beyond that point. And they find it most stressful when they are entirely economically dependent on their partners.'

[12]It roughly translates to: He may be as cold as a stone, yet he is your husband. He may be as weak as grass, yet he is your man.

with brutal family violence, including corrective rapes, discrimination, ostracization and even death…. Discrimination against queer women is entrenched in state institutions,' writes advocate Amritananda Chakravorty. 'In all this din, where is the opportunity to talk about desire, heart breaks, failed relationships, unrequited love, etc.?' Love is love, after all. It is just as elusive and paradoxical, irrespective of whether the partners involved are of different genders or the same. On the other hand, to break the taboo, there is the need to amplify successful queer love stories. In recent times, thousands of such accounts have surfaced across India. From the iconic love stories of advocates Arundhati Katju and Menaka Guruswamy, who led the struggle to decriminalize Section 377, to star athlete Dutee Chand acknowledging that she is in a same-sex relationship, real narratives are slowly breaking through the stigma against same-sex love. 'We fight like every other couple, but our fights are issue-specific. They never go beyond a day,' says Suchandra Das about her relationship with Sree Mukherjee, whom she married performing traditional Hindu rituals. Queer couples traverse relationship trajectories just as heteronormative ones, expect, unlike straight people, they don't have the privilege of falling back on friends to set up blind dates or family to arrange their marriage after harrowing break-ups.

'Forget meet cutes in bars or bumping into a fellow queer woman in a library,' states journalist Dipannita Saha. Apart from the fact that there still are many closeted lesbian and queer women who aren't using dating apps, there seem to be other, more fundamental issues with the design of dating apps themselves that reduce the chances of meeting potential dates. On Tinder, there is a 'very curious trend among the heterosexual female profiles which turn up when you opt to view only women,' writes Smita Vanniyar, a queer feminist working on gender, sexuality, and technology. 'It's safe to assume that they are on Tinder to meet men and would have opted to view only men… In most cases, they were women who said that they wanted to meet more feminists and become friends with them. …I cannot help but get a little irked sometimes. As it is, it's hard to meet queer women.

This just adds to the confusion. The least they can do is make it all clear during the initial interactions, just so that they don't lead anyone on unintentionally. And this does not happen on OkCupid, since you have the option of not viewing straight profiles there.' On the whole, some dating apps aren't as LGBTQIA+ friendly as they'd like to portray themselves.

However, idealistic love isn't non-existent. There are numerous couples who are textbook examples of good romance, cherishing one another with care decade after decade. But, still, passionate love does elude most. Once the fairy-tale period of romantic gestures ends, love enters an uncharted territory. A place where women often wonder how to go on staying in love with their partners. Blame it on the influence of tech, fate, or our busy lives, for scores of women, love is a phantom to constantly seek and behold. Date nights, holidays, and quarantines are the only times when love becomes a living, breathing entity for countless millennial wives/girlfriends mired in mundane work and everyday living. This is all the more so for women with children. Knowing this full well and not ready for their honeymoon period to end, many women delay, or deny, having children—choosing fur babies instead.

Oh, and there's this other thing about love: falling out of it altogether. Unlike in the past, women today aren't afraid to end relationships. Indian society usually stigmatizes those who choose to leave their partners, prompting them to be buried under tons of guilt. 'Being able to own every emotion you feel is not the easiest thing in the world. It takes a brave heart to honour your own feelings, and shatter someone else's in the process,' writes Tracy Ann in an article for *iDiva*, asking women to forgive themselves for falling out of love with their long-time lovers. Meanwhile, women who choose to get divorces are speaking openly about it. Some bold ladies even announce the end of their marriage on their social media pages just as they do at the beginning.

What's Consent Got to Do With It?

'A large part of Indian society is still conservative and orthodox with regards to their opinions about intimacy and their concept of consent,' declares Ayushi Murli, a Mumbai-based content creator. 'The issue with most people who sexually abuse someone is that despite knowing the consequences, and knowing the seriousness of the crime, they still go out of their way to do it. Maybe this is a way to show power, maybe they've been through some trauma, but none of it justifies this behaviour.' In the wake of #MeToo, Murli had written an open letter to the man who sexually abused her, in which she emphasizes: 'we've also learned that we cannot rely on the world to change for us. So, we're ready to start doing it ourselves. Our safety is in our own hands now.' When I ask Murli why this is the right time for women to assert their power and take control, she replies: 'Like most things, the #MeToo movement was expected to die down soon after it arrived. However, [the] conversation about sexual abuse is still going on and hasn't entirely come to a halt. A large part of our nation has developed a new sensitivity and opened itself up to uncomfortable, but important conversation[s]. Women, provided we stand together, are at a point where we have more power in this situation than ever before.'

What's so different about #MeToo? The feminist movement has fought against rape and sexual violence for decades now.[13] How are the stories of young women who were unable to report their harassers (on legal time) going to change Indian society? Moreover, several #MeToo stories are about sexual encounters with ex-lovers, colleagues, and friends. Surely, these men should be given the benefit of the doubt? Because naming and shaming is more akin to taking revenge than seeking justice, as soon as the floodgates of #MeToo opened, so did the victim blaming. Women doubting women. Women criticizing women. (Older) feminists questioning (younger) feminists' motives:

---

[13]Through a thousand petitions and marches, not only has mainstream feminism demanded and changed the law to remedy sexual violence, it has also highlighted the blight of sexual violence that permeates every section of Indian society.

especially since #MeToo stories often came from a place of power and didn't go along the usual discourse around sexual violence. Ladies who shared their experiences online framed themselves as fearless survivors daring to speak. They didn't view themselves as victims in need of justice, and so, instead of empathy, #MeToo elicited a wide range of reactions: from apathy to outright odium. There's a reason #BelieveWomen dovetailed #MeToo.

'One morning, when I was home and he had been shooting all night, Nowaz[14] sent me a text saying he was near my building. I invited him over and asked him to come and have breakfast with me. When I opened the door, he grabbed me,' wrote former Miss India and actor Niharika Singh on social media relating her #MeToo experience with a celebrated actor. 'I tried to push him away but he wouldn't let go. After a little coercion, I finally gave in. I wasn't sure what to make of this relationship. He told me it was his dream to have a Miss India or an actress wife.' Singh dated him for a while but eventually broke up as she realized he was seeing several other women and even had a wife. So, what happens when a woman accuses her ex-lover of sexual repression and toxic male entitlement? People suspect her intentions. Actor Kubbra Sait questioned Singh's motivations: 'You can't pull a relationship out of its personal space for your own purpose. There is a man's reputation involved.'

In a country where marital rape is a myth, society inherently doubts women who accuse men they'd been romantically or sexually involved with earlier. The distrust deepens when accused men claim they had no idea that the accusing women felt that way, because they thought that the sexual encounter was all hunky-dory, pushing the situation into the territory of he said/she said. As journalist Anoo Bhuyan writes earnestly in 'Women Remember, Men Don't': 'For men, there seems to be no concept of mind, body, and soul when they are with a woman. There is just the concept of body.' Most of society doesn't even acknowledge or account for the fact that men

---

[14]Actor Nawazuddin Siddiqui.

and women lead different psychosexual lives.

'Women and men differ not only in their physical attributes, but also in their psychological makeups,' says Dr Mitali Soni Loya, a psychiatrist who runs the Vayam clinic for women in Bhopal. 'The brains of men and women have differences in the way they are structured and wired due to which the way they process information and react to events is different. This accounts for the difference in which they communicate, deal in relationships, express their feelings, and react to stress.' An assistant professor of psychiatry at PCMS&RC, Dr Loya notes that despite women's education and entry into the workforce, 'men still assume superiority over women and maintain it through domination. This has led to underestimating the role a woman plays in the dyad of human existence.' Talking about intimate partner violence, she tells me that women who are subjected to 'domestic violence like beating, rape, or coerced sex are much more likely to require psychiatric treatment and are much more likely to attempt suicide. Common mental health problems for these women include depression, anxiety, post-traumatic stress, insomnia, and alcohol use disorders.' She also notes that traumatized women often cut themselves 'to alleviate overwhelming negative emotions, for self-punishment or to produce a physical sign of emotional distress.' When women are unable to sort out their issues through discussion with their partners, she suggests that they 'take the help of professionals like psychiatrists or psychologists who can help the couple in sorting out their issues with the help of various psychotherapies like Cognitive Behavioural Therapy (CBT), marital counselling, or couples therapy.'

As #mentalhealthmatters and #mentalhealthawareness traverses India's social media, women are beginning to call out men who have emotionally and physically abused them. The idea that sexual abuse can range from verbal sexual harassment to rape is finally being talked about thanks to #MeToo. What years of litigation for rights, sensitization drives[15], and reports about the alarming sexual

---

[15]The Ministry of Women and Child Development has conducted several gender

violence in the country couldn't do, this hashtag has done. There is nuance in the conversation about consent now. And women are no longer willing to stand by and watch. They have begun to speak for themselves when they feel their dignity has been compromised. Call out men who emotionally betrayed them for sex. Moreover, they have started to determine the nature of the physical encounters they've had with men, even reinterpreting past sexual encounters to decode every instance when they were touched inappropriately or when they felt threatened by a man's sexual overtures.

'Consent becomes a little bit of a grey area,' actor Sayani Gupta explained at the India Today Conclave. 'The fact [is] that I could begin the act, [and] in the middle of the act I could change my mind.... Being informed and knowing that you have the right to say no and step away at any given point is something we should all talk about.' In a postfeminist world, where women feel entitled to fully perform their sexualities, consent can appear like shifting sands, because a woman may change her mind at any time about what she wants to do with her body. And this is precisely where all men (including woke ones) lose the plot. Patriarchal societies code into all minds that a female body which indulges in sexual behaviour is an object of male pleasure. So, once a female body triggers the male pleasure switch, it's not entitled to turn itself off. If it tries to, the encounter may very well end in violence. For trans women, consent becomes an ever more challenging concept to establish (even laws are skewed against them[16]).

Body politics, then, is at the centre of women's empowerment. We must have control over how our bodies are treated, especially in

---

sensitization programs across the country, as have NGOs. There are hundreds of case studies on the internet that report on the positive outcome of such drives.

[16]The Transgender Persons Bill does not offer much protection to trans women. 'If a trans woman is abused and harassed, the strictest punishment is that of two years and a fine of Rs 10,000. If a woman gets raped, the minimum penalty is much more. This increases the chances of us getting targeted even more,' observes Shakti with regards to the bill. 'We feel that we're second class citizens who have no value like a regular person.'

our most vulnerable moments. This includes times where we may have consensually entered a space filled with sexual tension, only to realize that the man involved in the situation is quickly escalating it without our explicit consent and even while we're figuring out whether we're physically and emotionally comfortable with what's happening, much more happens than it should. When one comes out of a sexual encounter feeling violated rather than elated, it becomes a matter of abuse. Does this then mean that people can never have spontaneous sex? Sexual tension will fizzle out if people were to have lengthy conversations about consent before even laying a finger on each other. That argument, in my opinion, is BS.

Consent can be had in the most exotic of sexual encounters. As Shreya Ila Anasuya writes: 'One of the most common misconceptions about kink, and especially about BDSM, is that it's about making people do things against their will.... The Kinky Collective, an Indian group that tries to demystify kink, states on its blog, "Consent is at the heart of BDSM. It is not presumed, but actively negotiated, and can be withdrawn at any time, instantly and unconditionally."' Anasuya, who writes beautifully about exploring sexuality and what it means for contemporary society, ends the piece on a rather philosophical note: 'In a world that privileges violence over pleasure...the possibility that we are all on a continuum of sexuality, standing only some distance from one another' may seem dangerous. But if we accept our sexuality, 'there will be no more perverts, no more deviants; just people who reach out with both hands for their desires. And maybe this is among the most radical possibilities of them all.'

Our society does not like to talk about pleasure. It fears what might happen if it admits to its animalistic sexual tendencies. Perhaps it will become a carnal civilization wasting all its time indulging in bodily sin rather than focusing on high culture? But by making pleasure taboo, society has made consent non-existent. Men pounce on every opportunity to satisfy their bodily desire with or without the explicit consent of the woman in front of them (desperately, if I may say so). Sex has become a secret obsession in Indian culture riddled with guilt. Our curse words all stem from sexual adjectives. We simultaneously crave and abhor sex. We have become a perverse race that tries to deny its inherently erotic nature.

'I think the problem is that the way sex has been defined, it's always something for men to take,' suggests seasoned activist Bishaka Datta, who has constantly pushed the envelope in the national conversation about sexuality and promoted new thinking about women's rights in the age of digital media. 'In a gender equal society everybody would have sexual capital. It would be like a different form of currency. But in today's world, because of sexism, somehow sex is seen as something that women withhold and just give on certain conditions,' she says. The co-founder of Point of View (POV)[17], a non-profit platform that amplifies the voices of women working at the intersection of the internet, digital technologies, sexual expression, and identity, Datta talks about how all women use their sexual capital: 'Often you see in a relationship, when a woman might want something, say from her male partner, she might feel that the best way to get it is actually just to flirt with him a little bit. That's also using your sexual capital.' When I ask her why Indian society doesn't understand consent, she says: 'It's to do with stereotypes. Because if you dress a certain way, say in an office, it's assumed that you're available for the taking. So, there's that kind of assumption that you've dressed not to please yourself, but to put it out there that you're available. That's a complete misreading and very misogynistic.... The code is in the male gaze, where they make a gendered superficial assessment.'

Sex is under all our skins. We are corporeal creatures at the end of the day. And naturally, we all possess some form of sexual capital. Irrespective of whether a woman is modern or conservative, she is bound to use her sexual capital. In marriage and outside of it,

---

[17]POV has spearheaded several programs where women's point of view is at the centre. It has put forward the realities of sex workers in their own words, organized conferences on sexual expression, porn, and consent, published several important papers and reports, and made videos. More about their work can be found at www.pointofview.org.

women constantly trade in it. This may manifest itself in the form of harmless flirting or consciously leading one on in a game of sexual power play, and sometimes, even going all the way and sleeping with someone to get the job done. Now, a woman who does these things doesn't sound like an angel, and she most likely is not. But, because she chooses to trade with her sexuality, does it mean that she should relinquish control over her body in the process? Does this mean that at any point her body can be exploited without her explicit consent?

Actor Sri Reddy's protest of sexual exploitation by the film industry makes us tackle this complicated question. She highlighted the fact that several upcoming actresses are forced to sleep with influential producers, directors, and actors, with the promise that they'd be given leading roles. However, after sex, they are denied lead roles. When the affected actresses protest, they are told they are owed nothing as they willingly indulged in the sexual act. In such a scenario, where a woman goes through a sexual act in what may seem like her private life, only for the sake of her professional life, consent becomes a fuzzy phenomenon. The manner in which Sri Reddy protested is also something to take note of. She stripped outside the producer's association, as though to say: isn't this what you wanted to see? So, see it. Not only for the men, but also for judgemental women to see. Had she merely spoken about the evils of casting couches, not many would have printed her words in their newspapers, or made interviews to air (because she accused many big names of exploiting her). But by bravely[18] doing what she did, she got all eyes on her, and then everyone was all ears.

'Patriarchal hook-up culture treats consent like a game, something to be secured so that *technically* what follows isn't rape,' writes art and culture critic Kamayani Sharma. 'Many of the narratives that have emerged during #MeToo have revealed the hollowness of the

---

[18]Fun fact: feminists call body protests auto-sexualization or femmenism, because the protestor is reproducing patriarchal norms, albeit on their own terms.

distinction between illegal rape and unethical sex. There is value in making these distinctions because then we can arrive at some consensus about what a feminist theory of sex constitutes, one that is premised on care along with consent.' For sex-positive cis-het and trans women interested in men, sexual liberation is not easy to achieve unless their sexual partners are on the same page as them with regard to consent. Unfortunately, most men don't understand subtle boundaries. The very idea that a woman who is sexually liberal does not automatically renege on her dignity or her emotions is lost on Indian men. Be they clad in saffron robes, handloom kurtas, or dapper suits, their minds neatly divide women into those they could potentially start a family with (marked as sexually virtuous and safe for childbearing), while all others are libidinal vamps. I mean, how will any worthy man accept a non-virginal woman? You know, in India it's so easy to get a *reputation*. Sleep with one guy and everyone else thinks you're easy. Mind you, this isn't to do only with marriages. Honestly. How many guys want to seriously date a girl who's sexually experienced?

Ironically enough, it's not only men who have qualms with women who sleep around, so do many women's libbers. Remember the viral video *My Choice*[19]? Many feminists were aghast that it endorsed infidelity as sexual empowerment. And alongside their conservative (sanskari) brethren, they criticized the video and forced actor Deepika Padukone to dissociate herself from the script. This is in line with feminist tradition. As Professor Shubha Tiwari puts it: '[i]n India, feminism is and has to be welfare-oriented. A woman's right to drink wine is less important than her right to drink clean water. Her right to be in multiple relationships is less important than her right to say "No" to a relationship. Here, domestic violence, dowry, forced

---

[19]Released by *Vogue India*, as part of its empower women campaign, this video featured actor Deepika Padukone and made various anodyne statements, but also included slightly more daring ones: 'My choice, to marry or not marry, to have sex before marriage, to have sex outside of marriage'. Oh, how could director Homi Adjania assume all feminists were okay with infidelity?

marriages, dropping out of schools and colleges are the [real] issues.'

Can we not seek sexual freedom and justice for all women without denigrating each other? Unless we do this, we're setting ourselves up to uphold one person's rights while punishing another. Take the matter of sexual and reproductive freedom, for instance. Even while it may seem like all's well on paper, in praxis, there are a thousand problems involved. Laws drafted to protect adolescents from forced marriage or coercive sex can often work against those who are sexually liberal. 'The conflict of the Protection of Children from Sexual Offences Act (POCSO) 2012 and the Medical Termination of Pregnancy (MTP) Act 1972 is making doctors hesitant to provide services to girls under the age of 18 due to fear of prosecution, and teenaged girls apprehensive of seeking abortion services from legal providers, in turn, forcing them to seek unsafe abortion measures.' While it's not illegal to get an abortion in India, it isn't exactly easy. Especially if one is underage. In fact, all pregnant minors are considered rape survivors according to the POCSO Act—which means naïve boyfriends may be arrested for accidentally impregnating their girlfriends. Sexual freedom, then, is a double-edged sword in India.

For adult unmarried women, meanwhile, getting an abortion entails dealing with the supercilious judgement of healthcare professionals. Since pregnancy is considered a sacred rite of passage for women inside the institution of marriage, choosing to end pregnancies is no easy matter for married women either. Add to this the fact that in most cases, women bear the brunt of ending unplanned pregnancies. In fact, 95 per cent of Indian men don't like to use condoms, taking women's bodies for granted. Consent to have sex must then always be followed up with a discussion about contraceptives and possible pregnancies—whether one is married or not.

The Erotic Female Body (and Mind)
'Women need to take ownership of their pleasure,' asserts Priyanka Manikeri. 'If a man can tell you what he wants you to do to him, you bloody well have every right to direct him to your pleasure spots.

Men like direction, by the way, even if they don't like it while driving.' Co-founder of NODE workshops and a luxury brand manager[20], Manikeri is not a big believer in monogamy or the institution of marriage. A born and bred Mumbaikar, now living in Toronto, she lives by her own rules. 'I faked orgasms for a very long time,' she reveals. 'Even though I thoroughly enjoyed the sex, I just assumed this is what it was. I didn't even know the female orgasm existed in the first few years of my sexual life. Back then I felt very shy, embarrassed even, to show a partner how I could climax. Vaginal orgasms are so mainstream that so many men have no clue that there are women who are capable of multiple clitoral orgasms!' Never one to shy away from an honest conversation about sexuality, Priyanka has this to say: 'Please do not accept labels like slut, slag, or whatever the hell else people think up. If you have had 200 sexual partners, own it. No need to brag but it's a part of you. You've given yourself to someone and someone has given themselves to you. Sex is so much about vulnerability and accountability—we take these amazing experiences too casually.'

The fact that many women have the same sexual anatomy doesn't mean that their erogenous zones will be aligned too. Twenty-first-century men are as clueless as ever about women's bodies.[21] Can't blame them completely, for they've mainly been exposed to porn (created for a male audience) that reveres the timeless doggy-style, unctuous gang-bang, and of course, every man's secret fantasy: to have a woman on top. This is not to say that women don't enjoy partaking in sexual positions that are BDSM, where both sexual partners alternately play dominant and submissive. Sex, after all, is about shifting power dynamics and androgyny. The point I'm trying to make here is that most men end up simply replicating what they see done by one porn star to another, instead of fully delving into the individuality of the female body in front of them.

[20]Manikeri has been instrumental in the regional expansion of La Perla, Nirav Modi Jewels, Jimmy Choo, and Salvatore Ferragamo across India and Southeast Asia.
[21]Terms like periods, vaginal dryness, and female orgasms are like Latin.

I don't know if you've heard, but sex can get pretty monotonous with the same partner (especially with one who isn't interested in improvising).

'The women of Avanti hate kissing, marking with the nails, and biting, but they have a fondness for various kinds of sexual union,' reads the *Kama Sutra*. 'The women of Abhira, and those of the country about the Indus and five rivers (that is, the Punjab), are gained over by the Auparishtaka, or mouth congress.... The women of the Andhra country have tender bodies; they are fond of enjoyment, and have a liking for voluptuous pleasures.' These descriptions might appear stereotypical to us, but at least, men were told to please different women differently, and not expect a monolithic sexual response from all womankind. Honestly, this is more information about female bodies than contemporary sex education offers. Today's sex education hardly teaches women how to build their sexual capacities. At all levels, it only talks of the female body as one that is likely to bleed and bear children, downplaying the act of sex as a mere necessity to conceive (obviously there is no talk of anything beyond the heteronormative), while simultaneously freaking everyone out about the perils of sex: STD and pregnancy. There is no talk of desire or seduction or the clitoris.

Today, however, sex-positive ladies aren't taking things lying down. As active, pleasure-seeking sexual agents, they turn the tables. They now assert their hyper-individual sexualities. Declare that their female bodies don't exist to serve a single man's desire or bolster his fragile male ego. While this doesn't mean they don't want love no more, it does mean that they aren't averse to seeking sexual intimacy outside the norm. While infidelity and polyamory are definite possibilities, at the moment I'm thinking about masturbation. 'This practice, extraordinarily rich and inventive [is]...a veritable aesthetic activity, each stage of rapture inscribing a resonant vision, a composition, something beautiful. Beauty will no longer be forbidden,' writes philosopher Hélène Cixous. She holds that a systemic experimentation with the body will lead us to discover its erotogeneity. Of course, an adult woman seeking pleasure in her body will be shamed for her selfish, slutty, and disgusting desire[22]. Society views masturbation as a side-effect of desperation or an indicator of wantonness. But it is much more than a preliminary interlude to intercourse. A woman's inner sensuality is an intimate space where her fantasies and desires reside. By the act of touching herself, she can connect with her inner self, her soul.

'Self-love is important because my body and mind are the only things I really own,' Aratika Das tells *Homegrown* magazine. We 'have extremely complex relationships with our vaginas, since there's just soooo much going on down there', notes Disha in the same article, 'There's masturbation through direct clitoral stimulation, through penetration, through the G-spot...then there's combinations of these three. Then there's the whole multiple orgasms thing. And not to forget, before any of this, there's this hymen tearing stuff that can seem pretty terrifying. Oh, and we also bleed once a month.' Every woman, it would seem, has a unique relationship with her body. The 'notion of self-pleasure for women has become a beacon for sex-positive feminists all over the world,' remarks the co-founder of *Homegrown*, Mandovi Menon, who also wrote the piece.

Talking about masturbation, we must also talk about sex toys, sensual music, erotic literature, and porn—that which inspires new feelings, a tingle under the skin, or an arousal marked by wetness (women get turned on by porn, sexy music, and dirty words too). While successive Indian governments (from the left, right, and centre) banned several porn sites citing indecency and generations of mainstream feminists fought against the obscene representation of the female body, thousands of (libertine) women have relished that sort of dirty content in the past, as they do now. Nevertheless, anti-

---

[22]Watch Netflix's *Lust Stories* for a hilarious take on what happens when society finds out that you're masturbating. Megha (who marries a groom with climaxing issues, leaving her high and dry in bed) uses a vibrator to pleasure herself. All hell breaks loose in her joint family when she accidentally orgasms in front of them. There are perils for horny ladies living within Indian households where privacy and personal space are considered a luxury.

porn governments and feminists collude still to establish laws against obscenity, because they believe that hyper-sexualized and pornified depictions of women in mass media will lead to more sexual violence. How can one think depriving Indian men of porn (watching which they can do their business in private) will make the situation any better? With no outlets to relieve those blue balls, men will only get more desperate, not less. And as for the women themselves: watching porn isn't some self-deprecating activity.

'Porn can also turn upside down notions that we hold about ourselves…. Particularly disturbing is being turned on by fantasies involving humiliation, extreme objectification, coercion, or rape,' writes researcher Jaya Sharma for TARSHI. She suggests that when something is prohibited, it becomes erotic, a contradiction we should tackle head-on. 'Might this discomfort also be a productive place to be, one in which we can see that we are not as rational as we would like to believe we are? In keeping with the feminist mantra "the personal is political", might there be an invitation here to connect with the messiness of our desires?'

Porn isn't always made to cater to a male point of view—there is sexy stuff out there that depicts pleasure for all parties involved.[23] All in all, I'd say that porn is quintessential for social well-being: for people to turn to, to turn themselves on, for sexual inspiration. While hardcore porn is best-suited for those seeking better positions for hot, steamy sex, soft porn invites women to caress themselves— to find the spots that give them unbearable pleasure. In any case, feminism proper isn't entirely convinced about the use of porn in promoting women's empowerment, but it has largely accepted that

---

[23]'Back when I first came across shemales on *Sex.com*, I didn't differentiate between porn made for men and porn made for women. *Sex.com* featured almost exclusively the former, but that didn't get in the way of my enjoyment or late-night arousal,' writes Nadika Nadja in *Deep Dives* (an online publication that publishes longform narratives on big data, gender, sexuality, and bodies). 'But now, on *Crash Pad Series*, the porn I was watching showed me, perhaps for the first time, that pleasure could be experienced by *all* the people featured in a porn video—not just the guys.'

women's desire must not be repressed by society. Even so, it prefers to use the term erotica as opposed to porn. Obviously, porn is too raw for people with apparently refined sensibilities to promote. Erotica, meanwhile, is more artsy.[24]

This tendency to desexualize the erotic female body to make her respectable extends well beyond visual contraband and reaches all the way down to real women. As patriarchy has eroticized the female body for eons, many feminists feel that to erase the male gaze, we must desexualize ourselves entirely. Create a vision of womankind in the public imagination that is devoid of any sexual underpinnings. It seems like an ingenious approach to take, but isn't as simple as it sounds. How do you rip away sexuality from a woman's body? Whether she's performing femininity or masculinity or both, her sexuality is often apparent in the way she dresses, talks, and thinks. As long as we exist as women, we will be perceived as such. While it makes little sense to expect men to look at us without sex in their eyes (after all, like us, they're sexual creatures too), it's crucial that we fight for a society where men learn to respect a woman's body in spite of being turned on by it. Not touch a woman's body without her consent. Not proposition her in professional settings. Not gawk like an idiot. To be gentlemen.

For women from certain intersections of society, sexualization is not just based on their sex. It is also based on race, creed, and caste. Old prejudices are freely mapped onto contemporary women's bodies. 'Over the past few years, I have not only been sexualized as a woman, but as a woman from the Northeast,' reveals Samcha Lowang, a research scholar from Arunachal Pradesh. 'Apparently, there are nuances to being sexualized depending on your physical features.

---

[24]Author of *Cyber Sexy: Rethinking Pornography*, Richa Kaul Padte elaborates: feminists believe '[e]rotica has artistic and literary value, it can be beautiful and poignant and important for sexuality and society. Porn, on the other hand, cannot. The trouble with making this distinction, though, is that we replicate the very moral universe against which we are fighting.... It's easier to defend sexuality than it is to defend doggy-style, just like it's easier to defend erotica than it is to defend hardcore porn.'

When I went looking for flats in Delhi, I remember being gawked at by the landlords, and the landladies resenting us for their other half's behaviour. I was faced with questions like "Are you going to bring men?" and "Do you have any African friend?".' Women from the Northeast are regarded as sexy and erotic, the subtext being they're also sexually libertine. As a result, a large section of the Indian population fetishizes their bodies. Believe it or not, there are Quora threads and multiple listicles online that enumerate the benefits of dating women from the region. Some of the common benefits apparently include: '[y]ou don't have to worry about your girlfriend becoming fat. She believes in staying slim and fit' and Northeastern women 'LOVE having a great time…they know how to satisfy their men.'

DBA women's bodies, meanwhile, are simultaneously marked as erotic and tainted, even today. Bharat's casteist men still feel entitled to their bodies—after all, the *Manusmriti* ordains the rape and assault of Avarnas, and why change what works? Sexual violence and harassment are disproportionally experienced by DBA women in India. In such a scenario, most DBA feminists focus on the victimization of their women and radically desexualize DBA women's bodies. But DBA women are women too. Desiring women, women who're desired. As women from historically marginalized communities enter the urban space, how do they end the devaluation of their bodies and pursue lives as equals—when society is still stuck in the past?

'We should talk more about the personal—political, romantic, and sexual lives of Dalits and Dalit queers,' Ekta Sonawane, an activist currently pursuing her master's in gender studies at Delhi's Ambedkar University, tells me. 'Being a queer Dalit woman from a working-class background, it's really difficult to survive in these academic spaces.' She says jibes are routinely made about reservation, and Dalits are prodded to prove their worth. Seemingly liberal spaces in India are still casteist, she notes. 'There are indirect forms of oppression. It's not always about caste, it's about the caste–class intersection too.' When it comes to dating, Sonawane points out that these factors become strong influencers. 'I have a friend who is still single and a virgin. I asked him to try some dating app, but he said "it's not meant for us but for the monied". Should I suggest to him that he date somebody from the same caste/class? Is that the solution? No.' She has had the same experience as her friend. 'Actually, we don't know all the shitty etiquettes; we have our own basti culture which doesn't fit into their criteria. So, they are fine sleeping with us [but won't date us].'

Dalit women are increasingly asserting their rights and reclaiming their sexuality. Obviously, our casteist society is petrified by such outright rebellion—especially since Dalit women brazenly flout established gender norms that are sanctified by Brahmanical patriarchy. 'It is right that they think that Dalit and female bodies are dangerous, it is those bodies that have the power to demystify the caste system,' theologian Evangeline Anderson-Rajakumar once said. This fear of the Dalit woman not only exists in the political sphere, but also presents itself in the personal. Being an inter-caste woman, I've experienced the subtle bigotry that exists in the urban dating scene. Most Indian men are inevitably mired in their caste, irrespective of how liberal they are. I've always been viewed as attractive, but also been considered impure because of my Dalit ancestry. I've deliberately had to parse apart desire from bigotry in my romantic partners' eyes. Which part of my identity are you fetishizing, what part of me are you most afraid of?

Sexual desire is universal. It is meant to cut across all barriers. And it often does, bringing together people who are vastly different. But when relationships end and we are left to examine why, conflicts arise. For those of us with forbidden identities, the reason is often believed to be our blood. Since certain identities are indelible in India, it is hard to forget who you are as you fall in love with someone who is *not*. This makes us build walls around ourselves, to protect us from the vulnerabilities of falling in love, of desire. But then, isn't vulnerability an inherent part of the sexual experience?

'Can someone whose neck barely moves have lips that draw

passion? Can someone who needs support moving a single inch charm with her wit? Can someone whose fingers are stiff still flirt with her eyes and words?' storyteller and entrepreneur Soumita Basu pointedly asks in 'Can we ever have a conversation about desire without centring my disability?'[25]. 'Can someone with a "weak" body, a very "different" body, a disabled body still be desirable? I have frazzled many—confronting me; they have had to confront these questions.'

Since time immemorial, Indian society has only exemplified (and sexualized) neurotypical, able-bodied women with symmetric figures and perfect features in its art, literature, and cinema, not recognizing that almost all women (excepting ace women) seek sexual pleasure in their lives. It has viewed differently-abled women through the lens of sympathy; neurodivergent women through a frame of fear; and has never taken cognizance of the fact that their female bodies are just as sexual as any other. But times are changing. In the age of the internet, women with disabilities are speaking for themselves. They aren't waiting around for pop culture to destigmatize their stories (which in all likelihood won't do justice to lived realities) or creepily eroticize their bodies. On several online platforms, these women's bold voices confront cultural prejudices and clichés, articulating a much-needed critique of India's ableist culture.

The patriarchy has one main agenda with the erotic female body, after all. To impregnate it and prolong its pure bloodlines. This means that every woman who isn't high-born or physically 'perfect' is disqualified and her desires disregarded. On the other hand, however, this doesn't mean that women who do qualify for the honour of institutionalized motherhood are respected and their desires celebrated. During the course of a woman's pregnancy, her body may be allowed some respite from having to be erotic (unless, of course, her husband finds her protruding belly sexy). But just as this is so, young mothers are expected to bounce back into sex

---

[25]For *Skin Stories*, an online publication that features perspectives on disability, sexuality, and gender, several women wrote candidly about their sexual experiences.

as soon as they have children (or their husbands will stray, they're told). Sometimes, women are given the 'husband stitch' right after delivering a baby to tighten their vaginal opening (for the increased pleasure of their husbands, hence the name) without their express consent, as a result of which, they suffer excruciating pain during post-partum intercourse. Never mind that for most new mothers, their children often occupy all physical and emotional space during the early years, giving little space for sexual thoughts.

'After I gave birth to my daughter, I wasn't interested in sex for more than two years,' says Jas Kaur[26], a designer from Chandigarh. 'I was going through post-partum depression and was coming to terms with how my body was changing.' During this period, Kaur exclaims that she and her husband had many bad rows. 'Without physical intimacy, our relationship became very strained. On top of that we had to deal with being new parents.' Eventually, however, she did begin to feel sexual again. 'We're now sort of rediscovering each other.'

This brings me to the antipodal state of the erotic female body. Its disinterest in sex. For some women, asexuality is a permanent state of mind and body. While the demisexual or grey-a may choose to have sex once in a while, sex-negative women may not want to have sex ever, their idea of desire and intimacy being entirely different. Now, even for women who are sexual, there's no obligation that they must be interested in sex or even think sexually 24/7. It's a woman's choice to be sexual or asexual, for a day's time or a lifetime. In fact, in a society that has sexually objectified women for centuries, the fight for women's sexual liberation may be easier to win when we say women should be free to have as much sex as they like. The real struggle is when we say that women won't have sex when they don't like. Apart from asexuality, women have multiple other reasons why they don't want to have sex: pregnancy, post-partum anxieties, or when they discover they have sexual disorders like vaginismus and

---

[26]Name changed to hide identity.

dyspareunia[27]. Also, sometimes, all a woman really wants is to have a long bath or masturbate, but I suppose a female body that's not interested in sex is beyond patriarchy's schemata.

Kinky is Queer[28]

What is it to be a woman? Is it to do with identifying the body as feminine or being born with female genitalia? In a gender essentialist culture, every woman thinks about this at one point or another in her/zir[29]/their life. Woman 'itself is a term in process, a becoming, a constructing that rightfully cannot be said to originate or to end. As an ongoing discursive practice, it is open to intervention and resignification', emphasizes queer philosopher Judith Butler. This is true for all women. We rediscover ourselves every day and continuously transform—sexually, morally, and intellectually. The moment we stop doing this, or when society tries to stop us from changing, and we get trapped in a particular role or an identity forever, our liberty ends. True sexual freedom is one where we can redefine the boundaries of our bodies as and when we like.

'I'm not sure if this is a phase, or if I am truly bisexual, and I'm okay with that,' writes Shruti B. in 'Lessons in Self-Exploration'. '[U]nderstanding my sexual identity shouldn't have to come with a deadline. I am still exploring.' Jamal Siddiqui writes in '5 Things To Know About Dating Trans Men in India': As a 'queer demisexual trans man in India, my experiences of love and romance have been quite a journey. I have tried kink, I have been on online dating forums, and my love life has seen a lot....' More and more young Indians

---

[27]Vaginismus and dyspareunia are conditions where people experience pain during penetrative vaginal intercourse.

[28]Many people may disagree with this phrase—because they say straight people who are kinky can't take pride in being queer. In my opinion, the LGBTQIA+ movement should open its borders to include any and everyone who enjoys exploring their sexuality beyond socially sanctified heteronormativity. The idea is for society to become sexually liberal as a whole, right? Or are we now going to exclude those who aren't queer enough?

[29]Is a gender-neutral pronoun used by people who identify themselves outside the gender binary. Zie in the place of she/he; zir in the place of her/him.

are increasingly talking about their sexual experiences online, often through first-person narratives, and discussing how they discovered their sexualities (from cis femme to butch queer to transfeminine to genderfluid, and beyond). Now, the beauty about these first-person narratives is that they talk about sexuality in a nuanced manner—where sex appears alongside love and everyday life. Contradictions and confusions aren't ignored. These narratives break social taboos more effectively than any third-party account, which is likely to sympathize or judge. Exploring and discovering one's sexuality is a matter of pride. Only when people tell their stories in their own words will that sentiment shine through.

While women's studies have transformed into gender studies[30] in academic discourse to note the plurality of gender, sex and sexuality still remain at the margins of feminist thought. Queer/lesbian/bisexual/trans feminist writing hasn't flourished in India, even though the LGBTQIA+ movement has grown. One of the primary reasons for this is that often these sexualities are written about from a bland analytical or policy point of view, by heteronormative academics/activists/writers who primarily talk in terms of victimization. This is not to diminish the solidarity that cis-het feminism has shown the LGBTQIA+ community, fighting to decriminalize homosexuality and now asking for marriage/parenting rights. But I, as a bisexual[31] woman myself, have often wondered why feminism doesn't use daring language when talking about gender and sexuality. Because sexuality cannot be theorized or depicted without also indulging the explicit sexual acts that constitute it. Any talk about sexuality has to be raw, real, and powerful to make a lasting difference. Of course, there are some feminist platforms on the world wide web, where sexuality

---

[30]Drawing from philosopher Judith Butler's gender theory which postulates that we're all entitled to pursue masculine or feminine tendencies irrespective of the sex we're born into.
[31]I define bisexuality as the propensity to be attracted to both masculinity and femininity. Gender is immaterial here as a bisexual person may be attracted to an alpha man or a queer woman with a strong masculine side, or a straight man with a submissive streak, or a femme lesbian woman. All in all, my version of bisexuality is queer.

and gender are explored freely. However, only those in the know are aware of these exquisite online spaces. For everyone else, there's the more anesthetized 'right to sexuality'. The English word *sex* is a dirty word, as we all know. And it isn't that much of a surprise that postcolonial discourse about gender hasn't effectively rescued sexuality from the clutches of Victorian morality. I mean, how can prude English pedantry talk about sex for what it really is?

'Sex is empowerment, sex is gendered behaviour, sex is violence, sex is politics, but sex is so rarely, so infrequently, sex,' writes Paromita Vohra, creative director at Agents of Ishq. 'We talk about all the things that can go wrong, but we never talk about the things that can go right. Now if you don't know what going right looks like, if you don't know what consent looks like, if you don't understand that pleasure is a part of sex, how will you be able to act it out?' asks Vohra in an interview, and points out that even though we talk about sex, the only sex we really see is pornographic sex. 'In actuality we should have numerous accounts of sex in any culture—lived sexualness has to be part of our understanding of sex…. And this taboo on talking about sex as sex can be found across the [socio-political] spectrum. It is not about being right-wing or left-wing. Even those who advocate for a kind of liberated attitude towards sex will often speak about abstract concepts, and not talk about actual sex.'

In fact, academically vilified women's magazines are the first to have brought Indian women back in touch with their sexuality. True, the glamorous models who appeared alongside the content were perfectly manicured, but that doesn't negate the fact that these magazines spoke more plainly about sex and gave women tips that they could use in their sex lives. From reinventing the art of seduction for everyday life to guiding women to find their G-spots, women's magazines promote more feminist ideas than we give them credit for. They teach you not to suck his dick first, but to look him in the eye and kiss him. Own him. But then, magazines cross the line of good feministing when they promote corrective cosmetic surgeries to get better orgasms. Heard of G-spot enhancement? Anything for better sex, ladies. Don't ask, don't tell, and, most importantly, don't judge.

Ironically, it would seem that ancient and medieval India were kinky times compared to the present. One only needs to take a look at the carvings on the thirteenth-century Konark Sun Temple or sexy eighteenth-century Mughal miniature paintings to confirm this. Let's also not forget that tantric sex originated in this subcontinent around the first millennium CE. So, what happened? We can't really peg the blame on any particular historical moment, as neoconservative cultural moorings develop over long swathes of time. But we can definitely blame the British a little bit, for influencing us with their sexual prudishness. In fact, Section 377 is a colonial-era law introduced in 1864, which India decriminalized as late as 2018. Talk about colonial hangovers.[32]

'Sex is gender bending,' says Monisha R., a business analyst from Chennai. 'It can sometimes make us forget the sex we are born into.' A married mother of two, Monisha points out that women from all sections of society experiment with sex. 'I know many single and married women who knowingly push the boundaries of pleasure in bed. Experimenting with kink is quite common these days. We can now buy a lot of sex toys online which eliminates the embarrassment in trying to access these things in shops. Of course, everyone is not going to talk about this stuff on Facebook or at parties. For most people these are private affairs meant to be experienced in their bedroom. This doesn't mean they are boring in bed or have conventional sex.'

Being conservative or modern, feminist or postfeminist, doesn't determine what women do under the sheets. Who's dominant, who's submissive, who can tell? Desire is quirky, it takes many different forms. There's much more to sex than simple penetration. Ladies are exploring fetishism and BDSM with their partners, finding that even heteronormative sex doesn't have to be all that vanilla. Sexual

---

[32]Read Ruth Vanita's book *Queering India*, or Madhavi Menon's *Infinite Variety: A History of Desire in India*, for a fascinating account of precolonial notions of sexuality that were fluid and non-restrictive.

ambiguity is what makes sex sexy; and this is why kinkiness stands on the pedestal of sexual liberation. Women are rediscovering every passing day that possessing a female body or consciousness doesn't limit them from experiencing sex from a position of power. They interchangeably play dominant and submissive roles (sometimes with several partners; some couples even swing). They embrace the subversive nature of sex play and find new tools of pleasure. In fact, men crave to experience submissive sex much more than they let on. Perhaps they inherently fear that their wives/girlfriends might extend the idea of domination beyond the bedroom.

In any case, whether men like it or not, urban young women are living out their desires. This is the time of Sexcams and Dirtyroulette, where people from around the world watch one another have sex, live, while having sex themselves. It's like live porn, except, those we are watching are not porn stars, but real and horny people (like us). Then there're subreddit sites like R/IndiansGoneWild, where women upload nude images of their bodies for kinky pleasure. Female desire, for all practical purposes, is not a secret any more.

The age of female innocence has ended. The Mahabharata warns that women become 'corrupt and deceitful, and lasciviously fornicate with slaves.... They are aggressive and rude of tongue (krūravādinayh), easily unsettled emotionally, and are disobedient to their husbands... in Kaliyuga.' Well, we've all started questioning masculine authority and patriarchal social rules. I suppose the Kaliyuga has begun. And the more we women indulge in unbridled desire, the more we see, plain and simple, that in sex, all genders can bend, no matter what one's class, caste, or community. Of course, the patriarchy is petrified by the idea of women thinking about desire. What if women make love with men outside their clan or caste (or within the same gotra)? Now imagine how much more alarmed India's male-dominated society must be when women want to sex up other women. For dominant masculinity's primary task is to protect women from other dominant males, but what is it to do when women seek women? What happens when we all start questioning the boundaries of our queer bodies?

Lesbian and trans love especially confounds the patriarchy.

If it isn't violently coming in the way of queer love, the patriarchy tries to muffle all hints of queer sex in public spaces. Even though Section 377 has been struck down, excessive (queer) PDA is considered an offence in our country. Even while lesbian porn (made for a male audience) and tips (for homosexuals) about preventing HIV are freely available in India, there aren't many desi magazines or sites giving us tips for better queer sex. In a homophobic country that's just now coming to terms with the idea of queer love, where women have to resort to litigation to live with their same-sex lovers[33], talking about gay sex is taboo for the most part, if not entirely forbidden[34]. In mainstream media, meanwhile, LGBTQIA+ issues are often confined to Pride month or 'Ask the Expert' sections (where folks wonder whether all lesbians wear dildo harnesses or if they like to go full femme), instead of being part of Love & Sex in perpetuity. Where are all the full-length articles and videos about how to pleasure your lady lover, or how anal sex can be an equalizer in any sexual relationship?

'I think homosexuals and bisexuals are not uncommon but they are only hiding,' writes Sneha Sharma on a Quora thread 'What is it like to be a lesbian in India.' If we all came out, Sharma points out, 'then I can guarantee you that proportions of LGBT and straight people will not differ as many assume. There are many who live a very pretentious life.' I feel she has hit the nail on the head. Because we are all a little queer here. Not everyone explores this side of themselves—be it due to their own fear of the unknown or societal influence. A large proportion of homosexual men and women reluctantly enter into heterosexual relationships/marriages in order to conform to social moorings. But in the long run, suppression of one's sexuality leads to mental illnesses and poses a threat to one's sexual

---

[33]Recently in Kerala, the High Court ruled in favour of a lesbian couple who wanted to live together.

[34]Even the much talked about lesbian Bollywood romcom, *Ek Ladki Ko Dekha Toh Aisa Laga,* hardly sexualized the lesbian couple! The makers responded to this criticism saying that sexualizing would not help mainstream it.

health. Some such mismatches can even result in intimate partner violence. Only when we all open up our minds and bodies to the rainbow of sexual possibilities, can we ensure a life for ourselves in which we thrive. Moreover, only when this happens will gender equality become a lived reality.

Unlike much of feminism proper, where sexual rights are one among the many it seeks, in postfeminism, sexuality is quintessential. Mainstream feminism is not convinced that sexual liberation will help the ultimate feminist cause; and many secretly believe that women who are free to sleep around aren't truly empowered as they're unconsciously extending male privilege, if anything. Phallic ladies, to them, may as well be a myth. They support the LGBTQIA+ community because, like them, they're victims of the patriarchy. It's got little to do with pride.[35]

To fully liberate our female bodies from generations of sexual subjugation and conditioning, we must own our sexualities. If feminism in twenty-first-century urban India isn't about women's sexuality and sexual rights, then what is it about? If you say feminism's primarily about human rights, then it should be called human rights (a very noble pursuit, no doubt). Feminism—which sprung out of the fact that our gendered bodies aren't equal in a man's world—must now take the next bold step to fulfil its own grand agenda (instead of eternally performing allyship). To subvert the patriarchy altogether, we must queer feminism from the inside and out. We must, each one of us, own our sexualities in private, as well as in public.

Postfeminism is popularly criticized for reinforcing normative gender stereotypes, as it advocates that women pursue feminine pleasures whether they be socially conditioned or inherent, and reframe their traditional roles by positively acknowledging their choices. However, it is imperative to note that postfeminism is also

---

[35]According to a blog of Delhi Queer Pride: 'Queer Pride is about celebrating who we are, whether gay, kothi, lesbian, queer, dyke, transgender, bisexual, hijra, butch, panthi …whether sex worker or sex changer, Queer Pride affirms our diverse expressions and our everyday struggle for respect and dignity.'

about exploring a woman's masculine tendencies, or a man's feminine tendencies, or a gender-fluid person's sexual propensities, and so is quite open to interpretation. In fact, postfeminism is gender bending.

Mainstream feminists often argue that gender is a social construct (via Western queer theory), that we are socialized into believing we're a woman or a man. Taking the viewpoint that biology and culture are interrelated, they claim that by forcing women to perform certain roles in society for eons, their minds have been moulded a certain way—so maleness and femaleness aren't biological realities, they're genders manufactured by society. Biological essentialism is problematic for feminism and for gender theorists—because 'by admitting that there is a "natural" division between women and men, we naturalize history, we assume that "men" and "women" have always existed and will always exist. Not only do we naturalize history, but also consequently we naturalize the social phenomena which express our oppression, making change impossible.'

I would like to take a slightly different approach: I choose not to deny the biological differences between male and female bodies.[36] But this does not mean that I'm accepting the gendered norms imposed on my femaleness, nor does this mean that I believe only two gender identities can exist. Instead, I seek to expand the idea of gender through a discursive employment of femininity and masculinity. If we see these as oppositional energies that exist in all of us, much like yin and yang, we could begin to visualize ourselves as inherently queered beings constantly trying to find a balance. Not only between the femininity and masculinity within us, but with the biological markers of our bodies. This is a constantly fluctuating set of parameters. At times we may feel one with ourselves. But all of us are also gender dysphoric at some point in our lives. For many,

---

[36] As cultural anthropologist Margaret Mead writes, '[i]n our present-day culture, bedeviled by a series of *either or* problems, there's a tendency to say: she can't have it both ways, if she shows that different cultures can mould men and women in ways which are opposite to our ideas of innate sex differences, there she can't also claim that there are sex differences.'

this may pass. For some, this may be a permanent state of being and involve transitioning to affirm gender identities. While it is essential to understand that gender exists across a spectrum and we are all free to be who we really are, it isn't also necessary to deny the biological differences between female and male bodies—*because there is a difference*. Perhaps we could transcend this difference by locating the queerness in us all[37] instead.

The patriarchy has repressed sexual expression across genders and has reduced sex to an act performed for the sake of progeny. Now, it is important to ask: can we expect anything better from a matriarchy? Sex historian Dr Kate Lister opines that in societies where female sexuality is not shamed as a bad thing, societies are less rigidly controlled, because everything is not about paternal bloodlines. 'So, as you can imagine, sex and attitudes to women enjoying sex are vastly different from our own,' she notes, with women changing their sexual partners multiple times. So, am I now going to argue that women should rule the world for the sake of their own sexual pleasure? Well, why the hell not?

---

[37]Queer theorist Judith Butler herself has written that her work is meant to critique the political systems of gender that limit the possibilities of self-expression. Her theory of gender performativity doesn't essentially equate to all gender is performance.

3

WOMEN AT WORK

#MeToo has exposed the deep sexism that exists within all workplaces. It has brought to the fore how predatory, lewd men lurch between lust and power, carnality and clumsiness, all within the illusory confines of professionalism. Women from across the spectrum have now decided that silence is useless and the only way we can really bring gender equality to the workplace is by recounting the multiple horrors that men feel entitled to commit. Not only has this process been cathartic for many women but has scared the shit out of working men. Of course, the backlash against the #MeToo movement has already begun. Reports suggest that workplace relationships between men and women are strained since all this began. Many industries, especially those dominated by men, are trying to cut women out of the workplace altogether to prevent potential #MeToo moments. Takeaway: potentially lecherous men are everywhere.

But don't worry about the women's labour force falling because of #MeToo. It wasn't so high to start with in the first place: women account for only 19.9 per cent of the total labour force in India. In fact, we could add US$ 770 billion to the country's GDP by 2025 if women's presence in the labour force increases. However, apart from the problem of unsafe working spaces (even travelling to and back from work isn't always safe, leave alone working on off-site assignments[1] or in the rural sector where feudal norms still stand),

---

[1] In 2013, a Mumbai photojournalist was gangraped while on assignment. In 2017, an Infosys techie was murdered in Chennai on her way to work. In 2018, an Ola driver molested a female architect who had booked his cab to take her to the Bengaluru airport for a work trip.

analysts cite another ironic reason for the decline in women seeking work when compared to the past: the rise in women's educational attainments. A recent study pointed out that 'women with more education marry into richer families that enable them to withdraw from the labour force.' We can only wonder if every one of these women who chose to quit did so to acquiesce to the patriarchy, or to achieve their own personal agendas.

In any case, despite all odds, millions of Indian women do go out to work every day, creating a tremendous amount of economic, social, and cultural capital. But the powers that be do not make things easy for them to succeed: gender pay gaps continue to exist, there is no flexibility in the workplace, and motherhood penalties stop many from rising through the ranks. Governments and corporates routinely pledge their allegiance to gender equality, co-opting women's empowerment as fundamental to their agenda and pass policies towards achieving that goal, but nothing really changes on the ground. Every woman who dares to work outside her home is left to fend for herself.

Fortunately, fend she does. Hyper-connected and tech-savvy young women are brazenly circumventing sexism and shifting India's work culture today. They excel in diverse industries, from STEM, Medicine, and Business, to Media, Law, and the Humanities. Increasingly, more and more women are starting their own businesses. In fact, 34.7 per cent of urban women are self-employed[2]. A majority of female entrepreneurs, 51.2 per cent, start their businesses between the ages of twenty-five and thirty-five.

It would seem that millennial and Gen Z women are impatient for success. Known to constantly change jobs even after investing time and resources in an organization, these women are willing to take risks. They do not want to wait long years for professional acknowledgment as they believe that their time is now. Their aim is

---

[2] A report by Bain & Company and Google points out that enabling more women entrepreneurs to start up and scale their businesses can create direct employment for 50 to 60 million people in India. This, the report notes, is a great way to solve India's unemployment problem.

personal development and skill accumulation, and when they feel an organization is hindering their growth, they shift to a new one, or create a start-up of their own. A considerably easy feat for women with access to the internet (alongside plenty of socio-economic privilege and a number of networks).

Even while boss ladies want to get to the top and lead, several others want to lean out (going against Facebook CEO Sheryl Sandberg's advice to lean in and take charge). Women aren't a monolith after all, and we aren't all driven by the same motivations. Consequently, our aspirations differ and change constantly. According to a survey conducted by ASSOCHAM, 40 per cent of working mothers want to quit their jobs to raise kids. On the other hand, many stay-at-home mums want to start working and contribute to their family's income. Only, this isn't easy.

In a country with a slow growth of salaried jobs and sex-based occupational segregation within jobs, a woman's chance of finding the right opportunity, especially after a break (for homemaking, pregnancy, childcare, eldercare, health, or leisure) is low. Astute Indian women, however, have turned these obstacles into challenges. They transform their portfolios and become new avatars of their old selves, successfully merging past work experience, current interests, and future goals. Women-run start-ups like JobsForHer, myAvtar, SHEROES, and Her Second Innings help thousands of such ladies get back into the workforce with a bang. Meanwhile, many mothers turn mompreneurs, creating start-ups to sell fashion, lifestyle, food, and childcare products, often utilizing their networks (primarily consisting of other mothers) to promote their brands and drive growth organically.

While they're at the workplace, women demand everyday gender parity. They want their employers to respect their female embodiment[3], provide for holidays such as period leave[4], and not

---

[3]This has to do with the intertwinement of the female body and mind. Our bodies and bodily processes cannot be ignored by our minds, because there's a constitutive relationship between them.

[4]Granted every month by Culture Machine, a media house based in Mumbai, to all

cringe if they pump breastmilk between meetings. Some women want to discursively deploy their sexuality at work, without the threat of looming harassment. They want to dress how they please and flirt if they feel like. Others even want to talk about mental health: premenstrual stress and post-partum depression, without male colleagues rolling their eyes and dismissing these topics as women's problems that shouldn't enter the professional space.

This, however, is not to say that all young women become harbingers of radical feminist politics from the moment they enter the workplace. Many women are known to decouple their personal identity from work in the early months of a new job, projecting a 'positive front' even if they disagree with projects and methodologies, while being mansplained. But once they manage to get their work noticed, they capitalize on their strengths and shrewdly renegotiate terms.

Then, there's the matter of women who don't do paid work and are homemakers, free spirits, stay-at-home mums, connoisseurs of art, literature, gastronomy, and gardening, or philanthropists and thinkers. Before you inevitably use 90s feminist tropes to box every woman you encounter: as a fearless 'career' woman or demure 'housewife', let me introduce an alternative way of seeing like a feminist. Now, I know financial independence is one of feminism's major goals; and we're bound to imagine that in order for a woman to live a liberated life, she'd have to work outside her home and earn a living. But, honestly, do you think that every woman who doesn't work at an office doesn't work? Her contribution isn't considered gainful work because it isn't paid for[5], but she is working. In the twenty-first century, it's crucial we take feminism into our homes too and reckon with the importance of the work that women do there. Perhaps, fight

female employees on the first day of their period. There are several online campaigns across Indian industries pushing for menstrual leave.

[5]Women in India do almost ten times more unpaid care work than men. If this is valued and compensated as paid work, it would contribute US$ 300 billion a year to the Indian economy.

for women's financial rights inside the home and increase their legal access to family wealth.

Women (at home) influence society and culture more than they're given credit for. 'They have chosen to leave the paid workforce, but still want to be out in the world, contributing in ways that feel meaningful,' argue Hana Schank and Elizabeth Wallace in *The Ambition Decisions*. 'Opting out of a career doesn't make women less ambitious.' Many of these women build great networks and figure prominently in their communities. More often than not, they modernize pre-existing cultural and social norms from within, with the support of male allies. For others, ambition may solely concern the interests of their families. In any case, these women aren't oppressed, and actively choose to spend their time doing things that are of interest to them. And as for the matter of money, almost every woman knows its value, irrespective of her chosen occupation. Several homemakers routinely draw up budgets, think about variable/fixed expenses and optimize their investments.

For those who think of feminism as a radical act, one that rejects structures of perceived oppression outright, it might be difficult to find solidarity with women who choose to work within pre-existing social and economic structures. Funnily enough, this not only disqualifies 'housewives' from claiming feminism, but also women in the corporate world. 'Career women' who break down walls and ceilings every day within patriarchal corporate structures are often accused of being complicit in perpetuating capitalist greed.

But, it's important to remember that India is an aspirational nation with living cultures that have flourished over thousands of years, some progressive, others conservative, many fanatic. Altogether unjust. To survive here, you need to be on top of your game.

Fempowerment

'I cannot generalize but being a civil servant guarantees you a seat at the table by virtue of your position. But at times one might have to shout louder to be heard,' says Rupavardhini Balakrishnan Raju, a deputy director at the Indian Audit and Accounts Service[6]. 'In a hierarchical set up like the government where power is so clearly attached to job role, it is interesting to see how gender operates. Naturally when one goes lower down the hierarchy, gender bias and discrimination becomes more apparent. But speaking of women officers at my level of seniority or higher, I think largely our gender is blurred by power. This is not to say that gender ceases to matter. There are many structural barriers and biases that operate, and probably affect the positions one is considered for, how much access one has to decision makers who are male, or how the junior bureaucracy responds to female leadership which in turn impacts one's ability to work efficiently. There are irritants.' A Fulbright scholar with a master's from Harvard Law School, Raju is also a faculty member at the National Academy of Audits and Accounts, Shimla. When I ask her if young women officers have the power to make change happen, she replies that they do at the senior level, 'but whether that power has been channelled to create an impact in the area of gender equality as a whole is another question altogether. The real challenge is keeping the feminist agenda alive once women have gained access to the corridors of power. There is a danger of co-option. The ideal nameless, faceless bureaucrat is also genderless. So, factoring in gender in governance requires delicate manoeuvring. Balancing the need to be perceived neutral while being proactive about ensuring gender equality is complicated.'

To be a twenty-first-century leader isn't easy, for you must simultaneously be a team player while possessing influence and authority over others. You must be able to inspire without sounding crafty, you must play authoritative without force, and be able to rationalize your every move in public. All this in an unpredictable world where volatile factors determine the efficacy of every decision you make as a boss. This is true of the public and private sectors.

---

[6]Disclaimer: Raju's opinions are stated in her personal capacity, not from her official position.

Smashing the Patriarchy

Now, for women leaders, the game gets even more complicated. For women, amazing credentials and a treasure trove of experience are not enough to warrant them the freedom to employ power straight up, as in the case of men. Women have to become effectively genderless to be considered worthy of authority, constantly having to prove that their femaleness does not impinge on their ability to do a 'man's' work, for power remains a male prerogative. So, in all this sexist craziness, when we add another layer of responsibility to the female leader—her feminist duty to hold out for other women at the workplace—how many women pass the test?

'We may be exposed to academic ideas of feminism, but there is no manual or critique on how to be a feminist boss,' says Nilofer Shamim Haja, a digital editor based in Delhi. 'How do we show compassion and empathy to both men and women, juniors or subordinates or peers, and yet lead? I think women bosses need to introspect and develop a discourse on what being a feminist boss implies.' Haja has worked in the media, publishing, and non-profit sectors for over twelve years, has helped brand and build several reputed cultural institutions. 'I've had the worst experience with women bosses,' she tells me. 'My male bosses have been more than empathetic, hands-off, and let me do my work. They act as a counterpoint to all the neurotic, dysfunctional women bosses who have been an absolute terror to work with. I used to have a lot of anxiety going into work because they would yell, scream, and use people like punching bags.' Why do you think this is? 'The patriarchy is like a virus,' Haja replies, 'it mutates.' It can make women patriarchal too, she explains: 'I had a sense that my women bosses didn't know how to lead or how to be mentors. They thought that being bosses meant you control things, micromanage, and enforce things, becoming the very thing that we blame men for. I realized that's the kind of leader I never wanted to be.'

History illustrates that female leaders, like Queen Didda of Kashmir, were just as ruthless as men, if not more. They waged wars, exploited resources, and perpetuated inequalities. Just by virtue of their femaleness, they weren't inherently more humanist or morally superior. I would, however, like to point out that power has been a patriarchal preserve since antiquity, and when women took on the seat of power they were still working within the confines of a masculine structure. Hence, it is only natural that they'd channel their inner masculinity to make decisions that uphold their position. If power is vested in a feminine structure, the results may just lead to the creation of a utopian matriarchy.[7] But, who am I kidding; it's unlikely that a post-patriarchal world will essentially revert to a sinless matriarchy. Attuned to patriarchal ways, women are just as aggressive in the workplace these days (when meritorious/competitive individualism is valued, gender becomes immaterial beyond a certain point; big fish eats small fish through and through). Not to mention, female bitchiness is a real thing. Yet, I'd like to believe that all women possess at least an iota of (feminine) righteousness in them, which could help bring about positive change in the workplace—promoting equality and cooperation. 'We have to be more reflective about what power is, what it is for, and how it is measured,' writes English scholar and classicist Mary Beard. 'To put it another way, if women are not perceived to be fully within the structures of power, surely it is power that we need to redefine rather than women?' Feminist or postfeminist, we have to ultimately reckon with the masculine superstructures we are a part of, and we must work to shift them.

'Women are said to be more transformational leaders than transactional leaders,' Dr Saumya Sindhwani, who teaches at the Indian School of Business, tells me. 'Women need to acknowledge that they are different, they think differently, and hence they need to hold onto that difference and bring it to the table. Women's diverse

[7]'Matriarchal values grow out of a social philosophy in which the emphasis is on cooperation,' writes anthropologist Peggy Reeves Sanday, who spent many years observing the matriarchal Minangakabau people of Indonesia. 'Viewed from the Minangakabau perspective, matriarchy is not about "female rule," but about social principles and values rooted in maternal meanings in which both sexes work together to promote human well-being.'

perspectives are not only appreciated, but have also been shown to be beneficial for business.' Dr Sindhwani has written two books on leadership and creativity in business. She is currently researching women's leadership styles. Talking about women who occupy senior positions in the corporate world, she says: 'A lot of women have voluntarily transformed themselves into "alpha men" to be accepted in the bro culture. However, there is nothing that shows that it is necessary to do that. In my own research with senior women, some have said, "I don't remember when I changed myself, my younger self was very different." They attribute it to their experiences, but when asked could your experiences have led to a different behaviour, majority said maybe as against a definitive no.' When I ask her about women's role as agents of economic change, she says, 'Women entrepreneurship is on the rise, a lot of women are stepping out of the corporate world and starting their own ventures. Raising capital continues to remain a challenge, and that is because a lot of work needs to be done in riding over the bias investors have against women. However, I have a lot of faith in the millennial population, these women are far more feisty, courageous, and would go all out to change the narrative.'

Patriarchy has always held the key to the coffers, irrespective of whether its economic structure is capitalist, socialist, or communist. Women's access to capital has been minimal, almost forever. Let's not be naïve: every revolution needs funding. To smash the patriarchy effectively, we need to control the source of power. This not only entails women running organizations and businesses, but also involves forming economic policy. The International Monetary Fund (IMF) points out that there are very few female economists in the world. Apparently, this is because women are known to have vastly different views on important policy issues that men don't agree with. An IMF report points out that as 'women hold views at odds with the perspectives of more senior male colleagues on research and policy questions…[and are] less likely than men to be hired, promoted, and have their work published in top journals.' Female economists in India have constantly fought against the tide of men who fear women thinking about capital. Women in finance have also emerged as a serious force to be reckoned with, owing to their bright ideas and great credentials. Once they take over the reins of the economic beast, it is their prerogative to tame it or ride it, be intuitively bullish and bearish, as they make objective decisions based on empirical data.

'The gender pay gap is shocking and sad,' exclaims Ela Das, a tech entrepreneur and chief creative officer who lives in Mumbai. Towards the beginning of her career, when she discovered that a married male co-worker was being paid twice as much as her, she took it up with her boss. 'But why do you want a higher salary? You are taken care of.' He dismissed her claim, alluding to her well-to-do background, and added that her male co-worker 'had to earn more because he had to take care of his family,' and since she was single, she wasn't expected to have familial expenses. Even while women these days are considered 'far more equal' in the world of business, Das says 'you still need men to validate you in the tech industry, because initially people are sceptical about you.' But the situation is changing very fast, 'as young women are very upfront and ambitious. They collaborate and enable each other.' Regarding the matter of pay gaps, she stresses that 'women must negotiate'. It's telling of the patriarchal mindset, she says, that in most organizations, 'they send the woman for front-end presentations, but for negotiating money, they always send a man.'

We constantly see how women are pushed into apparently feminine roles within organizations, effectively curbing their prospects in male-dominated departments which are likely to be the ones where the actual power is. While a Grant Thompson report on women in business shows that 64 per cent of Indian businesses have adopted equal pay for men and women performing the same roles, it also points out that the process is slow and 'limited to the dated approach of ticking the diversity box'. Things don't look great. According to Monster India, a popular job site, the pay inequality in the IT sector is 26 per cent, in manufacturing it's 24 per cent, and even in women-intensive sectors like healthcare and social work, men earn 21 per cent more than women. 'Gender equality is a critical component of economic growth,' the World Bank's interim president Kristalina Georgieva said while launching a report on gender equality. 'Women are half of the world's population and we have our role to play in creating a more prosperous world. But we won't succeed in playing it if the laws are holding us back.' According to the World Bank report, only six countries around the world give women and men equal legal work rights. India is nowhere close to topping that list.

'[W]omen must learn how to question the most basic assumptions about feminine normality in order to reopen the possibilities for development which have been successively locked off by conditioning.' writes Germaine Greer[8]. It's important that we take another look at the distribution of power within every industry, because clearly, power is quintessential for change. I must also stress that the rise of women in male-dominated fields doesn't always equal radical policy change for the benefit of all women. For instance, let's consider politics. Though a male bastion, it features several powerful female political leaders[9]. While these women have done their share for women's empowerment as they see fit, (intersectional) feminist politics isn't on their agenda. Does this mean these women aren't feminists, or does this simply mean that female politicians are likely to work for the benefit of their own constituents/ideologies? Since no female politician contests elections on the mandate of feminism, it is hardly surprising that feminist politics isn't their primary agenda.

Feminist movements in the last era have been depoliticized and deradicalized by NGO-ization, where most of their efforts were spent

---

[8]This feminist icon is currently mired in controversy as she criticized the #MeToo movement: 'If you spread your legs because he said "be nice to me and I'll give you a job in a movie", then I'm afraid that's tantamount to consent, and it's too late now to start whingeing about that.'

[9]Tamil Nadu's J. Jayalalithaa, UP's Mayawati, Bengal's Mamata Banerjee, Rajasthan's Vasundhara Raje, the Gandhi women, BJP's Sushma Swaraj and Smriti Irani—women have been a powerful force in politics.

in negotiating international funding instead of contesting for positions of actual power. So, while feminists protested on the street, patriarchs sitting inside the parliament decided on their behalf (while female politicians remained divided along ideological lines). These days vocal feminists are also ministers. Bipartisan female politicians are rearing their heads to stand up for women. Non-partisan collectives like Shakti[10] look for ways to increase the representation of women in legislative roles, and lobby to pass the Women's Reservation Bill and to empower existing female legislators across party lines.

This is important, because political might is indispensable in achieving feminist goals. Sample Iceland, where since the 1970s female leaders have passed legislation and implemented policies to bring about female empowerment. Today, Iceland is the most gender-equal society in the world, thanks to its powerful female leaders who fought for universal childcare and generous paid parental leave: five months of maternity leave, plus five months of paternity leave, and two months of shared leave. During this time each parent is entitled to get paid 80 per cent of their average income. Any community that equally respects the time and efforts of women and men, of mothers and fathers, is definitely on to something progressive. Iceland's leaders didn't stop there. The head of the equality unit in Iceland's welfare ministry, Rósa Guðrún Erlingsdóttir, noted: equality 'won't come about by itself, from the bottom up alone.' So, her ministry enforced new laws. It's illegal in Iceland now to pay men more than women for the same role.

To create a gender equal society in India, then, legislation is quintessential. However, even in the presence of such legislation, women continue to face an uphill battle. They may lack an understanding of laws that benefit them or have no access to legal recourse. So, we need political leaders who're in touch with the pulse of their female constituents, and who will have the political will to

---

[10]Based in Bengaluru, Shakti is one among the few to promote women leaders across political lines.

inspire womenfolk to invoke the right benefits. Additionally, in a nation as large and diverse as India, urban and rural women's issues are vastly different. Political leaders, too, have to be as diverse in order to understand the issues of their constituents. This cannot happen with top-down politics. For real social change that cuts across populations, we need women from marginalized/minority communities to enter the political arena and speak for themselves.

'My community has been very supportive of my work,' says Urmilaben Baria, the first female Adivasi Sarpanch from Devgadh block in Dahod. 'Most women in my family work. Our male elders do not have a problem with women doing work for the community. In fact, it was my father-in-law who told me about the panchayat spot reserved for an Adivasi woman. Since I was the most educated among the women in my family, he suggested I file a nomination.' Baria is literate and has completed twelve years of schooling. A feisty woman determined to work for the benefit of her people, she has mobilized women to attend the Gram Sabha, helped villagers apply for social security schemes and get Aadhar cards—constantly interacting with the police and district officials to move things along[11]. When I ask her what challenges she faces as a female sarpanch, she replies: 'My community has been responsive and cooperative. The barriers I've faced have been from the side of the administration.' So, is there gender equality in her society? 'Not entirely. I do know that some men talk among themselves as to why being a woman I'm doing such important work as I may not know all the details. No one has directly said anything to me though.'

Every woman's experience of the patriarchy is radically different to another's. It's for this reason that it's impractical to expect any one woman to speak everyone's truths or fight multipronged feminist battles in India. Only when women from across the spectrum rise,

---

[11]Baria also took the lead in the case of the abduction of a migrant girl in her village (by an older man), and negotiated with the police and the girl's family to ensure she was found and rehabilitated.

can we even dream of finding a common feminism.[12] Until then, our efforts will only amount to appropriation. At the same time, it's also important to remember that every minute we spend trying to reconcile ideological differences with one another (through a lot of bashing), we're losing time in actually fighting to attain positions of power. We need to take advantage of every opportunity that exists in contemporary socio-political structures and pave our own paths to positions of dominance. It would seem that to make real change happen, we may have to think beyond tested feminist paths, such as promoting equality 'for women by introducing new social rights or asserting subordination of politics to a "feminine" logic. In both cases, they would be paralyzed.' To win against the patriarchy, we must also think inside-the-box, to achieve our outside-the-box aims. Several women's rights organizations across India have understood this need for a new rationale, and are working with women to empower individual lives in tangible ways.

'Unlike conventional women empowerment programmes that adhere to awareness classes, we devised a Gender Self Learning Programme (GSLP) to facilitate discussions that reflect on discrimination, violence, and inequality for neighbourhood groups,' says Manjari Asok, the communications specialist for the Kudumbashree State Poverty Eradication Mission in Thiruvananthapuram. 'Each woman represented in the network is regarded as a participant, information provider and knowledge creator.' Asok points out that 'these women are fighting back the worst of situations in life, yet making small but great achievements,' and that pursuing the GSLP approach with them has not only made them

---

[12]'Dalit men are the most discriminatory towards Dalit women when it comes to the latter pursuing leadership,' asserts Dr Aishwarya Rao, a public health expert and disability rights activist from Chennai. 'This is due to the misogynistic belief that women should not involve themselves in politics.' At a time when women rarely speak out against the sexism in their own communities (or political parties) for the sake of solidarity, Dr Rao's is a lone and powerful voice that calls out sexism and emphasizes the need for more women from marginalized communities to enter the political arena.

more aware of their rights and entitlements, it has also emboldened them to think about their individual selves. 'We encourage them to ask questions like "Who am I?", "What do I have?", and "What are my needs?" This has inspired them greatly and it is now being reflected in the gender politics of many women in their everyday lives.'

Feminism gains relevance not by reiterating old beliefs but by metamorphosing to accommodate the zeitgeist. Today, individual self-improvement is all the rage. Most people find it more advantageous to change themselves instead of devoting their lives to transforming the system, because the results are immediate. Across socio-economic strata, women have begun to negotiate power individually, in spite of society's constant effort to shame them for seeking it. This is a win for feminism. However, it refuses to see it that way because (according to feminist tradition) individual female empowerment does not constitute a social revolution. But only when a multitude of individual women take the power can a collective feminist future even be dreamed of. This is not to say that we shouldn't strive for what's perceived as collective (intersectional) women's issues—of course we must. In my opinion, if we are ever to agree on what constitutes collective women's issues (is it stuff like passing the Women's Reservation Bill and cutting the pink tax[13] or is it about formulating grand plans to eradicate inequalities of all kinds) it's crucial that we all feel equally empowered first to get into that debate. Otherwise, we'd forever indulge in rubbing one another's noses in a bottomless pit of feminist virtue signalling.

Reclaiming the Narrative
'Most young women from corporates live in fear of being judged for their lifestyle, attitude or attire,' reveals Beulah Moses, a senior corporate officer at an outsourcing firm in Chennai. 'When I first joined here, the women in my team thought of me as a "feminist"—

---

[13]Refers to women's goods like sanitary pads and tampons, which are taxed heavily as they are branded as luxury items.

with a negative stereotype—and judged me. They'd advice that I'd never find a man if I didn't change my ways. Well, I haven't really found my man but that's mainly by choice. What can I say, I'm picky!' she proclaims. 'It took me months to make these women understand the need for feminism and how important gender equality was, especially at our place of work. They had to stop judging other women. I now have a team of empowered ladies.' I ask Moses (who is known for never letting a sexist remark go undisputed) how men deal with her, a sexy woman, at work. 'I can't generalize,' she replies. 'But I've known men who believe that it's a deadly combination when a woman is smart and sexy. I think it turns men on. Smart only adds extra oomph to someone who is already sexy!'

In post #MeToo India, women don't intend to underplay their femininity and rein in their sexuality to be taken seriously (or avoid harassment). This is a time when women proclaim that they can be sexual, sexy, and talented[14]. Not only are men taken aback by the brazen attitude of these postfeminist ladies, but so are women. For let us not pretend that all women like each other. More often than not, they're bitchy to one another. Women who flirt in the workplace are considered 'loose' by men and women alike. Those who dress sexy or express their sexuality freely are judged as lacking professional integrity. In such a scenario, women at work not only need to find ways to deal with patriarchal men but have to constantly defuse tensions with antagonistic women with varying ideologies. Now, even while no woman can deny that body politics matter in the workplace, because the 'biological difference between the male and female bodies is the edifice…[on which] gender inequality is built and legitimated,' and this leads to sexual harassment, everyone may not agree on how to play out such a politic. Do we flaunt our

---

[14]'Shameless women are a powerful force,' writes *Guardian* columnist Suzanne Moore, referring to the likes of American politician Alexandria Ocasio-Cortez (AOC)—a Latina woman who takes pleasure in her female embodiment while boldly taking on the hypocrisy of the US Congress. AOC isn't an isolated phenomenon; around the world we see women who embrace their sexuality and take their sexiness to work with them.

bodies or erase our gender to be equal co-workers? Either way, a woman's female embodiment remains an integral part of how her professional performance is evaluated. This is true across industries.

'I usually focus on the sport and ignore all else that is said about me,' exclaims Sharmila Nicollet, a celebrated Indo-French professional golfer. 'Of course, there are instances when people discuss my persona, instead of talking about my talent. But when I win a tournament, things change. When I compete hard and achieve positive results people realize that I am an athlete and more than just a pretty face.' Nicollet is the youngest Indian to qualify for the Ladies European Tour and was the youngest to win the All-India Ladies Amateur Championship in 2008. She has a large fan following on Twitter and Instagram and is considered one of India's hottest sportswomen. Nicollet isn't perturbed by that tag. She holds that being glamorous comes naturally to her, and that she likes to look good to play well. 'My physicality, my talent, and my persona are one package,' she tells me. 'I'm sure women face this issue more than men do, in all fields. Women need to work twice as hard to prove themselves.'

Hiding away their femininity to fit into other people's ideas of what professional female decorum constitutes is not how young women roll. They're going to post selfies from their workspaces (like Mimi Chakraborty and Nusrat Jahan did from the parliament[15]) because they are an integral part of those spaces now. While it's true that women like to indulge in their female masculinity at work, this does not mean they are automatically required to give up on their feminine pleasures. Femininity 'here is powerful, playful and narcissistic—less desiring of a sexual partner than empowered by the knowledge of her own sexual attractiveness.'[16] From how a woman dresses to what images of herself she shares online, the contemporary woman self-consciously makes choices that boost her

---

[15]And they got trolled for that. Apparently, posing for photos outside the parliament in western clothes isn't sanskari/patriotic.
[16]Writes cultural theorist Rosalind Gill, about female subjectivity in postfeminist times, only to later criticize this aspect of postfeminist women. But I like this definition.

self-confidence and takes back the power. Women have always been told that their femininity is a weakness in the workspace. Men always equate femininity to enticement, irrationality, or toxicity. Women are not often appreciated for their achievements without also being congratulated for doing it *in spite* of being women. Such double-edged compliments belittle women, subtly implying that men are the superior sex.

'We all need to reflect upon ourselves as to why we equate womanhood to weakness,' states Amita Karadkhedkar, a Mumbai-based diversity evangelist and manager in the IT industry. 'Does wearing bangles take away one's courage and strength? Does wearing red lipstick malign one's character? Is only the privileged gender expected to be ambitious? This is for all women—trans and otherwise.'[17] A bold trans woman who transitioned while working and building her career, Karadkhedkar is a trailblazer paving the way for inclusion in the corporate world. 'When I decided to transition and embrace my true self, I applied my project management skills. I put together a plan with milestones and timelines and worked towards mitigating the risks involved. When it comes to workplaces, the fact is, people react differently due to fear and prejudice. I invested time and effort in helping colleagues get over these. I didn't take any impulsive decisions and had dialogue whenever required to get them on board. Also, I practiced acceptance towards dissent and let go of toxic people.'

Even though most organizations believe that inclusion and diversity are primary to promoting innovation,[18] it isn't always easy for women to express their sexuality and viewpoints boldly at the workspace. Often, this is because the more a woman plays up her sexuality, the more likely it is that stereotypical prejudices will follow her. Consider the matter of women and irrationality. 'The idea that

---

[17]She also says that presently trans and feminist movements intersect, but that feminism still has a long way to go to truly understand trans issues.
[18]Research suggests that having more female workers promotes innovation and productivity in teams, and drives revenue.

women are irrational is often paired with a notion that rational thought is superior to emotion, that reason leads to sound decisions and emotion leads to poor ones,' writes Jenna Baddeley in *Psychology Today*. It is unlikely that you will hear a woman lauded for her great EQ in a professional setting. But when an alpha male makes a brash (emotional) decision with successful results, he's celebrated as a fearless leader. There's a reason why women are routinely denied top managerial positions across industries—only those who match up to the masculine standard are allowed to hold such high-stress jobs. Women alternately make intuitive decisions and spend a lot of time thinking over said decisions, both behaviours that are seen as irrational in women, perceived as strengths in men. This especially irks me, because we all know who is most irrational when it comes to controlling their erratic urges. Male avarice in matters concerning lust and lasciviousness at the workplace is as real as it gets. #MeToo is proof.

'The #MeToo movement did shake things up, and I found myself sharing the collective outrage that followed after several women shared their stories of sexual harassment,' says Vrinda Agarwal, a Delhi-based corporate lawyer turned journalist, who called out the vile behaviour of her ex-boss, a legal bigwig who constantly harassed female colleagues and turned official meetings into boys' locker room sessions. 'Sharing a part of the story felt retributive. It also made me realize that I expect equality more in the workplace than at home…I am cautious about the battles that I pick at home—unless the stakes are personal and high, I don't call out anti-feminist behaviour. Workplace discrimination, on the other hand, evokes stronger feelings in me. This could be because we expect people to behave in a responsible way in a professional environment, regardless of their personal prejudices.' Agarwal doesn't consider herself a feminist in the conventional sense. 'I believe in equality of sexes in terms of opportunities and treatment but wouldn't call myself a feminist,' she notes, 'as I'm not actively engaged in bringing about change on that front. I am, at best, a selective feminist.'

Women lead complexly constructed lives. Are you a feminist only if you speak truth to power, can you not simply claim the power that comes with compliance once in a while? Most middle- and upper-class Indian families are benevolently patriarchal, with men in the family going to some lengths to support their daughters', sisters', and wives' ambitions. Men aren't a monolith either, after all. In a society that's simultaneously modern and conservative, many postfeminist women deem to make the best of both worlds: they might simultaneously uphold feminist values in the workplace while performing conventional roles at home. 'I hate that most workplaces in the country won't treat me as equal, but...I have to admit that it's a relief to have the freedom to fail professionally, or even choose to have a career at all,' writes journalist Sonali Kokra. 'And yes... upper-class women almost always do have that choice.' It's important that middle- and upper-class women (be we feminist or not) own up to this privilege. Many of us have an economic safety net to fall back on if things don't work out as planned. Only when we honestly acknowledge this fact can we begin to talk about women who opt out of careers with an open mind. At the end of the day, we all try to benefit from the patriarchy one way or another.

'Feminism to me is the power to create, nurture, and shape a better world where women are respected and supported,' says Apoorva Thumuluru, a homemaker from Bengaluru. 'Being a mother, there will always be children around who observe and learn. By creating positive impressions for them to imitate, we are generating change that will be taken forward.' Thumuluru worked as a senior consultant at Infosys before deciding to stay at home and raise her daughter. When I ask her who her feminist icons are, she replies: 'My grandmother who fought the odds in her early life with courage and shaped her own future. I look up to her confidence and ambitious journey. She was a forward thinker who rooted for women's education, work, travel, and individuality. Next is my mother who again despite several ups and downs in life, displayed poise and strong willpower to uplift the family together with my father.'

In conventional Indian society, the husband often takes on the role of the provider and the wife of the nurturer and overseer. For many educated millennial mothers (be they career-minded or not), this convention isn't the worst of evils, because it gives them time and space to focus on their children. While we may blithely argue that this is an outmoded convention that must be fought against, we must respect that some women do not want to work even if jobs are available, because they value their roles at home more. Some women don't want to have it all. But feminists everywhere will inevitably ask: when are you going back to work? Because a woman's choice to stay at home is seen as regressive, as one that replicates patriarchal norms. In an article for the *Economic Times*, Usha Shashikant[19] goes so far as to accuse young women of leaving the workforce because 'it has become somewhat fashionable to not go to work'. She asserts that many young women give up too easily, that 'women who went to work in earlier generations struggled through these problems. They also lived in more traditional households and did not compromise on their role at home for work.' Oh, the judgement that people feel entitled to make about young women's choices. And even while feminists belittle the lives of women at home, society creates its own caricatures of 'dented and painted' housewives. 'Affluent stay-at-home mothers are a cultural lightning rod for anxieties about wealth and privilege,' writes sociologist Rachel Sherman, because 'wealth is morally acceptable primarily when one works hard for it. But "hard work" turns out to mean "paid work"—work that men are more likely than women to keep once they have children.... The upshot is that our culture directs doubts about what it means to be a "good" rich person towards women, while making it easy for men with lucrative jobs to feel morally worthy of their wealth.' This is largely true in India, too.

'These days women are not influenced by what others think. They live life on their own terms,' says former flying officer at the

---

[19]She is a renowned author and financial educator.

Indian Air Force (IAF), Rupika Dhillon, who now works part-time in the private sector so she can spend more time with her son. When I ask her if her choice will be considered feminist, she replies: 'I made a personal decision to have a child and I believe it's important to spend time with him when he's young. My son has never been a hindrance to me. In fact, I started my postgraduate degree only after he was born. I'm pretty OCD and I plan my life way ahead.' Dhillon had to leave the IAF due to a back injury, but that hasn't thrown a spanner in the works of her ambitions. She tells me that her rigorous training will stay with her forever. 'I trained for two and a half years to become a pilot,' she notes. 'Our trainers never discriminated between men and women. The IAF is gender equal.[20] We were never made to feel that because we were lady cadets, we were special or that we'd get any discounts, nor did they make us feel that there were certain things we were not expected to do.'

Millennial ambitions transform constantly because they want the equal opportunity to pursue a career and fulfil their aim of self-realization. Sometimes their ambitions may coincide with society's (and mainstream feminism's) conception of success and purpose, but more often than not, it is about what one *really* wants to do, irrespective of how it appears to others. It's about looking into ourselves and figuring out our emotions. Whether we choose to perform one role after another, or balance them simultaneously, or sometimes find ourselves in situations where we don't have a choice but to perform one or all roles, we have to constantly deal with a million contradictory thoughts in our head. Millennials know this to be true: that ignoring our emotions in order to get work done will only lead to anxiety and stress. As we go on pushing our bodies

---

[20]While the IAF has inducted women fighter pilots, women in the army and navy are still not allowed to participate in combat. This is largely due to senior male officers' prejudice against female officers. An army chief publicly said that the army was not ready to put women in combat roles because women would complain about privacy issues like men peeping into their rooms while they're in combat zones. He also stated categorically that the army won't be able to give six months of maternity leave.

Smashing the Patriarchy

and minds, year after year, without a break to perform our roles to perfection, or spend our time lamenting about our inability to do so, we risk falling into depression or developing other mental health issues, not to mention psychosomatic problems. So, it's important to take a breather once in a while.

'Learning to drive, getting a job, and being financially independent does not complete the definition of freedom, for me it's more about being intellectually, emotionally, and spiritually free,' says Samar Hafeez, a consultant psychologist who specializes in cognitive behaviour therapy, women's health, and mindfulness. 'Self-discovery is at the crux of women's mental health. Women should break free from the confines of their own mind before they try to break away from shackles of any hierarchy.' She tells me that negativity and pessimism create a prison in our minds. The only way to break out of it is to become self-aware. 'It is the observation of one's own thoughts, feelings, values, beliefs, and behaviours in every sphere of life. It's about monitoring and being insightful about our inner world.' Bengaluru-based Hafeez has held several workshops on anxiety and stress management (both work-related and personal). She emphasizes the need for mindfulness in our everyday lives. 'Young women nowadays live either in the past or future. By failing to attribute importance to the present, they are living on the edge. This will always contribute to stress/anxiety-related health problems. Remember, there is no future without the present. Improving oneself each day will improve your relationship with others as well, making life less of a struggle. Young women should also pick out cognitive distortions. Change and challenge these thoughts to enhance your emotional reasoning.'

But feminism is not about personal happiness, some would say. Even while positive psychology is a central theme in postfeminist thought, where women constantly seek to improve the self in order to become emotionally autonomous, feminism proper disapproves of this self-improvement project. Consider sociologist Rosalind Gill's words: 'positive sentiments are disseminated through a multiplicity of "inspirational" aphorisms, from greeting cards to Facebook walls... These endlessly circulating feeling rules offer up powerful messages of hope and possibility, wrapped in a vaguely defiant sense of self-belief that communicates a postfeminist sentiment of entitlement—in this case to happiness.' It's like we aren't entitled to happiness unless our approach is approved by the Congress of Feminism first.

Rising Against the Odds

'Indian society has not yet come to a point where everyone agrees on gender equality, so it is very minimal across different professions. As a queer person (I identify myself as a lesbian), I believe there is hope for the LGBTQ community to flourish in the coming years!' declares Dr Poornima Josyula, who holds a PhD in applied mechanics from IIT. 'With the recent decriminalization of Section 377, the visibility of the LGBTQ community has increased, but wholehearted acceptance by mainstream society is a very slow process.' When I ask her whether gender matters in the field of science, she replies: 'Academic research is all about curiosity, interest, and passion. It is the mindset of a person which hinders them from achieving their goals, not their gender.' A devoted teacher at T.I.M.E. Mumbai, she invests equally in building strong concepts and mentoring students to handle life's challenges because emotional and mental support are crucial for success. 'Stereotypes and beliefs create a false "*idea*" or "*image*" about genders which in turn reflect *via* one's actions,' Dr Josyula tells me. 'In the current scenario, I believe that feminism is a construct created to balance out the chaos created due to these stereotypes and beliefs. But for me, feminism is breaking stereotypes about men and women. Our identities are built through our own beautiful selves and not through these stereotypes. When that realization dawns and respect creeps in, the word "feminism" may fade.'

The LGBTQIA+ community is driving a shift in metro work culture. Not only are queer women excelling across industries, they are also compelling their peers to engage in open-minded conversations about the importance of inclusivity. Until the decriminalization of

Section 377, many members of the LGBTQIA+ community were closeted at work in order to avoid discrimination. Now, times have changed, and women have begun to bring their whole selves to work. By taking a stand against discrimination, brave women are at once bringing queerness into the mainstream and highlighting the quintessential contribution of their community in the workplace. Every sector, be it creative, academic, or corporate, has gained from the innovation spearheaded by gender diverse people—the impact of their influence is visible either in the work culture of the organization they are part of, or in the manner the oeuvre has changed. In fact, gender diverse organizations are known to outperform their peers by 15 per cent. The economic side of this matters, because, until recently, several perks that were accorded to heterosexual partners of employees were not extended to queer companions. TCS was the first Indian organization to open this up and offer healthcare benefits to same-sex partners. This sort of proactivity is important, because discrimination takes many subtle forms in the workplace.

'The current feminist narrative of corporate India does not recognize caste as a factor,' writes Christina Thomas Dhanaraj, a business analyst and co-founder of the Dalit History Month Collective. 'In an Indian corporate context, although merit and performance are touted to be the only determinants, Dalit women hardly get chosen...the typical profile of a female colleague who is most often encouraged or promoted, is that of a non-Dalit who is fair-skinned, is generally regarded as a physically attractive woman, belongs to the upper- or the upper-middle class, and is visible to most people.' And this isn't an isolated story. Across educational institutions and industries, including the government, caste-based bias is persistent. For women from communities that have been historically denied access to power, wealth, and a dignified livelihood, entry into large organizations doesn't guarantee equal opportunity. This is especially so because bias based on one's identity plays out subtly in the workplace. While there may be no direct reference to it or overt discrimination, office politics have a way of singling out people who don't fit in. Power then, continues to reside in the hands of the upper caste. Ninety-four per cent of top jobs in the private sector are held by Brahmins and Baniyas, mostly Hindu or Jain. Bosses, one can imagine, will promote teammates who are cut from the same cloth as themselves (read: similar socio-cultural backgrounds). This is especially true of family-run businesses that aren't necessarily looking to improve their employee diversity.

Discrimination based on race, religion, or linguistic identity, and even political beliefs, isn't perpetrated by men alone. Women are equally capable of bias (sometimes in reverse). Ranging from casual casteism to exclusionary practices, thousands of Indian women live out their prejudices in the workplace. In India's current political climate, Islamophobia too has ossified across industries. Caste is contentious. Linguistic bias is everywhere. Political ideologies determine sisterhood. Even when peers are from the same economic or social background, their other identity markers are not forgotten. While this may seem like innocent association at first glance, the reality is stark. Women hate on women all the time. This became explicitly clear during the #MeToo movement, when all sorts of underlying rivalries played out on social media.[21]

'Most of my shaming came from senior female members of the industry, even those who claim to be feminists,' Chinmayi Sripaada, a Tamil playback singer, told *Huffington Post*, in the aftermath of accusing a well-known lyricist[22] of sexually harassing her. Several influential personalities questioned why she came out with her story decades after it had actually happened, smearing her character and doubting her intentions. Then came the caste factor. Since Sripaada comes from a Brahmin family and the lyricist comes from the

---

[21]Consider actor Payal Ghosh's accusation of director Anurag Kashyap. It is tempting to imagine that the accusation was part of a smear campaign orchestrated to punish Kashyap for speaking out against the Modi government. However, this assumption has unfortunately meant that many leftist-liberal women dismissed Ghosh altogether as an attention seeker and denied her a fair hearing.

[22]Vairamuthu Ramasamy, an award-winning Tamil lyricist, poet, and novelist.

politically-powerful Thevar community, people chose sides based on caste for the most part. Sripaada was routinely slut-shamed online, with men calling her a Brahmin prostitute, while women called out her caste privilege to undermine her. As her motives were examined under a microscope and her sexual history pecked apart, Sripaada tweeted 'Forget when I should have spoken. I have raised my voice now. What action will be taken against Mr. Vairamuthu since anyway everyone knows?' Well, the lyricist went on to receive honorary doctorates and Sripaada was banned by the (sexist) Tamil film industry. Yet, she continues to fight the narrative, online and in court.

From the film industry to the church[23], men sexually assault women while hiding behind the institutional power they possess. Toxic masculinity is everywhere. Author Ira Trivedi's #MeToo accusation against author Chetan Bhagat exposed the deep misogyny that exists even in men who make a living by posturing as woke bros. Women then, are forced to be extremely cautious with their male peers. This is obviously not something that's desirable in a workplace, where synergy is crucial for successful outcomes. Every day women across industries have to do the fine balancing act of associating with men (who in all likelihood are sexist) and getting work done, even while being careful not to let them get too close (for who knows how that will turn out). Obviously, none of this is easy to do.

'We have to deal with different people differently to get work done,' says Bhairavi Dhoot, an associate at Reasoning Instincts Architecture Studio in Ahmedabad, when I ask her about gender-based discrimination in her industry. 'The problem of gender only comes in when it comes to tactics.' Dhoot's architectural projects have won several awards and are expanding her footprint in the country. Raised by a strong mother, she is an inherently empowered woman who doesn't necessarily use the language of theoretical feminism to define herself or her actions. 'Clients judge my outlook and personality

[23]In 2018, a nun from the Syro-Malabar Catholic Church accused an influential bishop of raping her several times, which snowballed into a volley of sexual abuse allegations against the clergy.

as an architect. On-site labourers look at me as a woman primarily,' she says. 'It sort-of hurts their ego that a woman is telling them what to do. And I take full advantage of it. I often tell them: do I have to tell you what to do, or do you know what needs to be done? In fact, I have a good command on-site, and the workers tend to listen to me more.'

Working women deal with sexist prejudice of myriad varieties. Many cleverly circumvent the sexism and manipulate the situation to their benefit. Now here lies the Feminist Fault Line. You may argue that the only reaction to sexism must be outrage: hold the man accountable for what he says, call out everything sexist to fight for equality and educate the ignorant. But in reality, and you may hate me for saying this, many women let certain sexist remarks go in the workplace when there are larger stakes involved. Some may wallow in anger but choose to remain quiet, while yet others may not be so offended by sexist men—*because they expect nothing better from them in the first place.* These women are strategic and diplomatic in their approach to complicated situations. They effectively perform femininity to gain what they seek. This does not make them any less feminist. It only shows that they're postfeminist.

'I have a feeling I'd want to spend time with my baby at home when I have one,' says Anika Lodha Drolia,[24] a chartered accountant at a top firm, 'so I want to achieve certain things in my career before I take that break.' When I ask her whether women who take maternity leave are easily assimilated into the workplace, she explains: 'the promotion cycle is typically three years. If a woman takes a maternity break in between for six months, everyone expects her not to get the promotion. Especially the men who are also fighting for the same post. They're like we've worked six months more than her. Although there are policies to protect such women, the reality is this. People overlook the two and half years of work the woman did, simply because she took off for six months to have a child. If

---

[24]Name changed to hide identity.

she's out of sight, she's out of mind.'

Women with children are known to outperform their peers who do not. They are more efficient, empathetic, and better at time management. However, new mothers are often left out of the bro culture at work when they return after taking maternity leave (for up to six months[25]). Business cycles are short in the twenty-first century, and a lot happens in six months. It is for this reason that several millennial women postpone having children till they reach professional milestones (going against societal pressure). But this doesn't diminish the fact that women have to readjust into the workplace after a life-changing personal experience, one that involves a new gurgling living being. Some corporates have found a way to help new mothers get back into work by providing flexible work hours. Flipkart gives up to four months of flexibility, and even offers a year of career break without pay for new moms. All these are progressive steps. Next, one only hopes India makes parental leave gender-equal and gives paternity benefits like Iceland. Daddies, after all, are equally important in childrearing. If they take more interest in their children, mommies could go to work without guilt. The good news is that millennial men are fast becoming equal parents. A survey of 1,700 fathers across seventeen Indian cities found that 50 per cent wouldn't mind being stay-at-home dads, and 85 per cent are part of their child's daily routine activities. Multinational companies in India like Microsoft, Ikea, and Johnson & Johnson do provide longer paternity leave. However, these men and companies are not the norm, but the exception.

Whether socially-conditioned or inherent or individualistic or trendy, it must be noted that many millennial women believe children need the physical presence of their mothers in the early years. So even with flexible working hours and nannies and supportive husbands and

---

[25]While six months of maternity leave has been the norm in the government sector, the private sector has only recently increased the leave period from twelve weeks to twenty-six weeks. Many stakeholders have criticized the Maternity Leave Act, saying it will hamper the hiring of women, because businesses don't want unproductive employees.

childcare facilities, millions of women have #mumguilt. Managing it and turning up to work every day is the real challenge. Filter Copy's viral video 'Life of a Working Mother' portrayed many of these realities: judgemental male colleagues, dependence on babysitters, financial stress, approaching deadlines, and questions about personal ambition. Conversely, when a woman relegates childcare to family members or nannies, shows up to every meeting, and strives to live an ambitious life without guilt, she'd be judged at work for being a selfish mum—think of her poor unloved children! There's no winning if a woman pays heed to every unfair criticism that's levelled against her, by men, other women, and society at large. In any case, most women bear the mental load of home and family even while at work. During the Covid-19 lockdown, women did the bulk of housework and childcare. Most ladies end up multitasking in a perpetual superwoman mode because they have no choice. As a popular social media post says, 'we expect women to work like they don't have children and raise children as if they don't work.'

'When women try to balance a demanding career, motherhood, and family life, anxiety is very understandable and pretty common. When it is not attended to with self-care and care from others, it leads to depression,' says Radhika Sasankh, a counselling psychologist from Chennai. I ask her why self-confidence turns into self-doubt so quickly among young women these days. It is to do with how quickly their lives change in radical ways, Sasankh tells me. 'She is straddling three different spaces—here of work, marriage, and motherhood one after the other, with hardly any time to "secure each space". By which I mean the time and energy she invests in that space to first feel comfortable in it, and then grow with confidence there.' The first step we need to take to deal with these changes better, 'is to understand and appreciate the enormity of the challenges, and work on one's resources with compassion to the self.'

In the flurry of life, women constantly find themselves stressed out in the performance of their roles. Even while they pursue their ultimate aims with gusto, everyday failures rub off on their egos, and relentless work tires out their bodies. While many women are able to take time off work to balance their life, for single working mothers, who do not have a social or economic safety net, there is little space to think about health or mental well-being. Often, single working mothers have to push every nerve in their bodies to get things done. The matter of childcare adds to their stress. Single mothers who have no relatives, are widowed, estranged, or living away from family, have to do a tremendous amount of logistical planning to care for a child and go out to work daily. They also have to spend a large amount of money for nannies, day cares, and good schools. In metro cities around India, the lives of single mothers are still fraught with social stigmas. While most workplaces provide no special treatment for single parents, it is even more distressing to note that the Ministry of Women and Child Development and the NCW don't even have statistical data on the number of single mothers.

While it is tempting to imagine that every one of these women (single or married, parent or not, privileged or disadvantaged, stressed out or relaxed) is involved in a feminist battle, we'd be surprised to find that many don't see themselves through those lenses—they're simply living their lives as best as they can. In fact, what has surprised me is the positive attitude through which women see their lives. Even in the darkest situations, women work towards the light—utilizing every opportunity not only to build their own lives, but to ensure the future of their children. Some women even turn the lack of choice into a circumstance where they consciously choose.

'I had to leave my job after giving birth to my children,' says Latha K., a mother of four from Bengaluru who works as a domestic worker. 'My husband wanted me to stay at home to look after them. But his salary was not enough to support my children's education. He also drinks.' Even while Latha regrets that she did not receive a proper education, she is excited and devoted to the idea of educating her daughter on par with her sons. 'I do not want her to be dependent on her husband when she grows up. I want her to have a good job and earn well for herself.' As her financial situation deteriorated, resolute Latha decided to go back to doing housework despite her family's protestations: 'Upon my insistence, my husband realized that it was beneficial to our family to let me work. So, he finally agreed as we had no other option.'

Positivity seems to be the self-empowering mantra of working women everywhere. It fuels their ambitions and reinforces their choices, predicting a successful future. In Indian society, where women are often discouraged from having aspirations that extend beyond one's household, the fact that millennial women across social strata are pursuing their goals with confidence is an important change. While we may argue, like sociologist Rosalind Gill, that postfeminism exerts a regulatory force and expects women to cultivate the right kinds of disposition to survive in a neoliberal society—'confidence, resilience, and positive mental attitude'—it is undeniable that women have gained by developing this mindset.

'As women, we face many obstacles; not every situation will be in favour of us. Passionate aspiring women will face disappointments. Grit, optimism, and willpower will keep us driven and make life more joyful,' declares Dr Vaishnavi Prabhakar, a prosthodontist and implantologist from Chennai. A mother of two who runs her own dental clinic, Dr Prabhakar tells me why it's important to grow through our setbacks. 'I visualize each experience as a lesson learned. [The] greater the disappointment, the stronger I get. I begin every task with a leap of faith and firm belief that there's always something better and something more.' When I ask her about her feminist icons, she chooses Michelle Obama. 'She's a visionary, optimist, and full of energy, and gives without expecting much in return. She beautifully strikes a balance between work, home, and family.'

Will the Real Feminists Please Stand Up?
One can't generalize the intergenerational conflict between older feminists and millennials. However, it is true to a large extent that millennial feminism is criticized by older women who consider themselves the real upholders of feminist values. This isn't only with

respect to activism or academia, but also in the private and public sectors where women who have had to make many sacrifices to be 'career women' find the attitude of millennials as belittling the feminist agenda.

Take journalist Barkha Dutt, for instance, a feminist icon who inspired millions of millennials, including me, with her intrepid reporting, who now condemns 'the self-indulgent mumbo-jumbo of so-called post-feminists' in regard to the proposal of 'first-day period leave' for all female employees. In an article for the *Washington Post*, she writes that the idea 'may be dressed up as progressive, but it actually trivialises the feminist agenda for equal opportunity, especially in male-dominated professions. Worse, it reaffirms that there is a biological determinism to the lives of women, a construct that women of my generation have spent years challenging...for women to use the fight against menstrual taboos as an excuse for special treatment is a disservice to the seriousness of feminism. Stop this sexism. Period.' Well, hold on. Period leave is for those who want it.[26] It's not like postfeminists are asking that all women be monitored and sent home on the first day of their menstrual cycle[27]. Don't take period leave if you don't want to. Simple. It's called 'choice', something my generation swears by. *Kapish?*

The fact that millennial women talk so much about choice must be irritating for many from the older generations. It's understandable. They had to fight tooth and nail back in the day so we could have this choice today. But what's really bothering them is perhaps that we're using choice not only to fuck patriarchy, but many-a-time to do culturally normative feminine things that they worked so hard to overcome. Many of us have embraced motherhood to the point that feminist mothers-in-law can't understand what went wrong in their

---

[26]Like me, who, since the age of ten has had to take days off school and work once a month because I get severe cramps. And I don't even have endometriosis.

[27]Unfortunately, the practice of isolating women on their period is rampant in India. A college in Gujarat even forced its female students to remove their underwear to prove they were not on their period!

bahu's heads; female bosses cannot stand to see young women give up their careers for the sake of family or self-discovery. Young women who rebel against female authority are also a cause for concern: how could they disagree with the ideology of older women who pioneered to create the first feminist narrative? Comply, my lovelies, they seem to say. Be supportive of feminism proper and learn. As Indian society is one that venerates elders, not only because of their wisdom but simply because they're older people, it is very hard for young women to tell off their feminist female superiors without being implicated on many accounts: for disrespect, for being anti-feminist, for arrogance. This is not to criticize the previous generations of intrepid feminists. We sit on a platform they built for us. Nor am I trying to imply that all women from a generation think or act alike. However, there seems to be a tussle between older and younger feminists (and non-feminists) around what constitutes choice and activism.

The 'narcissistic reflexive thought process' of contemporary feminists (where one believes 'I define myself as feminist and so everything I do is a feminist act') obscures the seriousness of feminist ideology, argues Jessa Crispin, the author of *Why I Am Not a Feminist*. According to Crispin, feminism has now devolved into a marketable product that satiates itself with inoffensive slogans like 'the future is female'—toothless when unaccompanied by radical politics. Such criticism is made of Indian women by their more radical peers too. 'Of all the terrible things that have happened in the fight for equal rights, I am going to stick my head out and say, this current phenomenon of privilege masquerading as successful feminism is the most damaging,' writes Veena Venugopal eloquently about how 'Feminists Have Killed Feminism'. I find this somewhat uncanny, this dismissal of (privileged) women's individual empowerment as undeserving of feminist appreciation. In the 1980s, academic Madhu Kishwar, a polarizing figure in gender studies, argued that Western feminism inspired an extreme individualism in women which estranged them from their communities—making them selfish: '[i]n our culture both men and women are taught to value the interests of their families and not make their lives revolve around individual self-interest. Most feminists consider this world view a product of lower self-esteem.' Today, the problem that feminism seems to have with its young cadets is exactly the same: that they are extremely individualistic—to the point that their feminism is no longer collective.

'In society at large today, there's a focus on individualism,' says Professor Padma Rani, the director of the School of Communication in Manipal University. 'Young women aren't aware of the ground realities. They're talking from a very different pedestal. They're only looking at short-term goals, and not at the long-term. Take #MeToo for instance. It brought forth a lot of issues. Various people supported those issues. Action was taken against some of the offenders, it was not taken against others. Whatsoever. But when I spoke to senior recruiters, I saw that with all these movements they were worried about recruiting women. This is an issue as it may close many doors for women.' Professor Rani tells me that our lives are embroiled in larger gender inequalities that we don't recognize, and even the choice we claim to have made is actually still within a structure of oppression. 'Women from urban, middle-class Indian families live in a very idealistic world where they believe that everything is equal,' she notes, 'that they should get what they get and can make individual decisions.'

It is true that #MeToo has churned up the workplace. Male-dominated industries are shutting out women because they are likely to participate in campaigns like #MeToo—outing important men and bringing shame to their company. But I can only scoff at the cowardice of men. Trying to avoid women altogether like the sannyasis of yore who couldn't trust themselves around beautiful apsaras, for fear of straying away from their tapas and falling for their charms. So, what's new? I personally think it's crucial to let the #MeToo movement play out its course. Yes, I understand that there may be some innocent male casualties along the way. Decent men may be wrongfully accused, though this is also debatable. To protect the few good men in our society, we cannot let the beasts go scot-free.

(And then perhaps after weeding out all the offenders, we can start running short orientation courses on how to behave with female colleagues for newly onboarded men and grand old boys who are frightened of women.)

As for the matter of young women's individualistic ideas of empowerment and their hashtag activism, I have no qualms about them. 'We are at the brink of a gender equal world, the big change is social media,' the UN's deputy representative for India, Nishtha Satyam, said at a feminist conference. 'Never before was 140 words or a status on Facebook seen as a political opinion.' She's right. The advent of technology and social-media platforms are reshaping feminism and activism today like never before. Granted, internet feminism isn't inclusive of all Indian women, but that doesn't negate a seemingly privileged person's experiences or disqualify their version of feminism.

'Feminism to me is about a woman being able to express who she is freely and unapologetically,' says Elavarasi Manogaran, a researcher and computer science educator based in Singapore. 'It's the freedom to be our beautiful, innate selves and let our natural qualities shine through, in a world that is invariably telling us how to be.' Born in a small city in Tamil Nadu, Manogaran went on to get a master's from the University of Edinburgh and worked as an assistant professor at Vellore Institute of Technology, before moving to Singapore. When I ask her what she is most proud of about herself, she responds: 'My resilience and my ability to stand tall and grow out of every failure that I face and for being the woman I always wanted to be, rather than living up to others' expectations. Oh, I'm also a proud mom now. I've produced this wonderful compassionate human being who has added more meaning, value, and purpose into my life and I'm grateful for it.' While Manogaran's version of feminism revolves around self-empowerment, it does not shy away from social responsibility. She notes that feminists 'are the vanguard of change'. She believes that they must possess 'a sense of compassion for fellow human beings and treat everyone with equal respect, irrespective of their gender, caste, or creed.'

Even while millennial women's idea of feminism may be rooted in their lived experiences, this does not mean they lack humanity. Often, young women stand in solidarity with social issues that their hearts bleed for. But that's not enough for stickler feminists opposed to meritocratic individualism and cherry-picked solidarity. Unless a woman supports every issue that's a human rights issue, she will be disqualified from feminism by feminists. The fact that she may be helping to lift women less privileged than her in her private life will not be taken into account because she's not intersectional in theory. Take a step back, protectors of feminism. Talking about human rights in the abstract is all very well, but how does it play out in one's real life? What of all the underprivileged women you meet every day—do you treat them like equal humans? Tell me, do you all let your domestic workers sit on your couches and dine at your tables?

'Borders between countries are marked out by fences and guards, but borders between classes are marked out by where you sit, where you may go to the bathroom, and where and with whom you may eat,' writes Tripti Lahiri in *Maid in India*. The book reveals the underlying class tensions that animate most employer–employee relationships in the domestic sphere. 'Two-thirds of all domestic help employed by families are women and that share rises to 80 per cent if workers whose duties take place outside the house are excluded.'

We can talk all we want about intersectional feminism, but unless we start cleaning our own toilets and mopping our own floors, or pay those who provide us those services fairly (inclusive of paid emergency/sick leave) and treat them with dignity, we're failing. Of course, some feminists do practise what they preach, going out of their way to empower their female domestic workers, but I have met some feminists who train their maids like they're in a military bootcamp. As far as conservative women are concerned, there are Hindu/Jain ladies who'd never hire a Muslim or Dalit lest the purity of their household be tarnished. But I also know of traditional housewives who confide in their maids and take their advice (of course, only as long as they don't cross the line).

Inequality endures on the Indian subcontinent and in our everyday lives. Even for women who are devoted to #womensupportingwomen, it is crucial to remember that supporting peers is entirely different from supporting underprivileged women. Talking down to the women we're trying to empower and trampling over their ways of seeing to promote our version of naarivad is not an equal proposition. Many middle- and upper-class women feel entitled by virtue of their social position to guide working-class women on all matters concerning feminism. This tendency becomes even more problematic when urban women try to advocate for poor rural women. By focusing the lens on issues like domestic violence and dowry (she has a drunkard for a husband or that her community is backward in its treatment of women) middle- and upper-class feminists effectively ignore socio-economic issues that affect poor women's everyday lives. They sort of expect all women to begin their fight against the patriarchy by standing up to the men in their domestic life first.

'It's important not to reduce gender relations to the domestic sphere only,' says social work pioneer Sejal Dand, the co-founder of ANANDI[28], an innovative feminist organization that works with marginalized women in Gujarat. 'If a rural woman says that her husband is abusive, drinks or sometimes beats me, but I don't want to talk about that, I want to talk about water—I can't say she doesn't understand the reality. She is choosing what to foreground at what point and decides where she wants to act. Her primary enemy is not the man in the house, but structural injustice.' Unlike feminist organizations that instrumentalize poor women to promote their own agendas, ANANDI is unique in that it gives rural women the opportunity to set up their own agenda and decide the course of action. 'We decided very early on that rural women could set up

---

[28]ANANDI builds grassroots-level leadership, works towards ensuring that women from vulnerable communities get their entitlements and build sustainable livelihoods, organizes campaigns for awareness and conducts action-research projects to bridge the gap between feminist praxis and theory. More information about their work can be found at www.anandi-india.org.

Smashing the Patriarchy

their own agendas—we went with an open mind,' says Dand. 'We had long conversations with local women; we stayed at their villages and built agendas with them. Then we brought in interventions and programmes.' This approach allows one to understand where rural women seek change and what cultural values they cherish, explains Dand, who primarily works with Adivasi women. 'These women have intrinsic dignity and are magnanimous leaders. Their struggle relates not just to gender relations, but to the environment at large, including humans, animals, and the earth.' Most development policies are made using a top-down approach without taking into account the realities of rural women's lives, but Adivasi women have the courage to question the legitimacy of such policy. 'Who gets to decide what is a primitive and what is a sophisticated choice? While all Adivasi women want education, this doesn't mean everyone wants to leave their lands and find a thankless job in the city. Some women may want to work on their fields and grow their own food, while others may want to become a teacher or collector. Each woman is free to decide that for herself.'

Only a few women's organizations across India work in a bottom-up manner. For most others, feminist advocacy is an instituted top-down venture. While one cannot deny that such advocacy has had it successes, it is also a fact that 'such interventions are designed and delivered in increasingly disempowering ways, instrumentalizing poor women, and being distorted to serve other agendas.' Neither can we ignore the reality that subtle shaming is often used as a ploy to help underprivileged women aspire to something better. If you say that in order to get the feminist message through to an illiterate woman, a little bit of goading is okay, that's your (class/caste) privilege talking. It's not for nothing that urban working-class (Dalit and Bahujan) women's collectives have taken the mic to speak for themselves now because for the most part, middle- and upper-class women are entirely insensitive to DBA women's sensibilities. Empowered by the theories of anti-caste movements,[29] working-class women are creating a new feminism for themselves and advocating the idea to others using language that is relatable.

'Honestly, the first time I felt like I could take control of my own life was when I attended a meeting of the Magalir Sangam[30],' Prabha S., a domestic worker from Tirupattur, tells me. 'They made me realize my own worth. They encouraged me to go to work, earn my own money, and live well.' Born into a poor household, Prabha says it took her a while to realize that she couldn't afford to depend on the men in her family to provide for her. 'There have been times in my life when I didn't even have enough to eat. Only after I started to work could I manage to eat well. Standing on my own feet and working hard has brought my family to a better place. I want my children to be well-educated and not become like me.'

Working-class women's collectives in metros advocate for women to work with dignity. They sensitize women about their rights and protections, taking into cognizance not only class, but also caste. In Chennai, for instance, several domestic workers do not clean toilets or if they do, they charge over and above their regular wages for other domestic work, in an attempt to disrupt the historical practice of delegating menial work to the Avarnas as per varnashrama dharma[31].

But then there's the thorny issue of sex work. Is sex work dignified work? For most Dalit and Bahujan feminists, sex work is outright exploitation, because their women have been historically forced into prostitution or dedicated to temples as joginis or Devadasis, slaves of god. Most Savarna feminists do not consider sex work (or bar dancing) as a valid choice, either. Across lower-, middle-, and upper-class women's organizations, sex workers are not included as equals.

---

[29]Such as Periyar's self-respect movement or the Phule/Ambedkarite anti-caste movement.
[30]A local women's welfare organization in Tamil Nadu.
[31]The basis of India's caste system. As per varnashrama (the caste hierarchy), people are expected to follow their dharma (the work prescribed for their caste). Even today, around India, Dalits are primarily employed as manual scavengers, cleaners of drains, and as garbage collectors, while Bahujan women are employed for menial housework.

Since their work is considered undignified, they are seen as victims, not agents.

'I really feel proud to be a woman in prostitution,' asserts Shabana, a sex worker from Sangli. 'We have a right to speak. Whatever rights you have as citizens in a society, we also have those rights. What is the matter even if we are women in prostitution. Are we not women?' Shabana did not enter the sex business out of coercion and freely chooses her clients. She notes that she is empowered in several ways and points out that married women are more vulnerable to contracting HIV from their husbands compared to her, because she insists that her clients wear condoms. Shabana is a member of VAMP/SANGRAM, a revolutionary collective that mobilizes sex workers to improve their working conditions and proclaim rights. 'VAMP members don't want to be "saved" by foreign organisations; they want to be respected as human beings,' writes Professor Andrea Cornwall for *The Guardian*. 'To see them as "prostituted women" is to treat them as not fully human, incapable of determining their own destinies or, indeed, of working together to claim justice. It's precisely that kind of attitude that perpetuates the abuse sex workers experience.'

In fact, it is a myth that all women in sex work are trafficked into it. In her book *Intimate City*, sociologist Manjima Bhattacharjee goes deep into the discourse of sex trafficking. She illustrates how most sex workers do sex work out of their own volition, and how they are routinely arrested and sent back to the communities/societies they once escaped, completely undermining female agency. The narrative of trafficking is problematic because it further adds to the stigma of sex work, when what sex workers really need is for their profession to be decriminalized and theirs rights protected. Only a handful of organizations across India work to empower sex workers and help them live a life of dignity while pursuing sex work. The Durbar Mahila Samanwaya Committee is one. Based in West Bengal, it recognizes sex work as an occupation and works to protect the rights of female, male, and transgender sex workers.

Traditional feminism's approach to sex work extends to other work that involves trading the female body for money as well—including surrogacy. In recent times, there has been much debate about surrogacy. The 2019 Surrogacy (Regulation) Bill criminalizes commercial surrogacy altogether (thanks to women's rights groups calling out India's rent-a-womb racket). Now, surrogacy can only involve Indian parents, can be done only for close relatives, and no money must exchange hands. Surrogate mothers earned between ₹400,000 to ₹1,200,000 per birth—a lot of money for a woman trying to break the shackles of poverty. Instead of regulating this exchange, our policymakers repeatedly end the means of such livelihood, while also not providing an alternative source of income for these women.

The word *choice* continues to have umpteen connotations and drastically dissimilar consequences for women from different socio-economic situations. In this scenario, who gets to decide who's a 'real feminist' and who isn't?

4

DEMYSTIFYING THE FEMININE

Is femininity a transhistorical phenomenon or is it a myth that the patriarchy made up to imprison women for its own masochistic delight? In most phallocentric cultures, femininity has been chiselled out over millennia to represent the attributes of an ideal woman. From the lofty qualities of selfless nurturing to self-effacing humility, its often misogyny veiled as virtue. Femininity has also become representative of suffering, submissiveness, and spite, a codification that is still a part of our lives. India is an exception in that it has also nurtured the quality of justified wrath and feminine rage, in the form of Kali. However, even She, who is eternal time and death, is forced to bow down to the fount of supreme masculinity. It is no surprise then that the contemporary woman has become somewhat jaded with the concept of femininity.

Every woman contemplates the femininity within herself at some point or another in her life, defining herself either by embracing or rejecting it. But no matter what her choice, it remains a phantom in her mind that doesn't fade away. There's an unconscious lingering. A perpetual procession of ifs and buts. Perhaps, this is because femininity transcribes itself not only in our sexed bodies and our performance of it, but also in how we experience life. Most women know it to be true that their minds and bodies are intimately entwined. As inherently transgressive beings whose bodies can shift from being motherly to erogenous, from sexed to sexless, women's thoughts are boundless too. They are conscious of every sensation, every thought, everything unthought. Femininity is that quintessential element which gives a voice to the unconscious. To discover our complete inner selves, its significance is tremendous.

Even so, femininity and feminism share a difficult relationship. Since most theory is logocentric, *feeling* is often negated as regressive. And especially since emotion is central to the feminine experience, it is of little value to the socialist or Marxist feminist who seeks political change, because individual desire isn't compatible with collectivising. As literary and cultural theorist Leela Gandhi points out: 'This prejudice against feeling is sustained partly by the assumption that the condition of "interiority"—required by feeling—presupposes a receding away from the social into the narcissistic pleasures of fantasy and the imagination…. Thus, female subjectivity [is]…"the site where the opposing forces of femininity and feminism clash by night."'

It's undeniable that the female *self* is fluid. Zie is capable of perceiving the world through a multiplicity of self-states. Zir thoughts are polymorphous and do not fit neatly into ideological agendas. The patriarchy has always been suspicious of this aspect of femininity. From a masculine perspective, this propensity to shift inherently ruins a woman's capacity to uphold abstract ideals. After all, empathetic women are known to make ethical choices even when they are in conflict with the ideal.[1] On the flip side, incensed women are capable of seeking retributive justice and toxic femininity. In effect, women are considered lesser beings who are bound to the contradictions of earthly life. Men, meanwhile, are capable of transcending the everyday to espouse superhuman objectives. And what do you know, the patriarchy locates this ability in masculine steadfastness and reliability. Women, we are told, are prone to feminine instability.

The patriarchy is obsessed with every supposed female flaw. No woman, not even the chaste Sita, is exempt from being accused of feminine failings[2] because ladies tend to cross the line, and do things

---

[1]Psychologist Carol Gilligan illustrated this phenomenon in her book *In a Different Voice*. She found that women seriously considered their responsibilities to others while making ethical choices, while men tended to blindly submit to abstract ideals.

[2]Her fidelity is questioned. She's blamed for being abducted. For carelessly crossing the

their lords bid them not to. There's something wild and primitive about women. How can their minds then be expected to contemplate rational or metaphysical thought, stuff that only the masculine mind can do? 'Within the male centred conception of the world, woman is Other, that against which the transcendence of the male subject is contrasted, an immanent thing, a body, an object characterized by its sex,' writes Karen Green. So, the woman who tries 'to affirm her status as a transcendent subject confronts the temptation of theorizing herself as masculine and denying her status as woman.'

Women are the creators of the continuum, the inheritors of both masculinity and femininity. We may as well abandon one in pursuit of the other. For all we know, female masculinity may be the tool that emancipates us from the shackles of feminine compliance. And here we find ourselves in a quandary. Femininity doesn't exist only in relation to masculinity. It exists in itself. Whether we meld our femininity with masculinity, or deny our femininity to assert our masculinity in order to create newer ways of seeing, our self-reflexivity doesn't let us forget our roots. Traces of primeval femininity exist in us all, be we hetero-, queer, bi, homo-, trans, or asexual, irrespective of how we perform our gender. Femininity taps into the Imaginary,[3] it is a cosmic way of knowing. We cannot, try as we may, extinguish it.

Our liberation as women does not come from denying our very own existence, but 'consists in refusing to be "the Other" and asserting instead "I am"—without making another "the Other"' as philosopher Mary Daly writes. Masculinity is an inherent part of the female universe and always has been. Unlike men, who locate femininity in females, women have always known that they hold both aspects within them—women, after all, birth all sexes. So, it

Lakshman Rekha, for disobedience. Even while the patriarchy celebrates her feminine devotion, it also is suspicious of her femininity.

[3]As theorist Brownyn Davies writes, due to 'their otherness to masculinity, women are also constituted as other to conscious, rational thought…and are able to include in their range of considerations the emotions, feelings, and other "irrational" elements of their being that have been relegated to the unconscious by men.'

makes little sense to distance ourselves from femininity in order to be accepted in the masculine world. We must reclaim the femininity in ourselves, for ourselves.

In a land like India, possibly the most dangerous place in the world to be a woman, you'd think women would give up on their femininity. But no. Contemporary women are taking back control over their bodies, sexuality, and *feeling*, and reinforcing their femininity. We see this across the spectrum as young women guiltlessly channel their femininity online and offline: in their words, attires, thoughts, art, and action. But why is this happening here? Why are they seeking inspiration from the life of their spirit; from primeval femininity. Is it because women are unconsciously falling back into patriarchal traps?

In the West, where everything is seen in binary opposition, there is little space for nuance. The feminine aspect has been completely culled out from its memory, because it is the unnecessary Other. Cultural feminists can only speculate about the attributes of the divine pre-Semitic feminine,[4] because all *Her* trails have been erased. In India, however, the feminine aspect has always held sway. Its influence may have waned and waxed, but it persisted in our collective imagination. The fact that countries like the United States are still unable to accept the idea of a female president is indicative of Western culture's contempt for the powerful feminine. At least, in India, thanks to the Mother Goddess cult, female leaders are accepted by men. They only need to relinquish their sexuality altogether and become Amma or Mataji, the respectable feminine. Our battle with the patriarchy, it seems, is then somewhat different. It involves expanding the idea of feminine respectability. Undoing patriarchal definitions and tapping into indigeneity to discover the raw power of an all-encompassing femininity, one that merges with and detaches from masculinity at will.

---

[4]Cultural feminist Matilda Joslyn Gage believed that the Bible did not contribute in any way to women's rights. 'In one of her most intriguing ideas, Gage borrows from occult theories to postulate that the notion of a "lost word" or a "lost name" is really the lost memory of the divine attribute of motherhood—of the feminine. When that is back in its rightful place in the cosmos and in the culture, the lost power will be restored.'

Perhaps it will do us well to decouple with mainstream Anglo-American feminism in our quest to know the feminine. If we need some inspiration, we can find it in French feminism, in the écriture feminine, which provides a new language, a 'feminine syntax', to explore our own selves. Or better still, we can look for flashes of knowledge in Indian proto-feminisms. As Jasbir Jain envisages in her book *Indigenous Roots of Feminism*: 'Draupadi deconstructed the notions of chastity and sati; Sita, of power and motherhood; Kali, of violence; Puru's young wife, of sexuality; the bhakta women, of marriage and prayer.' There is a trove of feminist thought in Indian epics and mythologies. All that really needs to be done to identify the brazen heroines of our past is to peel away the layers of mansplaining. As historian Wendy Doniger does in *The Hindus: An Alternative History*, 'the later Brahmin imaginary greatly played down Sita's dark, deadly aspect and edited out her weaknesses to make her the perfect wife, totally subservient to her husband. How different the lives of actual women in India would have been had Sita as she is actually portrayed in Valmiki's Ramayana (and in some other retellings) been their official role model.' India's proto-feminist heroines aren't all mythical, by the way. Remember the royal courtesans and ganikas of Buddhist times, like Amrapali and Vimala, and their legendary artistry? Not only did these women amass wealth and power, they also donated to the Buddhist order, and pursued a life of self-realization, seeking nirvana. And what about all the accomplished women of the Mughal period? Empress Nur Jahan led a vast empire with her political acumen,[5] while Hamida Begum rode into battle with her husband, and Jahanara wrote Sufi treatises.

Femininity has many meanings in India. It always has and always will. It holds the secret of flight. Tells the story of creation. Gives the power to sustain. To love and raise. It is the rage that ends all evil. Our foremothers have whispered it in our ears and infused it

[5]Read Ira Mukhoty's *Daughters of the Sun: Empresses, Queens and Begums of the Mughal Empire* for such empowering stories.

in our blood. Their grit was a revelation. Your thoughts are your inheritance. Cherish the contradictions, because in it, you will find the feminine truth.

Performing Gender

'I thoroughly enjoy and prefer "genderless" characters,' says Kanchi Kamatchi Thangadurai, an intrepid performer who has worked in theatre, mime, stand-up, improv comedy, and burlesque across India and Europe. 'By this I mean scripts or monologues written in such a way that male or female [persons] could perform them. Or, the character is so exaggerated or large that it doesn't matter whether a woman or man is playing them.' But then, I ask her, don't you think there's any difference between a man and woman's performance, even if the character is genderless? 'We are each trained differently either in movement styles or by being a male/female—we do come with our own baggage which colours the way we perform. So, yes, in that sense, women and men perform differently, as every performer is unique.' However, she says, performance training is about letting go of certain habits. As concerns tapping into feminine emotions, Thangadurai believes both male and female performers can access them if they choose to. Trained at the London International School of Performing Arts and at the Comedy Café Berlin Training School, she is a seeker of the pure art of performance and has experimented with various forms. 'I tried burlesque to help me overcome issues around my sexuality,' she discloses. 'Growing up with parents from conservative backgrounds in places with conservative lifestyles and attitudes, coupled with my sensitive nature, has had a negative effect on my sexuality—ranging from shame, anger, sadness, injustice, disbelief, and denial of femininity, to feelings of not owning my own sexuality, feeling ugly and undesirable.' Performing burlesque acts is like putting on a comfortable mask, she tells me. It lets her view her journey with personal issues as a work in progress.

We all put up masculine or feminine (or genderless) acts every day to conform to or rebel against societal norms. But performing our gender a certain way doesn't eliminate the contradictions within us. For even when we perform femininity as codified by the patriarchy, it doesn't necessarily erase the masculinity within us, and vice versa. We're always either both or neither. There's a certain queerness inside all of us that manifests ever so often. Judith Butler argues that gender is an 'identity tenuously constituted in time' and 'instituted through the stylization of the body.' Irrespective of our sex, we can perform *woman* or *man* because these genders are constructed through specific performative styles (femininity = female; masculinity = male). In theatre, we constantly see women push the boundaries of gender in performance.[6]

'So I, warrior, man, woman, and in-between, I Shikhandi, ask nothing, except that you leave Bhishma to me!' Actor Mahnaz Damania's voice rises towards the rafters of the National Centre for Performing Arts in Mumbai. She is Shikhandi, a woman-turned-man, the earliest trans character mentioned in Indian mythology. She'd earlier played alpha female Chitra in *Sundays with Chitra & Chaitali*,[7] which drew from the story of Chitrangada. Why is she drawn towards performing such gender-fluid characters, I ask her, to which she replies: 'I've acted in glamorous Bollywood films and played several conventional roles but finally felt at home playing Chitra. The confusions that she has about love, sexuality, and identity are so relevant even today.' Dusky and tall, Damania has had to constantly defy society's conception of beauty and femininity to get to where she is. 'I've been told I have aggressive body language for a female,' she says. Has Indian theatre come of age, to accommodate the diversity of performances that female actors are capable of? 'Things are changing slowly and we're definitely getting there,' she assures me. 'The structures of stories are changing. Female actors now have more space to experiment. We have to take control of the situation.'

---

[6]In thespian Anuja Ghosalkar's *Lady Anandi* (a documentary theatre performance), she plays everybody: man, woman, man as woman. It's a fluid exploration of transition.
[7]This play was written and directed by Isheeta Ganguly. *Shikhandi—The Story of the In-Betweens* was written and directed by Faezeh Jalali.

Inside and outside theatre, members of the LGBTQIA+ community constantly redefine gender. They express their femininity and masculinity interchangeably. In fact, Indian historians argue that in precolonial times, the expression of this inherent gender fluidity wasn't curtailed entirely, even if frowned upon. Only after Victorian morality took hold of us did we mark out imperious gender boundaries. It isn't impossible to imagine this former world, where even as our sex determined our roles in society, we could traverse the spectrum of sexuality and expression. Somewhere along the way, this fluidity disappeared. Art historian Niharika Dinkar locates this at 'the confluence of two significant factors in colonial modernity... the development of a print and cinematic culture.' She writes that these mediums 'amplified and distributed the female body in ways unimaginable previously...recasting feminine identity through the lens of colonial codes of respectability and morality.'

Since cinema has visually recorded the feminine ideal since the 1950s, we can see how the codes of gender performativity shift. From vintage heroines who exemplified Edwardian feminine dignity alongside daring, to the 1970s and 80s where we saw them typified as femme fatales or demure domestic women, and, later, the 1990s when women became mere eye candy and femininity crystallized into glamour, we see the archetype change, not in the form itself (for the ideal female body is always fair and skinny) but in its presentation. Even today, feminine performance for the big screen is codified. Women who don't fit the prototype are masculinized and othered. Queerness only exists on the margins of mainstream cinema. Trans and homosexual characters are stereotyped. Plus-size women are presented as unattractive and unfeminine or, sometimes, as raucously feminine. These typecasts have fused with the Indian psyche. And because femininity, femaleness, and beauty are intricately entwined in our culture, women who don't fit into the mould of the ideal are often left questioning their own desires.

'Plus-size women must not shy away from their wish to look alluring,' declares Bengaluru-based Anuja Pandey. 'Every woman essentially is beautiful and feminine. She just needs to become aware about it. Once she embraces herself in totality, nothing can stop her from looking great.' Bullied and body shamed as a child, Pandey went on to become a consultant for top beauty pageants including Femina Miss India, thanks to the strong sense of self-respect that she says her mother instilled in her. On her blog Lofty Spectrums, she provides beauty and fashion hacks for plus-size and rich-skinned women, among others. 'I believe that if you are a woman, you must not be afraid to experiment with your beauty and experience yourself. All of us have one attractive feature on our face and we must highlight it. Make-up is like an art, a play of tones, rich and dark, expressing your mood of the day.'

Society celebrates the performance of femininity among women it classifies as beautiful, but denies its pursuit to others it considers unattractive, and young women are calling this out. Feminine performance, they have rediscovered, is an act, and admiring oneself, a pleasurable prospect. Everyone is entitled to it. To look into the mirror. Put on that red/blue lipstick. Wear that sexy dress/blazer. Do whatever feels right, no matter what one's body type or gender identity. Femininity is narcissistic. It is not meant for the sole purpose of pleasing the male gaze, it's primary goal is to increase one's own self-esteem. Lesa Lockford argues that the modern-day woman is fully aware of what she's doing: '[s]he takes femininity out of the bedroom and makes it public. Hers is not an accepted feminist politic, but step by step, she makes it more difficult for anyone to presume her sexual availability. Incrementally, she makes femininity another possibility for performing feminist woman.'

Feminists have consistently denounced the pursuit of femininity among emancipated women. Since femininity is inherently associated with passivity, they are suspicious of its subversion as well. The reasoning is that when a woman in a male-dominated industry performs overt femininity (comprising charm or humility, apart from beauty), she'd inevitably be viewed as a (submissive) woman, not as the performer of a particular professional role that is meant to be genderless. But then, we must again ask, what role in the world is genderless? Even if a woman chooses not to perform her femininity, she doesn't become exempt from gendered expectations. In the *Journal of Professions and Organization*, Swethaa S. Ballakrishnen writes that while women are expected to be masculine to get things done, they're also required to be ladylike with their peers. 'This coinciding expectation and undervaluation of what are coded to be "feminine" traits remain persistent and more recent research confirms a continuing expectation on elite professional women to be "chameleons",' she writes. They need to 'embody masculine traits (defined as aggressiveness, assertiveness, and confidence) while also being able to "self-monitor" their behaviour in expected, gender-conforming ways.' This is true of most countries around the world. Everywhere, the patriarchy persists regardless of whether we choose to perform or reject femininity. So, then, why not reclaim our femininity as we see fit?

'As a woman, femininity to me is about poise, confidence, and charm,' says Anusha Balivada, a software engineer based in Los Angeles. 'Any man or woman who exudes these qualities is feminine. As an engineer, my focus is the solution and the process by which I arrive at it. Femininity has no play there.' Balivada likes gaming, reading, learning new languages (spoken and technical), and playing tennis—in that order. Has she ever been discriminated against because she is a woman? 'Yes, I have. I've been talked down to. That doesn't bog me down. I have enough mentors (men and women), who are supportive and encouraging. No matter which field you work in, you are who you associate yourself with the most. On another note, when I came across the idea of "mansplaining", I was oblivious to it. Then I started noticing the pattern after a couple of meetings at work. It's rather funny! So, I just started working on improving my communication with the team. No one needs an explanation any more.' Do men and women think differently when it comes to science? 'I don't believe gender matters in the field of science. Variation of thought process is applicable to everyone.'

Since gender mainstreaming has happened on a policy level in most workplaces, and as women increasingly turn gender stereotypes upside down, the emphasis is not on denouncing femininity or performing neutrality, but the democratization of gender. We see this across male-dominated industries, where contemporary women perform a range of gender identities instead of simply becoming alpha to kick with the bro culture. In many cases, women cherish their differences, yet perform masculinity when it suits them. This is all the more so in workspaces where there are more female workers than men. While critics are quick to label spaces like call centres 'female ghettos', other theorists argue that there's much more freedom in these spaces for women (and men) to redefine femininity and perform gender the way they like. Anthropologist Mathangi Krishnamurthy explores the 'steady and shifting structures of gender differentiation' at call centres in her book *1-800 Worlds*. She writes: 'Even as gender discourses are conduits for the reproduction of existing structures of power, in many instances these complex iterations also prove to be remarkably dynamic in their ability to disturb these very accounts of power…they nevertheless produce confusion, possibility, and hope.'

When we say that the future is female, we don't necessarily mean that men will be vanquished. After all, they are also caught up in the patriarchy and are affected adversely by it. The fact that not all men are as masculine as the patriarchy wants them to be leads to a number of psychological issues. Boys aren't allowed to cry or explore their feminine *feelings*. They're forced to repress their emotions. As long as the superstructures remain masculine, this shall be the case. In a female future, however, men can be as feminine as they like, if they like. Just as women can be as masculine as they like.

Female masculinity isn't some futuristic possibility that doesn't already exist in India. While elite upper-caste society adopted the English code of heteronormative femininity and mandated that their women relinquish every ounce of masculinity to become sophisticated, superficial refinement meant nothing in the face of the nefarious gender injustice meted out to women from oppressed communities. For them, femininities and masculinities have always been interchangeable. If gender identity is performativity constituted by 'expressions', then caste has instituted varying gender norms for Indian women, based on positionality. Especially when we discuss femininity, it is so very important to consider what that term means to DBA women. As inheritors of their foremothers' inherently complex gender performativity, contemporary DBA women are giving voice to 'othered' sexualities and ideas that have been suppressed for centuries and pushed to the margins. *Dalit Feminist Theory: A Reader* looks into the 'complicating processes of shifting masculinities and femininities by which Dalit radicals departed from upper-caste femininity to forge new constructions of a masculine Dalit womanhood, vernacularizing and claiming universal ideas of human rights, education, individualism, daring, resoluteness and emancipation.' The book's editor Sunaina Arya emphasizes the need to theorize Dalit difference from a Dalit perspective. She calls for 'a dialectical process of collective articulation'. We will remain oblivious to the infinite possibilities of performing gender until we learn to view femininity through the eyes of DBA women.

'Dalit femininity, if that exists, is seen as crude or fetishized. Its adjectives are bold, brave, courageous, never beautiful, divine, pure. Even today, dark skin and [a] non-skinny body is associated with being "lower" caste. This is not true. There are plenty of Dalit womxn who are fair and skinny,' says Rachelle Chandran Bharathi, a research scholar working in the field of aesthetics and neuroimaging. 'Femininity thus exists as a privilege which Dalit womxn who look a certain way are unable to grasp.' Bharathi, who writes about intergenerational trauma, intersections of caste, queerness, and gender,[8] further explains: 'Femininity in our culture has been dictated by men and we cannot discuss this question without acknowledging them. We know the harm Savarna men have caused Dalit womxn,

---

[8]For various publications including *Round Table India, Skin Stories, Antiserious, Gaysi,* and *Forward Press.*

as most historical casteist violence tied with misogyny occurs on Dalit womxn bodies. One would expect Dalit men to understand our struggles—because it is natural that when one is threatened, one turns to those most likely to show support and nurturance. However, this doesn't occur,' zie points out. 'The Dalit man like any other man in Indian society carries the same patriarchal, misogynist training and adheres to the same standards of beauty and behaviour as their Savarna counterpart. As much as caste separates these two men, it's the ideal Savarna woman they desire. Desire is irrational and powerful, it is performed in different ways.' Bharathi notes that this gives cultural and social capital to Savarna women. When I ask what femininity means to zir personally, and how it manifests, zie replies: 'My rejection of femininity and my hesitation to abandon it completely arises from certain childhood incidents. My experience of masculinity feels more innate as if it existed, latent, expressed maybe after the trigger.' Sexually abused and harassed as a child, Bharathi says zie (un)consciously superimposed the psychological trauma on the site of violence: zir femme body. 'The psychological trauma is intangible but it arises from a tangible site, a dualist question that has often driven philosophers insane and much too early for any child to reconcile. Within this struggle, is the imposed idea of being feminine or masculine. Because of my experiences, perhaps, it may never be easy to distinguish if my gender identity was influenced by my experiences or if I didn't have the experiences I had, would I claim this gender identity?' Zie adds: 'And, let it be amply clear that I am not resorting to the dangerous argument that trans and enbie[9] persons have had psychological or violent childhoods, hence, the reason they become the way they are. My experiences are unique to me.'

We're all always becoming, forever getting to know ourselves based on what we live through, trying to negotiate an identity that reflects

---

[9]Abbreviation of the non-binary tag used by people who do not identify as male or female primarily. Also written as *enby* or *enbee*.

who we feel we are. Gender performativity, then, comes to be a highly individual practice, informed by conscious and unconscious factors.

Of Transcendence

'I do not think of myself as an artist or my work as art,' Alyen Foning declares. A resident of Kalimpong, she designs and creates textiles, makes dolls, and illustrates. Every object she creates tells a story inspired by her heritage. Foning has exhibited her work across India and her pieces are sold in cities like New York. 'I am questioning what art means to me,' she states. 'For me, the message, essence and spirit are important to share. Through what medium it is received is something I do not hold onto.' Her work seamlessly converts ancient wisdom into pieces of art that provide visual solace in a hard and fast world. 'For me, most of the times, the journey to those expressions [is] internal and require me to question a lot and dig deeper. This process is very intense, challenging, and exhausting most of the time. I'm looking at my roots, my ancestors, Mother Earth and her kingdom, and to myself.' There is a profound sense of spiritualism in her work that draws one back to the question of existence itself. One that is beyond femininity and masculinity. 'The feminine does draw me but it is not the only point of reference. What is femininity and feminism I truly do not understand yet. But in all the spaces my expressions are received at, I have always found some deep connections with people with similar or same songs.'

Outside the realms of duality, in cultures that preserve the oneness of all creation—femininity isn't the Other, to start with. In the Northeast, for example, every community has unique stories to tell about Mother Earth and the nature of human existence. Among the Khasis, Mother Earth is referred to as Mei-Ramew, and She is the creator of the sun, moon, fire, air, and water, the source of all life. 'It is about time we reflect on the all so popular metaphor "Mother Earth",' writes sociologist Rekha M. Shangpliang. 'Metaphorically speaking, the term should evoke our human minds to the spirituality within ourselves to respect and revere nature. We may not expect a miracle to happen through some "divine spiritual interventions" but we can definitely bring a change by closely examining the environment around us and understand what is our role in it.' In a time of ecological destruction, where governments and corporates plunder natural resources, it is quintessential that we seek to understand indigenous epistemologies and its value in the contemporary context. Also, it's important to acknowledge that women from tribal communities across India have consistently fought for the earth and all its creatures, and among them are our original ecofeminists[10].

'I love that dance allows me to experience the unknown; feelings and expressions that may not be a part of my everyday life,' says Sathvika Venkatesh, a Bharatanatyam dancer from Hyderabad. 'The power of art transcends boundaries of gender. It has the ability to be masculine or feminine, both or none in its varied forms and expressions.' Venkatesh, who currently lives in Chennai, where she heads PR and marketing at Aalaap,[11] tells me that 'Bharatanatyam draws from literature and storytelling several thousand years old, from eras when women were rulers, custodians of art forms, lawmakers, warriors, poets, and so on. I am constantly inspired by these characters in literature and poetry.' She talks of Andal, the ninth-century saint-poet. 'Her poetry and life are very often used in Bharatanatyam. She illustrates a woman's freedom to proclaim love and desire.' Venkatesh also speaks of the historical court dancer: 'She was wealthy, the custodian of a very rich art form, she had privileges and rights in the kingdom and was highly respected as a performer, and as an individual in society.' In modernity, women have redefined and revived various art forms, she points out, from 'Balasaraswati, Rukmini Devi Arundale, M. S. Subbulakshmi, Gauhar Jaan, Chandralekha, Padma Subrahmanyam, and Anita Ratnam. All of their stories are examples

---

[10]The likes of Soni Sori, Sukalo Gond, and Agnes Kharshiing have defended the environment against all odds. Younger activists like Kuni Sikaka are fighting against large corporations today, speaking truth to power.
[11]An arts management company bringing professional practices into the Indian classical performing arts space, Aalaap also creates a dialogue between the artiste and the audience.

of how women use art to fight for their choices.' Venkatesh holds that Indian art forms stimulate women 'to feel stronger, to desire, to inspire and be inspired, to fight, to act, and to take control.' Then she adds: 'Our history is filled with stories of female change-makers. Why are we today fighting to be heard and to be respected for our choices, in the name of feminism?'

Indian feminism has hardly considered classical performing arts an instrument of gender equality. Nor has it represented contemporary female performers as those who embody the potential to transcend the bounds of tradition and codified gender norms. What it has done, is locate the sexuality of the female body performing the art form and reduce it to something that attracts the male gaze[12]. However, this isn't a problem that's unique to feminism, but something that permeates all of postcolonial society. Scholar Royona Mitra situates this calamity of thinking in the nationalist and colonial discourse of chastity. She investigates the 'dilemma that has been projected upon Indian female dancers' bodies by contemporary Indian audiences when female desire occupies the centrality of a performance and projects the female body as sexual, articulate, and independent of the discipline and propriety of classicism.' This is interesting to consider because it embodies the eternal conflict that accompanies every activity of the female form. A woman is always viewed through the prism of femininity and desire, even when she performs masculinity or androgyny or nothing. Today's performers of classical arts are exceptionally aware of the contradictions that arise in their audience's mind. To transcend it, many expand and reinterpret their art forms to engage and inspire the modern-day rasika (connoisseur of rasa/aesthetics). It is important for us, as feminists, as women, to consider classical female performance through a different lens and contemplate its potential to exemplify gender fluidity. Learn to admire its tenacity to desire, to create, to perform sexuality, and explore the divine.

---

[12]Which it does do, but why is that wrong? Just so you know, it also provokes the female gaze, that is, for those who seek and relish.

Although female sexuality has been relegated to the dungeons and classified as unholy today, this was not always the case. The Harappans represented the female aspect in all its manifestations. Not only did they honour the female aspect as mother goddess and the possessor of fertility, but also seem to have admired female sexuality in itself. The famous bronze sculpture of the 'Dancing Girl' from Mohenjo-Daro continues to fascinate us with her sassiness. And her sexiness. Femininity, it seems, was unabashed and supreme. Through waves of migrations that populated India, with people bringing diverse cultures and new conceptions of patriarchal femininity, the power of the female aspect declined somewhat, but it still survived as Shakti. The angry, sexual, (un)sexy, divine mother—capable of both the erotic and the esoteric, unique to India. Even Vedic religion had to accommodate this fierce femininity into its repertoire, which otherwise visualized demure, benevolent goddesses like Saraswati and Lakshmi. But then, this has led to an inherent contradiction in our way of thinking about the feminine, which lasts to this day. Historian Nupur Dasgupta writes that the question of celibacy 'lay at the centre of all early Indian religions and demanded a marginalisation of the feminine.' Since the female body and her femininity attracts the masculine male, she is cursed for it, and shorn of her right to seek the sublime. But this hasn't stopped women from seeking the truth through various mediums, albeit a different, multidimensional truth. Something that's worldly and otherworldly all at once.

'Women not only use their sexuality, but also the innermost core of their spirituality,' says Professor Ranu Uniyal who heads the English Department at Lucknow University. 'They are not necessarily writing only for women, as women. A woman writes because it is essential for her to do so. How else would she be able to capture the multiplicity of her being?' An established poet herself, Professor Uniyal asserts that 'the sharp tone of her desire, the touch of her innate drives, her madness, her sanity, her silence, her quiver, her courage, her anger—all gets reflected in her writing.' When we speak about feminist literary criticism and its tendency to judge some female subjectivities as more progressive than others, she points out: 'If critics like de Beauvoir saw motherhood as an impediment, we have French feminists like Cixous and Kristeva who find pleasure in women's bodies, celebrate mother's milk and blood, express solidarity with women's multiple identities, her jouissance, her joie de vivre is reflected in her body. As suggested by Cixous, woman is writing herself and her body is being heard. Having said so, the binaries will continue to haunt us as long as we refuse to acknowledge and accept the Other as our own self. Difference should never invite discrimination. Difference is to be welcomed, assessed, and assimilated with an open mind. I may not agree with all that you write, but I must respect your freedom to write. Taslima Nasreen is a case in point.'

Contemporary Indian women writers are a feisty lot. They speak their own sexual truths and discursively construct multiple versions of the female self, unafraid of criticism. They rage at one time. Desire at another. Soothsay. Enchant. Philosopher Luce Irigaray suggests that when reading a female writer, we must 'listen with another ear, as if hearing an "other meaning" always in the process of weaving itself with words, but also of getting rid of words in order not to become fixed, congealed in them.' Because there exists a 'female syntax' that subverts patriarchal language. I wonder if this holds true not only for writers, but all women. Everyone's language shifts as we discover our identities and constantly subvert meaning as we speak. Talk is a 'third space,' according to cultural sociologist Shirley Anne Tate. It allows us to see women's 'identifications in process: as multiple, dynamic, fleeting with every passing word, whilst at the same time reproducing a contingent essentialism.' Women's voice, then, is a portal through which we may briefly comprehend the complexity and hybridity of the female self. But where do we hear these unedited voices?

'I'm a spoken word poet and have performed at open mics. I realized quite soon that there aren't many spaces that are easily accessible to women,' notes Vani Venugopal, co-founder of Anderooni Open Mic, a non-judgemental space where women perform for women in Bengaluru. 'At an open mic with women performers and a women audience, the atmosphere is so different to that of other open mics.' Anderooni stages comediennes, poets, performers, storytellers, and artists who use other modes of expression. Their aim is to develop a community that supports women's creative endeavours. 'A female audience is encouraging and supportive,' Venugopal tells me. This environment is important, 'especially for those who are performing for the first time, it's very difficult…it's an act of great vulnerability.'

Standing up on a stage and talking about your life, your insecurities, your identities is a brave thing to do, to unfold your image and then make yourself whole again in front of an audience. More and more, across the country, women are mustering up the courage to do this. For some, this experience is a form of catharsis, for others, a form of art, and, for many more, it is an act of protest. In all these cases, women are looking to transcend what they know about themselves, to go beyond the tags that society has labelled them with.

Another forum where women insolently speak their minds is the internet. Here we see and hear refreshingly raw, politically incorrect, and sexual words—whispered, shouted, engraved into the deep chambers of the web. Despite all its faults, the internet is 'quintessentially female technology'[13] and it is the space where women talk. Here, on TikTok, YouTube, Instagram, and other such platforms, we see women be their multiple selves. They perform a meta version of themselves—from living the life of a domestic diva and being their own reality TV stars to becoming knowledge creators or activists who stand up against injustice every day. Millennial and Gen Z women, known to be true to all their emotions, often discuss their feelings on these platforms too. All along, the patriarchy has asked women to supress their individual emotions to maintain the higher order of rationalism. Be selfless so we can be good (and emotionally stable)

---

[13]In the words of philosopher Sadie Plant. The values 'of the Internet, like the free exchange of information, the lessening of hierarchy, and the nurturing aspects of virtual communities, are female values,' she writes in her book *Zeroes + Ones*.

women. This just doesn't cut it any more. According to research by dating app Tinder, 'being myself' is the top priority in the five-year horizon for women between the ages of eighteen and twenty-five. This means that not only are young women discussing their positive and aspirational thoughts, they are also speaking of the darkness inside their heads. After all, to truly discover oneself, one needs to explore all aspects of the self.

'Something that is negative for me may be positive for you, something which is positive for me may be negative for you. These are perceptions. But general emotions like anger, hatred, jealousy or revenge, all these are also ours. Somehow, we don't accept these emotions,' says Nupur Sandhu, a practising psychologist and author. She points out that this is the case not only in India, but all around the world. 'Society teaches you to behave,' she tells me, 'but nobody teaches you to accept yourself totally. To deal with your emotions, you need to accept your emotions first. Instead of dividing your emotions as negative and positive, we must accept them all as they make us complete.' In her book *NUMI: The Guarded Loop*, Sandhu explores the ideas of self-realization and transcendence, concepts that she regularly helps others realize through her workshops and therapy sessions. A certified teacher of the 'Serenity Surrender' modality, her approach to healing involves discovering the relationship between the body and soul. 'Here we talk about the subconscious. We all have a past,' she explains, 'some of our past we remember, some other parts we don't even remember. Yet the past remains and it plays its role in our life.' Talking about traumas bygone, she holds that when we assume that we are over certain experiences but continue to talk about them, it means 'that past hasn't yet passed'. 'Serenity Surrender is about vibrations, energies, and the cosmos. Through past experiences, we can understand our present relationships.'

All our minds and bodies seek existential transcendence. To go beyond the burden and duty of positive thinking, of happiness. Of having to hold it all together. Let go of our sorrows. We want to be free. Being the complex creatures that we are, this is not a straightforward process. Each woman has to create her own individual path, with the right guidance. From psychotherapy, spirituality, a shift in one's philosophy of life, meditation, and medication (some of us need drugs to regulate our skewed emotions at times), millennial and Gen Z women pursue different paths to reach an inner balance. The starting point to healing, however, is the moment when a woman realizes she needs to spend time with herself, without guilt. More often than not, our emotional imbalances result from our lack of understanding ourselves. The more time we devote to building a relationship with the self, the more resilient we become in the face of adversity. Because, whoever you are, you will have to walk through the darkness at some point or another in your life, in your body and mind, all by yourself. Better to prepare. Young ladies these days strive for that kind of independence through many means.

'There is a certain kind of liberation that solo travel brings about, and that involves leaving one's comfort zone and being on the move, in a world full of strangers,' says Trisha Bhattacharya, a fiction and feature writer. 'Solo journeying engenders a sense of self-sufficiency and independence. It eliminates or lessens any feelings of inadequacies and enhances one's ability to differentiate between right and wrong. Although, all this depends on how calm and meditative one is. When one is travelling by themselves, there is automatically a need for quick decision-making for tracing routes and roads, and this power to depend on one's own judgement makes one feel like a free spirit. Then one can say: I made this possible.' Why do you think young Indian women are making this choice to travel alone? 'Because it gives them the ability to micromanage itineraries without indulging in co-dependent tendencies and also because it encourages devising and alacrity,' she replies. 'Travelling alone helps develop one's intuition and self-reliance, which in turn develops one's self-esteem. A woman becomes fearless when faced with a multitude of situations because courage brings with it the capacity to handle pressure and detours. She turns hawk-eyed about minutiae and develops a lone wolf's instincts as though traversing forests and dense lands.'

The Art of Reflexivity

'Self-reflexivity is a way of looking at the lenses through which we view the world, develop our self-concept, ideal self-view as well as our worldview,' says Sarbari Dasgupta Gomes, an OD practitioner, transformational coach, and diversity consultant. 'The practice of self-reflexivity through dialogue and reflection makes us aware of our own lenses (in this case gendered lenses) and review what is contextual and what is not.' Gomes is the co-founder of Reflexive Lenses Consulting at Bengaluru, and has helped scores of corporate leaders sharpen their leadership styles. She channels a Jungian framework and the masculine and feminine aspects of the self and the system simultaneity[14]. 'Most organizations have a notion of managerial competence which is heavily tilted towards masculine traits like analytical, decisive, dynamic, rational, assertive, knowledge-centric, etc.,' Gomes points out. 'Both men and women who show these qualities are noticed and promoted.' However, she notes that women are expected 'to display all those values as stated above in their behaviour, but also at the same time must display overt or covert "feminine" qualities that do not make them intimidating to others.' She says that in this scenario, 'developing self-reflexivity provides the individual with clarity about how they perceive themselves, the lenses through which they view authority and power of self and of others, and limits of their influence within the organization/social structure they are part of. Without such insights, I have often found women executives to wait for their good work to be noticed, or believe that they are not ready yet, or simply take on roles that they are offered.' She explains how we need to make a mental shift to let go of our own prejudices even while tackling those of the system we are part of: 'for instance, an abusive experience may turn

---

[14]Based on the work of Ashok Malhotra.

a person into a suspicious vigilant and increase their propensity to be afraid, with a worldview that no one, especially "men" (replace with "authority"/"women") can be trusted. However, that may have been true at one point of time, the current context in the person's life may actually not pose those threats. But since our body and mind remembers and we unconsciously act out our innermost beliefs and assumptions, the person may juxtapose the same belief on another system where those fears are minimal.'[15]

We're all acutely aware of ourselves and our varied contradictory thoughts. But how many of us take the time to reconcile them? Do we consciously explore our minds scarred with ancient traumas and let go of what isn't helping us achieve our goals? Or do we bury our experiences, letting them subconsciously influence our choices, making us angry and resentful? Naysayers may dismiss this sort of self-analysis as overthinking, one that is likely to further complicate our thoughts and lead to analysis paralysis. Especially since women are already accused of fixating on strange thoughts and obsessing over everything, asking them to think a little more may sound circuitous. Expecting women to reconcile their conflicting thoughts may also be criticized by feminists who argue that we must not diminish our rage against the patriarchy by turning the reflexive lenses onto ourselves. But it is imperative that women investigate themselves and find out why they think the way they do. Only when we understand ourselves and our thoughts more tangibly, can we engage positively with the structures that we are a part of and bring in real change that makes our systems more equal.

Moreover, self-reflexivity is also a quintessential tool to find a balance between how the world sees us and how we see ourselves. In

---

[15]'At the same time, there are needs to review how women and men both look at systems and what unconscious lenses are being used to look at systemic inequity and lack of mutuality,' Gomes adds. 'Unless both are looked at simultaneously, the pressure will be on women to change from a "victim" location to be more "assertive" and without systemic changes, the frustration [will] only build up as [a person keeps] banging one's head against oppressive or silent forces.'

the patricentric world, masculine qualities are considered superior to the feminine. We are all conditioned to perform our gender one way or the other, based on the sort of social environment we grew up in and our own natural tendencies. And depending on how we express our femininity or masculinity, we face varied barriers. We already know how female masculinity is not easily accepted by society—we have to fight tooth and nail to effectively express that side of us. But let's consider the other end of this spectrum for a moment. What happens to women who cherish their femininity and refuse to let go?

'Femininity to me means a certain quality of kindness,' says Anvitha Pillai, a Kochi-based filmmaker, 'a certain sensitivity, an intuition that can scratch beneath the surface and understand interpersonal relationships better. I have been lucky to be myself and trudge down the wedding filmmaking path and still achieve some success. I am definitely soft-spoken in the workplace and I don't like having loud confrontations. Some people take advantage of that,' notes Pillai, 'and make payments later than promised. But I have been lucky to have mostly educated, well-meaning clients who don't differentiate and respect me for what I bring to the table. I have also noticed people feel safer and comfortable with women around to shoot their weddings, especially for the bride. It's very reassuring when septuagenarian matriarchs at weddings come and tell me, "We are so proud to see a woman holding a camera today. We never saw this in our times." I think it's perfectly possible to exude charm and make meaningful work.' With a degree in art history from the Aegean Centre in Greece, Pillai founded The Marigold Company and has made scores of wedding films that are at once aesthetically pleasing and emotive. 'I feel as an artist in the film industry at large, people tend to take us less seriously if we are more feminine, soft-spoken, and put some attention to the way we dress, for example. We are definitely taken more seriously if we are affirmative, loud, and exude a mock-toughness. If we dress-down, not wear make-up, we are perceived as more committed to the project. But I hope that's changing. I hope people realize it has no correlation.'

On the one hand, feminine qualities of empathy, grace, loyalty, and nurture are considered unsuitable for the workplace. On the other hand, women who do not channel these attributes are judged. This scenario has pushed several feminists to abandon the pursuit of femininity for its inherently contradictory effects. Some take this a bit further and altogether negate the transformative nature of female experiences like motherhood, and regard the 'rejection of motherhood as a pre-requisite for overcoming women's subordination'. This is the position that Simone de Beauvoir takes in *The Second Sex*, and this continues to be upheld by many feminists. For a while, I held this position too, for fear of losing my individuality. And later, when I did decide to have a child, I was determined to not change in the slightest because of motherhood. Since becoming a mother is considered a rite of passage into womanhood by Indian society, I rejected its potentially transformative power. However, becoming a mother changed my whole life. For one thing, I learned to love unconditionally for the first time and that opened me up to the idea of acceptance. Suddenly, I found myself looking up to different women for inspiration; to other mothers who were ideologically opposed to me. I began to see how love could unite us all. 'Giving birth becomes a moment in which the most terrible pain is transformed into great joy and tremendous strength...a process endowed with the power to effect mental transformation, changing anger and violence to love and tenderness...' writes social critic J. Devika in *Womanwriting=Manreading?* '[I]t becomes a means of recreating oneself, freeing oneself of one's lacks...Motherhood becomes a basis on which the collectivity of Women may be imagined.'[16] Just as it's crucial to emphasize the choice of a woman to not become a mother, it is imperative that we don't belittle the experience of giving birth, or of motherhood. Only when we do this, can we begin to talk about

---

[16]To experience the transformative power of motherhood, one doesn't necessarily need to birth their children. Mothers of children born through surrogacy and adoptive mothers equally experience its magic. Author Mridula Koshy writes beautiful fiction and non-fiction about mothering adopted children.

the vulnerabilities we feel no matter what our choice.

'When it comes to dealing with pregnancy, childbirth, and babies, the impact on a woman's mind is immense,' says Rakhi Kapoor, a physiotherapist and antenatal counsellor. 'Most females of any species are more sensitive to threat; they are aware of their surroundings and quick to react to danger when there is an offspring involved. When we take this caring, loving, childbearing woman and put her in an urban jungle where she has to share responsibilities like earning and having a full-fledged career, it can get too much for her.' At Dwi Maternity Studio in Chennai, she has helped hundreds of expecting mothers prepare for childbirth and parenthood. 'Because of the basic design of life, a woman is more prone to emotionally heightened reactions and the popular term: mood swings. From being in a calm state of mind, a woman can swing to chaos in no time. This is her strength and not her weakness,' asserts Kapoor, who has also authored several books dealing with women's mental and physical well-being. 'Women are programmed for emotional upheavals and mental issues; they are designed to overthink so they can anticipate threats and avoid danger. This is a life skill which reflects upon a woman's interactions in every situation beyond her maternal responsibilities.' In her studio, Kapoor combines meditation, yoga, and physiotherapy with Zen, Sufi, and Vedantic thought to create routines that help women reimagine their lives as they enter a new stage of womanhood. 'Emotions are a sudden surge of feeling that comes with a lot of energy and intensity. It is important for women to unburden themselves of resentments and hurt that they hold. They must understand that it is natural to feel this way and let their steam out through crying. It's absolutely fine.' On the other hand, she states, to keep a check on one's emotional well-being, one must always keep oneself physically active and mentally occupied. 'Pursue a hobby or passion,' she urges, and then adds: one must understand that one's 'state of contentment and bliss is not entirely dependent on another person or external stimulus.'

While motherhood is a life-changing experience, it is critical to recognize that a woman remains an individual with her own desires, even after becoming a mother. Unlike the Indian metanarrative that peddles the idea of the self-sacrificing woman who devotes her whole existence to her child, real mothers have many other interests. The problem is that society scoffs at those who pursue them, especially if they aren't overcompensating in their role as mother. Since mothering is the primary role expected of women, those who choose not to have children altogether are in for some pointed social judgement, which includes detailed analyses of their sexuality, health, and intimate relationships. It takes a special kind of zest to show the middle finger to everyone and do what one likes. After all, the art of being ourselves, living our lives the way we want, is not an easy thing to do in this patriarchal world. Since we 'are living in a male power structure… our roles become necessarily a function of men. The services we supply are services to the male ego. We are rewarded according to how well we perform these services.'

Historically, only the pursuits of women that satiated the male ego were recorded as commendable. Everything that women may have done for themselves, their art, words, and thoughts, have all been lost to the expanse of time. While we are told that ancient Indian women were knowledgeable, we don't know what they did with all that talent except be good wives and procreate. Apart from some saintly prose and memories of philosophical debates, nothing else has survived the onslaught of Brahmanical patriarchy. In the medieval period, however, women[17] in the zenana wrote and painted and sang and danced, and brazenly recorded their (her)stories in their own words. This is an illustrious period of our proto-feminist history that is seldom talked about. What we understand to be femininity in today's age is not only defined by India's ancient scripts, but equally, if not more, by how women performed gender in medieval times. Women from this period held illustrious public offices, signed decrees, composed music, led armies, designed architecture, and fostered

---

[17]Like Gulbadan Begum and Zeb-un-Nissa.

fashion. Gender performativity and conceptions of femininity took on new meanings: influences from the Arabic, Persian, and Central Asian worlds intermingled with Indo-Iranian, Vedic, and native notions. It would seem that India has always been multicultural and global in its exchange of ideas much before we encountered European modernity. Surely, women throughout history (belonging to various classes of many communities) must've self-reflexively adapted to imbibe these influences. Their minds must have been rich retrieves of imagination.

'I find it very fascinating to look at women's lives closely, because there's not that much access to their thoughts already,' says Afrah Shafiq, a Goa-based artist. 'Whenever I find something new[18] regarding women, I'm immediately interested.' Shafiq is the creator of Sultana's Reality, an interactive multimedia web-story that explores the transgressive nature of women's work within the house. It's like a game, where you enter to various rooms filled with medieval/ early modern archival imagery of Indian women cheekily performing everyday activities. With every click you can see pop-ups with hidden notes, jokes, and GIFs, creating a window into the impudent minds of these women. Sultana's Reality won the Bulgarian 'Art in Mobile Applications' award and was exhibited at the Kochi Biennale in 2019. 'I'm a feminist, but it's not like I set out thinking I'll only make work around women and that's my specialization,' Shafiq tells me. Sometimes she questions herself about the whole idea of gender: 'I do feel we are living very specific lives where we identify through a particular gender, but what does that mean? I make choices and have desires that are more masculine in some ways. I really look at gender more as a spectrum or a choice.... Maybe gender doesn't have to define the way you interpret a person or a life.' So, in her work, even when she's telling a story through women's lives, which are inherently gendered, there are several other universal ideas in her art that are just as, or perhaps even more, relevant. 'When I look

[18]Shafiq was awarded a fellowship by the India Foundation for the Arts, through which she was able to access archival images of women at the Centre for Studies in Social Sciences, Calcutta.

at domestic work,' she tells me, 'I'm trying to break it down into a mechanized state of being. Tying art with science, I'm looking at robotics and artificial intelligence, and the mathematical potential of all this…. If you're doing a lot of domestic labour then the body is engaged, but it's not the kind of work that you need to keep your mind alert. So, I'm trying to imagine where the mind travels…'

The manner in which each artist experiences their gender is thought-provoking and eye-opening. It provides an avenue for dialogue with and interpretation of an artist's work. But then, what sense does it make to try and decode a female artist's work through the lens of gender, when the artist herself claims not to consider gender as uniquely relevant to her work? Those of us who wish to feminize every canon may seek to analyse female art or literature through feminist yardsticks, especially because patriarchal benchmarks often cannot fathom the depth of a woman's mind (whatever the patriarchy doesn't understand, it either dismisses as narcissistic or inconsequential). However, most feminist critics analyse female subjectivity through an apparently progressive framework, panning every other woman's work that doesn't obviously reform the female experience. But post-structuralism has undeniably demolished the idea of an Absolute (be it patriarchal or feminist), because all our realities are fragmented, contradictory, and discontinuous. It would seem then, that in the world of I, feminists must always self-reflexively make space for subjectivity: one that questions the very idea of feminism.

'Race, caste, class, colour, nationality, generation, and so on are constantly at loggerheads fighting for supremacy and inclusion,' articulates Dr Yamini Dand, a literary researcher and co-curator of the Kala Ghoda Arts Festival in Mumbai. 'With sexuality being questioned existentially, feminism, with all due respect, seems to be less a pressing need to assert, appropriate or disseminate.' A propounder of humanism, she holds that 'we have reached a stage in the urban strata where we should be able to pay back idealistic masculine chivalry with our own version in lieu of effecting empowerment.' Dr Dand, who is also an adviser to the Board of Studies at Ramnarain

Ruia College, talks about our collective 'colonial amnesia' in various disciplines, saying: 'I think it's about time we erased the colonial stooge mindset and the reinforced abrogation, comprehend our denial of being made into a worlding. We must undermine Western hegemony, accord agency, subvert nativism, and make it a starting point; step out of the civilizing mission and focus on' the revival of ancient Indian heritage. I firmly believe that this history on which we seat ourselves in a garb of "understatedness," this thin layer of dust needs to be shrugged off.'

Colonialism has had many deleterious effects on the Indian subcontinent, but none as lasting as the damage done to our collective self-esteem. We're all now colonial subjects who question the cogency of our own heritage. While we're quick to call out every 'regressive' aspect of our culture, we are doubly reluctant to espouse anything native—unless of course, it is considered 'woke' by Western standards. As for the matter of women's empowerment, most of us see it through a colonial, postcolonial, or post-postcolonial lens. We're inevitably caught up in the quandaries of Western binaries, unable to extricate ourselves from its masculine cogitation. Also, it doesn't help that we locate the beginnings of Indian feminism in the independence struggle, which was largely led by men who romanticized the feminine to embody suffering. While nationalists fervidly imagined their new nation as a mother, they simultaneously (further) demoted women to the position of 'the Other' using Western tropes. They pondered over 'the woman's question' and took it upon themselves to improve their condition. Femininity and femaleness were trapped in a cage yet again, to be scrutinized, modernized, and saved by a new benevolent patriarchy. Women's private and professional lives were then measured by masculine yardsticks.

'With the wake of nationalism in India, a newly constructed code of masculinity iconized the modern, while women became the forebearers of the traditional,' explains Shrinjita Biswas, an arts researcher and writer from Delhi. 'Art, during the early decades of the twentieth century, became a reflective medium for both the nationalist and the modernization project, taken up by the upper-class bourgeoisie men. It was in 1922, when the Bauhaus art exhibition was held in Calcutta. This event can be marked as the birth of modernism in Indian art history, an avant-garde artistic expression, which acted as resistance to the established colonial art in India. While the canon of this avant-garde movement was led by the urban male intellectuals and artists, female artists were eclipsed and criticized, in the course.' Biswas has worked with several platforms for the arts, including the magazine *Take on Art*, the online platform Sahapedia and the Alkazi Foundation for the Arts. In 2019, her experimental sound project was a part of the 15th Asian Women's Film Festival. 'A popular example of this sort of criticism faced, would be by artist Amrita Sher-Gil, a modernist whose works were often dismissed by her nationalist contemporaries. Coming from Indian and Hungarian parentage, Sher-Gil could never comfortably identify herself as Indian. Though her works gained some recognition during her times, it was never solely judged by her art itself, but mostly with the tag of a "woman" artist. Author Partha Mitter mentions an instance where Sher-Gil was awarded under the tag, the "lady artist" in the All India Fine Arts and Crafts Exhibition held in Delhi,' says Biswas. 'While her male contemporaries were free to criticize art, an outspoken and critical woman artist, Sher-Gil was dismissed of such behaviour. By 1939, Amrita Sher-Gil, the first professional woman artist in India, started feeling demoralized in the male-centric modern art world. She wrote, "Funny that I, who can accept a present without the least pang of conscience, should not be able to say that a bad picture is good even if it is in my interest to do so."' Biswas also points out that Sher-Gil was nobody's muse. 'She was free-spirited and her blurring of self and art becomes reflective in her self-portraits, however, often regarded as narcissistic. Her works mirror her subjective observations of people and the social environment that she is surrounded by. One shouldn't fail to realize the inclusion of the perceptions of gaze, female sexuality, and gender identity in her works, as a feminist trope against an exclusively elitist and patriarchal artistic hegemony.'

Whenever a woman refers to herself, subtly or overtly, she is marked as narcissistic, and not much has changed since the twentieth century. From self-referential female politicians to artists, actresses, YouTubers, theorists, and writers, everyone whose work draws from their own ilk are characterized as self-absorbed and therefore unworthy of universal commendation. As we all know, only that which is masculine or neuter (not feminine) is capable of being universal. Since antiquity, women have been accused of possessing the proclivity to let their individual egos overshadow the collective good or the higher truth. As women are bound to their bodies, they are considered incapable of imagining anything beyond it. They are constantly indicted for their vanity, for using their bodies and beauty to lure men into committing sins. Eve tempts Adam to eat the apple, Menaka seduces Vishvamitra and breaks his meditation. We women, we are seen as a vain lot.

The Female Narcissist

All of us express some behaviours that may be classified as narcissistic, don't we? Some of us obsessively overthink, going off on endless mental tangents. Others intuit and impulsively trust themselves. Most of us anxiously assess (and reassess) the flaws of our bodies. The self-assured take excessive pleasure in their beauty. At times, we doubt this reality. Tread into the surreal. Some summon up the courage to interrogate instituted conventions, especially when they infringe on personal freedoms. We're all a little selfish. Try as we may to think in the collective *we*, we end up using the pronouns of I, me, myself quite a lot. Not so long ago, selfish women like us who thought too much of themselves or asked too many questions were burnt at the stake as witches or branded as madwomen and locked up in dark rooms. These days, self-indulgent women are still called all those names, although we aren't incarcerated for our crimes as much. Speculation about the instability of our minds, however, persists.

We're still looked upon as beings inclined to bouts of melancholia or hysteria—terms that men made up for female behaviour that they couldn't fully comprehend. They also promptly dismissed our sick minds for faulty cognition and marked our unruly behaviour as madness. 'Relying on the imagery of men's lives in charting the course of human growth, Freud is unable to trace in women the development of relationships, morality, or a clear sense of self,' ethicist and psychologist Carol Gilligan writes in her book, *In a Different Voice*. 'This difficulty in fitting the logic of his theory to women's experience leads him in the end to set women apart, marking their relationships, like their sexual life, as "a dark continent for psychology".' Although many of Freud's theories have been discredited, the sexist prejudices that informed his ideas have remained in modern society's subconscious. Women's mental imbalances are assumed to stem from their sexual inferiority and their innate propensity for narcissism. Women's psychological problems are located in the realm of 'penis envy' or 'castration complex', even a woman's excessive love for herself is considered to be a convoluted ploy to make men love her, to make up for the lack she feels within herself, because you know, essentially, she is a hole. She is nothing. Nada.

'Women have served all these centuries as looking-glasses possessing the magic and delicious power of reflecting the figure of man at twice its natural size,' writes the brilliant Virginia Woolf. All around the world, women are still expected to magnify the egos of men, not bring their own into play. Whenever a woman has the audacity to be egotistic, she's accused of toxic femininity. Of narcissism. Now, narcissism isn't considered a virtue for anyone, you may say, so there's nothing wrong in calling out conceited women. Hold on though. Female narcissism and male narcissism are two different things. Men are socially conditioned to think and act in a whole lot of self-centric ways—so much so that they do not see themselves as being narcissistic when they act self-important. Society doesn't hold men up to such scrutiny. Women, on the other hand, are supposed to be selfless. Even the slightest spark of self-admiration or arrogance will set off cultural alarm bells. Also, a woman's narcissism will always be linked to her sexuality, her feminine charms or lack thereof, sensationalizing her pursuit of individuality and making it seem particularly devious.

Fortunately, contemporary Indian women are having none of this nonsense. In a society fraught with gender expectations, ladies are making choices that are self-empowering even if they are pigeonholed as selfish. Guilt, you see, is a dated concept to the postfeminist woman. She dismisses all the shade that's thrown at her because she knows that no matter what her choice, someone or the other will denunciate her for being selfish. On the other hand, ambitious women do not shy away from using all their faculties to achieve their goals. This may include skill. Scheming. Even sexual capital. As sociologist Catherine Hakim argues in *Erotic Capital*, women, these days, demand a higher return on their erotic capital, which includes qualities like beauty, sex appeal, social grace, liveliness, social presentation, and sexual competence. Is this a sign of female narcissism? Perhaps. Is it moral? Perhaps not. But morality is a socially-constructed concept too. Who is to say that women cannot use their sexuality to pursue their own ends? Not all women are saints, after all.

In any case, no matter how an egotistic woman performs her gender, be she sexy or sexless, she has to fight against the tide of judgement every step of the way. It is no exaggeration to say that as she strives to live a distinct life in a patriarchal world that seeks to generalize femaleness, her mind is bound to traverse a range of mental states. She'd experience anxiety, depression, bliss, mania, paranoia, and schizophrenia, in varying degrees, throughout her existence. While some may manage to maintain a balance in their minds, many of us skid far off the edges of light, falling into the darkness and sinking in our own thoughts. Society tells us that it is because of our narcissism that we suffer so. Had we been the ideal selfless mother, wife, daughter, saint, we wouldn't be writhing in agony. It is because we choose to exalt our own self over others that we lose our minds. But the problem is that in the tangible world, if we don't have (excessive) self-esteem, we're likely to be taken for a ride. Treated as doormats. Told what to do and what not to do.

So then, is the self-loving modern woman cursed? Is there no way that she can escape the emotional traumas of existence unless she conforms to the codes of selflessness? Let's explore this idea of selflessness a little. In India, the contradictions of being and nothingness have been explored since antiquity. While the path of renunciation has been held as supreme, more men than women have chosen to pursue that course (as a full-time vocation) through ancient and medieval times. This may be because women have historically been denied this option, but also because some women may not have wanted to go down that path in the first place. For one thing, to renounce worldly existence, a woman would have to undergo twice as many hardships as a man, owing to her messy periods, menstrual stress, the flesh and blood and gore of childbirth, all the things for which she is considered impure by saintly men. Take the Mahatma, for instance, who 'believed menstruation was a manifestation of the distortion of a woman's soul by her sexuality'. Tell me, why should women strive for the sort of selflessness that punishes them for their female embodiment? The patriarchy understands this conundrum. Which is why it decreed that women could achieve moksha by being selflessly devoted to the men in their lives. How convenient.

Call me a narcissist, but I'd say that the only place where you can find the truth is within yourself. In your female body. With your female mind. And this truth is inherently plural. Unlike the masculine absolute, the feminine truth is dynamic and ethereal.

'When we assert intuition, we are…like the starry night: we gaze at the world through a thousand eyes,' writes psychoanalyst Clarissa Pinkola Estés in her book *Women Who Run with the Wolves*. 'It's not by accident that the pristine wilderness of our planet disappears as the understanding of our own inner wild nature fades. It is not so difficult to comprehend why old forests and old women are viewed as not very important resources. It is not such a mystery.' Around the world, prehistoric myths and archetypes of women tell a story different from ours, tales of the power of the feminine. Women of those times are spoken of as clairvoyant, possessors of magics, and androgynous bodies. We seem to have forgotten what we are capable of. Even while we resist the patriarchy, we are bound by its ways of seeing, for we define ourselves in opposition to male definitions of femininity. In doing so, I wonder if we're erasing our own primeval consciousness, denying our bodies the ability to draw from the enchanting realms of femininity. Is our ultimate aim to become masculine subjects who wrest the power from men in their ways, or do we subvert the patriarchy by self-reflexively performing our androgyny, upholding our inherited femininities, enjoying its pleasures, and feeling its pain?

As much as I've tried to look at the feminine truth from different points of view, through other women's eyes, I'm bound by my own subjectivity. My experience of the world informs my politic. My narcissism exists in the innermost kernel of every word I write. So, perhaps, I should tell you a little bit more about myself and the contradictions that define me, so you can judge me for better or worse. I haven't always been a champion of femininity or femaleness. In my adolescence, I was very dysphoric. Hated every feminine part of my body and mind. When my breasts started to develop, I bound them with tape in an effort to hide them. My first menstrual cycle was one of shame. Every thought that I believed was gendered, I painstakingly erased from my consciousness. On the whole, I denied myself my femaleness and channelled every ounce of masculinity within me to toughen myself. But then, magic happened. I fell in love at sixteen. With a girl. Between us, sexuality was a fluid experience and in that space, I encountered my femininity without self-conscious pretension for the first time. I realized that I was hiding a big part of myself for the fear of being trapped in female convention. Slowly, I learned to claim all the ambiguous aspects of my bisexual body and mind. With men and women, I experienced completely conflicting, interchangeable desires. As a mother, the very same breasts that I once wished away took on surreal significance as I breastfed my daughter. All their erotic sensations transformed into tender affection. And now I as write this, my breasts are insensitive.

My post-partum body somehow feels more masculine than feminine. My relationship with my body shifts and changes. I still catch myself in moments where I feel like I'm pretending to be a woman. But such is the performance of femininity. As for my mind, my bodily experiences have inspired incompatible thoughts that linger eternally. Essentially, I'm lost in a loop of self-doubt.

'She can be jarred out of ambivalence by an intense, and often painful, emotional event which inverts or resolves the ambivalence. I'm not sure exactly how. The work takes places underground—subconsciously. It is work that [the] soul performs,' writes queer theorist Gloria Anzaldúa in an essay about contradictions and self-consciousness. 'That focal point or fulcrum, that juncture where the *mestiza* stands, is where phenomena tend to collide. It is where the possibility of uniting all that is separate occurs.' It'd seem that to transcend the corporeal, we need to engage with our female bodies and minds acutely, narcissistically experiencing our lives and thinking through all our thoughts. This phenomenology has been true in my case, at least. Somehow all the moments of intense agony—emotional and physical—make me see through the nebulousness that surrounds me. I find meaning piercing through all transitory delusions. My female body, it appears, is irreducible in my pursuit of the infinite. Of course, it's arguable whether what I experience is psychosis or spiritual awakening, but that's another story for another time.

Like a madwoman in the attic, I write these words. I know this little section of the book contains my vanity. My bias for the feminine. This, despite the fact that my masculinity has held sway through most of my life. But the moments that matter to me most, the ones that have defined me, are those that I believe emanated from my femininity.

5

SOCIETY, SANSKAR, AND CHOICE

Izzat (n.) honour, reputation, or prestige is quintessential across Indian cultures. Men are its guardians while women carry it in their flesh and blood. The enigma of femininity puts women in a difficult position. What with the magical powers of virginity and the nurturing touch of motherhood, women are seen as prized possessions to be cherished and protected, like cattle, gold, and skewed history. We are not expected to be reasonable; nor are we trusted to make the right moral choice. However, we can lose our izzat quite easily. We could wear jeans[1], have opinions, watch porn, fall in love with a man from another religion (falling prey to love jihad) or worse still, fall in love with another woman—all protests against tradition. And how do Indian men react to such dishonourable acts? Depending on how deluded a patriarch is, it can range anywhere from mild violence to rape and honour killing. It's not very encouraging to know that domestic violence is on the rise among the educated middle class. Moreover, if it takes the Indian judicial system over two years to 'allow' an adult Hindu woman[2] to move in with her

---

[1]Uttarakhand's (male) CM recently criticized women who wear ripped jeans, worrying about the sort of values they'd impart to children. After the media took him up on the comment, he clarified that he was only against women wearing 'ripped' jeans, not jeans per se.

[2]In 2016, a twenty-two-year-old Hindu woman, Akhila, converted to Islam to marry Shafin Jahan. But her father got the courts involved claiming she was brainwashed by anti-Hindu propaganda and kept Akhila (now Hadiya) in house arrest for over two years. In 2018, the Supreme Court finally intervened to 'allow' Hadiya to move out of her father's home and move in with her husband.

Muslim husband, all's not well in the world of choice. Yet, Indian women continue to make choices that are sure to piss the hell out of patriarchs everywhere.

Mind you, they are also getting on the nerves of aunties. In a Gurugram mall in 2019, a middle-aged woman told a girl that she should get raped for wearing a short dress, prompting the girl to make a video of the incident on her smartphone, which went viral. People across the country were outraged. Public shaming got her to apologize. Is this a (post)feminist win? In the same video, the girl and her friends are seen shaming the aunty for her weight, her looks, and beliefs. By posting the video on social media, did they invade her privacy? Did they police her in return, only on a larger platform that the aunty had no understanding of? If we're okay with shaming men online through #MeToo, why not use the same stratagem to bring judgemental aunties to book?

Of course, aunties are women too. It's important to acknowledge that they are unconsciously caught up in their own prejudices and realities. We shouldn't judge them too harshly. Except, just as patriarchy intended, older ladies (from honourable families and institutions) often become the repositories of outmoded traditions, often going great lengths to ensure that younger women follow in their footsteps. It's not for nothing that the older women in Gilead who emotionally and physically abuse the handmaids are called Aunts[3]. So, to fight the patriarchy, young women in India have to fight some tough aunties along the way too. Like the doctor aunties (a.k.a. gynaecologists) who judge you for having premarital sex and make abortion feel like homicide, aunties at weddings who make it their business to give you marital advice (especially if you are not married), and meddling mothers-in-law who take you to medical check-ups to ensure your reproductive parts are in place (their sons are assumed to be fecund), making reproductive choices an extended family affair where the copulating couple have little to say or do

---

[3]Fictitious characters from Margaret Atwood's dystopian novel *The Handmaid's Tale.*

except, well, copulate. Also, let's not forget that cool aunties can be judgemental too. Like the older women at work who judge you when you take leave for the sake of family, or a high-achieving aunty who calls you out for practising attachment parenting while sacrificing efficient time management.

That brings us to the other side of judgement. The feminist kind. Not only older but younger women who consider themselves modern, liberal, and progressive focus the lens of judgement on women whose choices seem parochial. Women who get married according to their religious traditions are mocked for gullibility, those who let their husbands win an argument in public are considered to be enslaved, housewives are regarded with pity or scorn (or both), believers who are against women entering the Sabarimala temple are considered anti-feminist, the list goes on. The primary judgement here is that these conservative women are victims of patriarchy. There is no consideration of these women's subjectivities. This, I believe, is because of how Indian feminism blindly follows the standards of the West where women's progress is largely plotted on a linear graph (in keeping with their histories). But we know that Indian history is not so straightforward. It dips and curves and throws up progressive sentiments a thousand years old. In a country with a veritable treasure trove of proto-feminisms, it's important that we decolonize our minds and reframe the idea of Indian feminism.

I suppose the problem is that the idea of feminism came to us with its attendant reasoning through British colonialism. In spite of trying to integrate its terminologies into the Indian context, we have not really been able to rescue it from its Eurocentric roots. Indian feminism shall always remain a consequence of Western feminism.[4] And as products of the imperial outlook which ridicules anything

---

[4] 'Feminism is not a "pure" ahistorical ideal that only one or another perspective realizes…' notes Maitrayee Chaudhuri in *Feminism in India*. 'At issue…are two related themes: one, our ambiguous relationship to the *westerness of feminism*. And two, the linked phenomena of a persistent desire *to search for indigenous "roots" and the problems of defining the indigenous in a plural society*.'

that's traditionally Indian, we are all colonized on some level. We think of Indian culture as fundamentally flawed, as one built on gender inequalities, primed to mortally punish women for their existence. The almost paranoid suspicion with which we view minor rituals and sartorial accessories stand as testament to this prejudice. Take the purdah for instance. As distinguished professor Rajeswari Sunder Rajan notes: 'Purdah, in certain western feminist analyses, has been equated with "rape, forced prostitution, polygamy, genital mutilation, pornography, the beating of girls and women," as instances of "violation of basic human rights"..."the institution of purdah is ...denied any cultural and historical specificity, and contradictions and potentially subversive aspects".' Rajan also deliberates about the speech/silence binary and wonders whether they fall within the same sphere. Sometimes, when women are silent in the face of tribulation, it cannot be assumed that they have given up on themselves—what goes on in the minds of women is enigmatic.

In our quest for collective progress, we often trample over individualism and subjectivity. We do not view 'feminism as a mode of analysis [that] leads us to respect experiences and differences, to respect people enough to believe that they are in the best possible position to make their own revolution.' We refuse to acknowledge that a woman's resistance originates as a response to her individual circumstance, and that her fight is to ensure her own survival. Even though the mode of her resistance may not be similar to ours, or perhaps even too miniscule to be considered feminist, she may be 'operating from the vantage of strategic resistance', as criminologist Karlene Faith suggests, 'watching for openings and coalescing the fragmentary forms of resistance which, in combination, articulate a potential challenge to the status quo.'

Analysing the choices of women who take the idea of self-empowerment too seriously can prove to be counter-productive as well. 'Freedom, choice, and self-responsibility—key tropes of positive psychology, neo-liberalism, and post-feminism,' writes sociologist Suvi Salmenniemi, 'subscribe to the grammar of individualism by advancing the notion that our practices are all freely chosen and that we are all autonomous agents, unconstrained by any structural inequalities.... However, making choices becomes an ethical obligation for which one must bear full responsibility.' Obviously, even free will isn't free will, as we are all operating within several superstructures. Even the choices we make are just choices that we have access to. We could then argue that self-empowered women are not really empowered, but only assume themselves to be so. If a woman makes an acceptable feminist choice, likely from the position of a victim seeking justice against the patriarchy, then she'd be lauded for her bravery. But when a woman who claims self-empowerment makes a choice that isn't considered feminist per se, then she'd be called out for her solipsism, even if that choice poses resistance to the patriarchy. Both these women have to take responsibility for their choices, so then how do we decide who's more feminist than the other? After all, aren't all versions of feminism a bit hypocritical?

When we view women as victims, feminism becomes a creed that fights against injustice, not only for women but for all marginalized communities which also politically employ the idea of victimhood. However, as young women move away from this self-view, and begin to visualize themselves as inherently empowered survivors, their allies change. Unlike their idealistic peers who espouse all issues that are (apparently) a matter of human rights first, self-empowering feminists only stand in solidarity with stuff that matters to them or when their personal demands intersect with another individual or group. Does this make their practice of feminism more selfish and opportunistic, or self-aware and realistic? Never forget that mere allegiance to human rights does not make every feminist the beacon of equality. Upper-caste and Hindu bias against other castes and religions are as intact as they were before Independence, if not more perspicuous (and vice versa), both inside and outside feminism. In this scenario, collective feminism is a myth. After all, feminism has been around for a while in urban India and has gone out of its way to claim legitimacy to speak on behalf of minority communities. Not only has there been little change on the ground, it has only served to further divide womenkind on the basis of tera feminism mere feminism se zyaada safed nahin hai, your feminism is not fairer than mine.

Feminism is altogether mean to conservative[5] women who consciously avoid the feminist tag, choosing to pursue a seemingly traditional life. They are immediately pigeonholed as feminist failures, especially because they do not tread radical lines but work within the boundaries they are socialized into. Many theorists have persistently pointed out the discord between the sort of social change advocated by feminism and India's family culture. Sociologist Suma Chitnis 'emphasised that Indian culture places greater value on accommodation and compromise, as opposed to confrontation and categorical choice'. This does not mean these women do not have 'choice'. They do, but how, when, and why they rebel against kin is for them to decide.

For women of all ideologies, meanwhile, ambition is a subjective term. Even while feminism considers financial independence a marker of empowerment, many women don't want to push themselves outside their comfort zones to be considered a legitimate feminist subject. 'Stop asking the worn-out question, *Is it possible to have it all?* Whether or not it's possible is irrelevant. Instead, ask yourself, *Do I want to try having it all in the current climate?* writes Monica Pierce in *Working Mother.* 'If your honest answer is yes—if you truly don't mind the midnight emails and the urgent phone calls from your CEO who somehow eschews resting and recharging and expects reports to do the same—then by all means, lean in! But if you've been pretending you have ambition to run the world because you feel like you're supposed to, it's OK to lean out. You don't have to try to have it all. Instead, try to have just what you want.'

Today's women are self-aware. This does not mean they have no insecurities, they do, possibly more than any generation before them, because their heads are muddled with ideas and full of information.

---

[5] I do not use this term with a negative connotation.

Nevertheless, they seek to achieve what's best for them. Mowing through all the negativity that's flung their way, women are heading towards that elusive thing called inner peace. This may be regarded as selfish or futile, because happiness is philosophically impossible to achieve in reality. In any case, women are in it to win it, one way or another.

A Woman's Place

'Patriarchy is ingrained in our society, but it's very subtle,' says Kimde Marak. This surprises me, because Marak, a historian and curator at the Tura museum in Meghalaya, also belongs to the Garo tribe, one of the world's few matrilineal societies, where property is handed down from one generation to another through the youngest daughter. 'Of course, it depends from family to family, but it's usually the uncles and the brothers who make the decisions. It's like the woman is there for the property to be handed down,' she discloses. 'Especially when a marriage happens, because we are a clan-based community, the clans will gather and it is the men who do the talking.' I ask her if there's social pressure to marry in her community. 'Honestly, I get asked this question every day to the point that I'm fed up. I go out anywhere and people are like, when are we going to get [to] eat at your wedding and all that rubbish. And I can't even be mean because in a small community, you know everyone…' Marak holds a master's in History and has done much to retrieve ancient anthropological and historical items that'd help create a record of Garo traditions, which is often eclipsed by the Khasis of the state. 'I have many friends in my social circle who are all single, and when we all get together, we have so many other things to talk about. But the moment I hang out with someone who's married, the first question they ask me is: when are you getting married?'

In India, and around the world, a woman's success is measured by the presence or absence of a husband beside, or before, her. And when every other older man is an uncle and older woman an aunty, single ladies are expected to be eternally respectful and listen to unsolicited advice about the benefits of matrimony. This custom takes a turn for the worse when gender prejudice amalgamates with apparent goodwill. Unfortunately, this proclivity to invade another person's personal space isn't confined to older generations. Young women (recently married and in the flush of love) unintentionally cross boundaries when they prod their single friends about finding the one. Singledom, rather than being seen as a choice, is treated as a consequence of a hitch—something that can be fixed.

On the other hand, once married, a woman isn't exempt from judgement. If she married within her community, she'd be assessed on tried-and-tested bahu parameters that have been around for centuries. If she married outside her community, especially if she hypergamy-d and married a man from a higher caste or class, then her entire past history would be assessed to find ulterior motives, because she's obviously a social climber. But, once these initial assessments are made, then the common judgement begins. Is she working, not working, why hasn't she had a child yet (perhaps the marriage isn't working out)? So, she has finally (after fertility treatment) had a baby, now has she hired a nanny? What, she has moved out of her in-laws' place? After all they've done for her, how could she, the callous home-breaker? Yada, yada. You get the picture.

While gender expectations in social circles nag women and push them to the brink, they seem to get no respite at work. Here, women are expected to take on affairs that could benefit from feminine beneficence. Anthropologist Mary Mills points out that the 'new demands for feminist "caring" in corporate cultures exist in uneasy relationships with longstanding metaphors of "cowboy" competition and related modes of masculine aggression in global business practise.' Not all women are Mother Teresa. Some driven women may have aggressive tendencies, aligning more with alpha males. Any attempt on their part to adapt to an approach that conforms to workplace expectations of womanhood will only leave them in a double-bind. Being too feminine at work is equated with coquettishness and being too masculine is considered pretention. Women are observed through a microscope; colleagues wait with bated breath to see when they trip up in their performance of gender, so they can be called out and belittled over a steaming hot cup of cutting chai in office crannies.

'Societal perception of working urban middle-class women, especially married working women and working mothers, plays an important role' in determining the challenges they face at the workspace, says Dr Murli Desai, a former professor of social work at the Tata Institute of Social Sciences and National University of Singapore. 'One interpretation is that her husband may not be working or earning enough. Another perception is that she does not need to earn but is not housewife material and likes the independence from household work. The implication of such perception is that she must be a dominating woman, playing a dominant role in her marriage and family.' However, if such a woman faces male domination or violence in her own marriage, 'society has no sympathy for her, as she is considered privileged to start with', notes Dr Desai. 'These women are also made to feel guilty of making alternative arrangement of childcare if they are mothers.' Among the other challenges that working women face in urban India, she tells me, is the 'double shift, that is doing paid work in the workplace as well as the unpaid work at home, before and after the official work hours. On the other hand, men generally do only the office work. Of course, this seems to be changing….' Dr Desai has also been part of several United Nations policy committees and has written acclaimed books about social development and ideology. When I ask her whether Indian workspaces, which are still mostly masculine, are looking toward gender-neutrality or gender-equality, she replies: 'The emphasis today is to discourage gender-neutrality and bring gender awareness. Similarly, the policy emphasis is on gender equity which emphasizes gender differences as well as similarities. It is no more on gender equality which emphasizes only gender similarities.'

A woman's place in society then is determined not only by how she envisages herself, but by what people around her expect her to be. Unless communities and families change their perceptions about womanhood and what it entails, feminism can never really succeed. Because if feminist women spend all their energies in dissenting and resisting social codes at large, they cannot concentrate on realizing their full potential in their personal or professional lives (to achieve their feminist goals). This is probably the reason why (post)feminist women cherry-pick what battles they want to be part of; instead of investing in the lofty and enlightened scheme of transforming society as a whole. Issues like sexual harassment and gender equity at the workspace unite them, while anti-corporate or anti-state agenda don't necessarily incite everyone. The postfeminist woman too understands the need for (progressive) change across the board, but instead of investing in traditional modes of collective feminist dissent, she often takes on the path of a personal struggle, carefully choosing how and when to contest the social, cultural or political order such that she benefits from the intervention in a real and tangible manner.

Treading this fine line of thought, we could argue that millions of young Indian women participate in online campaigns like #IWillGoOut because the result of participation is immediate. By posting #IWillGoOut on their social media feed, they are sending a message out not only to society at large, but also to their immediate social circles: to protective brothers, uncles, male friends, and acquaintances, and, of course, aunties who ban nightly outings as sacrilegious to feminine dignity. Remember, this campaign began in the wake of the mass molestation incident in Bengaluru on New Year's Eve 2017. Multiple women were groped on the streets. The home minister of Karnataka blamed the women for dressing in Western outfits and instigating the men. Of course, poor men, what can they do when faced with bare skin but act like wild animals and pounce, right? Basic instinct. Well, not really—even wild animals have elaborate mating rituals, and I'm sure they would resent being compared to sleazy men. Violent male behaviour among humans is more psychologically rooted than biological. In India, men are socialized and conditioned (often by older women) to believe that they are to zealously guard female chastity and associate with good girls only (even the much-adored Raksha Bandhan celebration traditionally prompts men to protect their sisters from all harm). So, when a woman steps out of the boundaries that she is bred to uphold (that is, instead of being prim and coy, she flaunts her skin and invites men to look at her), these men take it upon themselves to teach her a lesson (of course, only if she hasn't already tied them a rakhi, because Indian men would never sexually hurt their sisters[6]). And what better way to insult and leave a mark on a scarlet woman than groping, something that isn't rape but will surely scar her forever.

#PinjraTod, too, appealed to young women across India. What began as a petition to the Delhi Commission for Women in 2015 by students of Jamia Milia Islamia, grew into a movement that protested the arbitrary and sexist rules that Indian educational institutions practice: such as enforcing strict hostel curfews on female students, curtailing their mobility and freedom, and the moral policing and patriarchal protectionism that staff feel entitled to propagate, invading female students' personal lives. The Pinjra Tod collective also asked that universities enforce the Vishakha guidelines issued by the Supreme Court of India, to take actual measures against male students/staff who sexually harass female students, instead of dismissing complaints as harmless and not serious enough to be considered actionable. The movement spread its wings to campuses around the country. However, most universities and colleges from South India stayed away from participating in it—perhaps the words Pinjra Tod (Hindi for 'break the cage') didn't click with them[7]. A day of feminist reckoning in South Indian professional colleges is much needed though, because they are known not only for producing the highest number of female doctors and engineers in the country, but also for their institutionalized sexism and exacting dress codes for

---

[6]However, they may kill for the sake of izzat. Police registered 251 cases of honour killings in 2015; I wonder how many brothers have since killed their sisters for falling in love with the enemy.

[7]India is not a Hindi-speaking rashtra, theriyuma?

adult women: salwar kameez paired with pinned dupattas[8]. Anyhow, within the Pinjra Tod movement of the north, fissures began to emerge in 2019. 'Pinjra Tod is an organisation of Savarna Hindu women and like all other Savarna organisations it has failed women from marginalized race, castes and religion,' claimed a group of DBA women in a statement. 'We have time and again raised the issue that in many cases our oppressor within universities has been Savarna women.' But the Pinjra Tod leadership don't seem to have found merit in including these issues in their official agenda. This led to women from minority communities leaving the Pinjra Tod collective en masse.

Brahmin-Dvija feminists 'grab the mic from us, and talk about us, and get global recognition for their work, on us', proclaims Divya Kandukuri in a BuzzFeed video about intersectionality and feminism. A Bahujan activist, Kandukuri was a signatory to the statement issued to Pinjra Tod mentioned above. 'Intersectionality is not a sub-theme of feminism. It is what feminism is and should be,' asserts Kandukuri, who is also a freelance journalist. To the upper-caste intersectional feminist, she proposes: 'Acknowledge your privilege and stop occupying all the space. Redistribute the sources that you have to the marginalized without acting like a saviour. Use your social capital for amplifying the voices of the marginalized and pass the bloody mic. Reform your own casteist, racist, transphobic, and ableist households.'

Caste is a complex issue. Saying one is anti-caste doesn't make one an obvious ally of DBA women. Because while a privileged Savarna woman may denounce her caste (due to conviction or convenience), a privileged Avarna woman cannot do so. For the latter, the social prejudice that comes with being Avarna will precede her personality and achievements throughout her life. Her student peers will casually wonder whether she used the 'reservation[9] quota' because she looks

---

[8]Because future female doctors and engineers should not be wasting their time inadvertently showing their cleavage to their male peers, lest they distract them from more noble pursuits.
[9]Reservation quota for marginalized communities has been a thorn in the side of the

like she's from the creamy layer, her professional colleagues will constantly ask veiled questions to deduce what caste she belongs to (as by this point she has most likely hidden her caste identity to escape negative bias). Meanwhile, the Avarna woman who wears her caste proudly on her sleeve will routinely be suspected of identity politicking and extremist agenda (read anti-caste, anti-Hindu, anti-capital, anti-establishment, anti-everything). It takes a tremendous amount of courage to identify as an Avarna in today's India (where the politically-charged debate about caste has eclipsed the moral debate about caste). This is not to say that Avarna women don't hold negative bias against (well-intentioned) Savarna women. In all likelihood they do. Given how Savarnas have historically suppressed the Avarnas, it seems quite natural to be suspicious. There's a trust deficit both ways. How then do we build real solidarity among women?

Men, meanwhile, are guarding the borderlines. They literally kill the women who dare to cross the line and fall in love with the enemy. Only 11 per cent of marriages in India are inter-caste. The rest of the time, people are making endogamous matches by choice or persuasion. Whether they be liberal or conservative, Savarna or Avarna, Hindu, Muslim, Christian, or Sikh, they're perpetuating caste by socializing and breeding with their own. I'm not suggesting that this is a crime, just that this is the nature of caste. It's a social code that people live by. And make no mistake, we're all prejudiced one way or another because we've all been exposed to the radioactive rays of caste all through our lives, whether we know it or not. The side-effects are permanent.

---

upper-caste since independence. Routinely the upper castes accuse the lower castes of appropriating educational/government seats that they do not deserve (saying merit is being ignored for political gains). However, the debate about reservation has come full circle, as over 80 per cent of SC/ST/OBC students now clear the general category cut-off in entrance tests to professional engineering and medical courses, while Dalits top the UPSC exams—proving that merit isn't a preserve of the upper castes. Meanwhile, the upper caste (lower class) has been granted reservation under the auspices of the current government.

The Identity Matrix

In *Seeing Like A Feminist,* political theorist Nivedita Menon explains that 'the success of feminism lies precisely in its capacity to motivate "people" to affirm themselves *as* feminists in different kinds of contexts.' She writes that 'we may respond to different kinds of political challenges, as "Dalit" or "Muslim" or as "women" ...a Dalit activist or a Marxist will have to recognize the defining feature in some situation as gender, not caste or class.' However, this isn't as easy as it sounds. While a privileged upper-class Hindu woman may freely choose to momentarily view the world through the lens of class, and the next day swap that lens out for gender or caste, a woman who is Dalit or Muslim cannot simply separate her identities. In India, a Dalit is always a Dalit, rich or poor. A Muslim is forever Muslim first. So, it's critical to point out here that there's a fundamental difference between the identities that we choose for ourselves and those that we are born into. While we may choose to be liberal, feminist, Marxist, socialist, humanist, environmentalist, (Hindu) nationalist, Gandhian, whatever, knowing that we have the privilege of changing *our* minds, Other identities remain permanent in India. Muslim, Dalit, Adivasi, disabled, lesbian, queer, transgender—everyone cannot shift and change their identities as they please. In a deeply inequitable India where Brahmanical patriarchy has held sway for centuries, one's identity becomes a dilemma of existential proportions. Identity still determines one's access to resources and knowledge (both constitutionally and socially). Moreover, our identities create the bioscope through which other women view us.

'Most often we are seen as victims,' writes researcher Pradnya Jadhav in 'From Victimhood to Power'. Dalit women's 'assertions have never been taken into serious consideration except for branding them as outrageous, emotionally driven, irrational, and violent. In fact, our assertions...to take lead of our struggles is also important, as outsiders can never understand our issues the way we do...[we have] to organize and learn-unlearn ways of dealing with it.' Dalit women do not need self-righteous Savarna feminist intervention in their lives. They need platforms and resources to help amplify their voices and improve their livelihoods. Educated urban Dalits need affirmations like #DalitWomenThrive, not endless talk of their victimhood. As Gayatri Chakraborty Spivak emphasizes in her work, in the dichotomous relationship between the oppressor and oppressed, the position of oppression can shift into a position of power. This can only happen when women speak for themselves.

Identity politics, then, seems crucial to proclaim power in any situation, especially in a representative democracy where influence is directly proportional to identity. However, this sort of politicking may take bizarre turns. Sample the US, the UK, and India—all diverse democracies where far-right politicians have captured the imagination of the people, by making the privileged majority (read Christian white/ Hindu upper-caste) believe that they're the truly marginalized, the real victims who have been forgotten by the state as it went on with its humanitarian scheme of protecting and advancing minorities, by sharing apparently unwarranted privileges and rights. While the US and UK hate on new immigrants, India hates on its rather imaginary immigrants (Muslims) and natives (a.k.a. Dalits and Adivasis). Now, the position of gender within this scenario is puzzling. In India, young Hindu women have turned activists fighting for the political goals of the BJP, while in the US and UK, women (especially white women) are very much part of Trumpism and Brexit. Should this alarm feminists everywhere? Or does this show, yet again, that all women aren't inherently liberal, nor do they all believe in the sort of empowerment that leftist feminists envisage for all womenkind because it often infringes upon other identities that they hold dear?

'I argue against identity in politics,' says Dr Yasmeen Arif, a professor of sociology at the University of Delhi. 'Currently, the grounds for identity in politics, i.e. solidarity of the excluded and marginalized has been appropriated by or extended to people who emphasize more on boundary making processes that exclude, not unite against exclusion.' While the need to recognize and assert difference, individually or collectively is one thing, 'arranging difference in competition with one another is a whole different thing', notes Dr Arif, and the added problems of 'caste and religious assertions leads us to absurdities of competition. Once governmental policy gains the upper hand in aligning resources and justice to identity collectivities, the incentive to constitute collectivities by exclusion is and will be the name of the game.' In her book *Life, Emergent*, she challenges the conventional understanding of biopolitics and propounds a politics of life[10], one that looks at the commonalities that are yet unsurpassed. True to her theory, she does not identify as a feminist. When I ask her whether identity politics within feminism only serves to reify identities already defined, she replies: 'The impulse that will remain in this kind of fine tuning of identity in feminist politics will involve splitting hairs about how my concerns are different from yours, resulting in smaller and smaller fractions.' But what about identities that we're born into, that have caused us suffering due to social bias? 'Suffering based on socially sanctioned or ascriptive identity will change only when society changes—reifying those identities, in a way, seems to be about reifying that society itself. Having moved through an epoch of identity in politics, it seems more useful to understand what that suffering is, rather than classify the identity that bears that suffering. Identity need not move out of politics, that is not my suggestion. But, we do need to recalibrate what identity in what politics based on what history might have shown. We need to understand what humiliation is, what dignity is, what power is, if we are to be a society that sustains life per se.'

In an India of diversity and deep-seated inequality, perhaps identity politics will only divide us further. We've already become

---

[10]Extending her bio-political work to India, Dr Yasmeen Arif later tells me that 'governmental ability to co-opt social difference produces populations for control, leading to self-regulatory identity practices—this is troubling to say the least. When the commonality of flesh and blood, of life and its vulnerabilities are fragmented with socially sanctioned difference and prejudice, and when that difference is hierarchized in government sanctioned competition, identity in politics will have done away with any hopes for social equity.'

so hypocritical that we often feel compassion selectively—for those we consider marginalized based on our ideological frameworks. We don't value life per se.

Oh, but feminists aren't like that, some would say. They're devoted to intersectionality and fight for the rights of all women, religious and caste minorities, LGBTQIA+, disabled people, and the economically marginalized (even men). But people from these sections of society can be on the right (and the fence-sitting centre) too. To be truly intersectional, then, one has to reach out to folks who probably do not share the same ideology. This is a difficult proposition, of course. How can we, as feminists, collude with those whose values aren't (seemingly) as progressive as ours? Academically speaking, intersectionality is great, because you can read intersectional theory and literature and become aware of other people's realities. But what does it mean in practice? How can it be implemented in a world where ideologies are porous?

Intersectionality, after all, isn't simply an idea meant for the cathartic purposes of the privileged few. For it to have a real effect in the world, marginalized folks have to be brought into the mainstream. It's all very well to claim that you're not feminist if you're not intersectional, but what does that mean if you're not consciously changing your practices in life to amplify the voices of the marginalized and share your resources with them? To just be bookish about the concept of intersectionality isn't being intersectional at all.

'To me the intersectional metaphor is not particularly useful,' says Dr Manisha Desai, a professor of sociology and Asian studies at the University of Connecticut, 'because I think it was a very particular term for a very particular US context. When you think of intersection as a road, you see two separate roads coming together. But in terms of our identities, we are not separate. It's not like one day I'm a woman and one day I'm an upper-caste woman, one day I'm a Dalit woman. You are all of those things all of the time. So, the intersection metaphor is not a particularly good one.' Dr Desai has written extensively about gender and was awarded the title of

Distinguished Feminist Lecturer by Sociologist for Women in Society (SWS) in 2015. When I ask her if one can put intersectionality into practice, she replies: 'Trying to be intersectional in one's organizing and one's thinking is important, because the moment you think about any issue, you have to think what would the impact of that be for women who are gay, or Dalit, or disabled.... when you think about all those things for any issue and make sure that all of those are addressed, then you're taking into consideration a really systemic view.' How does one's identity play into all of this? Dr Desai holds that identity politics is currently important inside the feminist movement, because 'we need to recognize that feminists have been, for the most part, upper-caste and upper-class. People often dismiss identity politics, but I think only privilege allows you to dismiss it. Because your identity has always given you the privilege to do [this] and speak and represent others. But now that the others are challenging you, you're suddenly calling it identity politics. What was it when you were speaking on behalf of everyone? You also had a particular identity. However, identity politics does have limitations' she explains, 'it needs to go back and forth to construct a new idea of *we*.'

Indian feminism today is essentially a collective of identities. Diverse groups and individuals have their own definitions of what it means to be feminist. 'I have not found a discourse or discussion on what the definition of modern feminism is. Right now, everyone has some idea of what it is, some are afraid of identifying themselves as one,' says Sukhraj Vimal Kaur, a senior project manager from Delhi who has worked for many years with NGOs. 'But really if someone wants to call themselves a feminist, they should believe and fight for the emancipation of all women[11]. It's as simple as that.'

Now, we must spend some time contemplating this idea of *all* women. Millions of Indian women, be they caste Hindus or Avarna, Muslims, Christians, Sikhs, Parsis, disabled, transgender or queer, do

---

[11]As the civil rights activist and feminist Audre Lorde once said: 'I am not free while any woman is unfree, even if her shackles are very different than my own.'

not identify as feminists for various reasons. Shouldn't feminists fight for them too? However, feminists often think that in order to fight for someone, we must first proselytize to convert that someone to our ideology. If they don't convert, then they're not sisters, but the enemy. Because, more often than not, feminism tends to bully women whose ideology or belief doesn't match its (often leftist) agenda. When I say left, I mean it more than in an economic sense. Leftism is also atheism. In a country of believers, how can feminism be for *all* women, when one of feminism's primary adversaries is religious faith? As for the economic agenda of leftism, in a country of endemic poverty and middle-class distress, a socialist approach for universal minimum guarantees makes sense, but not a radical redistribution of wealth. Honestly, that agenda is empty rhetoric when primarily propounded by an elitist upper-caste, high-class leftist leadership even as it eats the fruits of its ancestral privilege.

Feminism in India suffers from an image problem. It needs to update itself to include women across the political and ideological spectrum if it really wants to represent all women, instead of co-opting the struggles of the marginalized simply to appear intersectional. In the India of 2021, this may seem almost impossible. For how many liberal feminist women are willing to identify or show solidarity with a conservative feminist (who possibly voted for the BJP)? Not many I'd presume. Identities are more polarized now than ever.

'Conservative feminists rarely identify themselves as feminist at all, often believing that feminists must necessarily be irreverent outliers. Liberals, on the other hand, find it impossible to extend the feminist label to someone who swears by social, traditional, and conservative family values,' writes Sanya Dhingra for *The Print*. 'At a time when liberals confront several dilemmas as they seek to make space for themselves in an increasingly conservative Indian society, liberal feminists must acknowledge the rise of the conservative feminist on the political and social landscape. Without acknowledgement and dialogue with the conservative feminist, the liberal feminist could risk becoming redundant.' What conservative feminism is she talking about, you wonder? Seen those neo-traditional ladies who take the power, while subverting both patriarchy and feminism at the same time? They are postfeminists in action.

While Hindutva may have won in 2019, feminism did not lose. For what would you call Smriti Irani's historic win in Amethi? It's a feminist act through and through. She won against a politician whose family has ruled India for quite some time now—and she defeated him at his family bastion (wah, wah, what a way to end feudalism-masquerading-as-progress). In a party of many (controversial) men, she has held on to power shrewdly, deliberately, and with spectacle. Still, Irani isn't applauded as a feminist by liberal women. In the past, most liberal feminists have not even bothered to call out liberal men for using misogynist language when talking about Irani. Her acting career, personal life, educational qualifications, and physical appearance were all routinely targeted, deconstructed, and made into memes. It was sexist and abhorrent. But as we all know, women who wear sindoor and invoke motherhood can't be feminist, because if they're conservative then they must be secret enablers of patriarchy (and fascism). Granted, Irani's contribution as HRD minister towards the calibration of Indian education to Hindutva ideology, and stifling free speech on college campuses are not progressive deeds becoming of a secular democracy, but that does not then mean liberal feminists should look the other way when a female politician is attacked by liberal chauvinist men. Sexism is sexism, right?

On the other end of the conservative spectrum are Muslim women. In the protests against the Citizenship Amendment Act (CAA), Muslim women in burqas were at the forefront fighting for the rights of their community and the idea of secular India—all while invoking Allah's name. Are these women not feminist? Many secular feminists (previously opposed to religious rhetoric by principle) found themselves on the same side of the political divide, and started to see the fearless determination of conservative Muslim women. Only time will tell how this will change mainstream feminism's perception of the traditional woman. Will it continue to view them through the lens of victimhood, even while lauding their courage? Or, will it open up its mind to regard female empowerment using a different yardstick?

That brings me to the problematic of political women from the Hindu right (again). Isn't it beneficial for the feminist collective to engage civilly with these women who actually have the ear of patriarchs, with the potential to bring change? You may think that this is an absurd or naïve suggestion—how can political women who support Hindutva ever be trusted to work for the benefit of all women? Let me remind you, that no matter what your ideological choice, you're still very much within the patriarchy. Even though certain ideologies may appear more gender egalitarian, they're really not. Not even democratic secularism is the ultimate vanguard of female empowerment. In her book *Sex and Secularism*, historian Joan Wallach Scott argues that although modern Western nation states stand for equality and liberty to all, they were built on notions of biological differentiation with regard to power. It seems that no matter what the ideology of the ruling elite, the plight of everyday women will remain the same because sexist bias is deeply rooted in our society as it is elsewhere in the world.

In such a scenario, isn't it worthy of the sisterhood to involve all women in conversations about feminist futures? Trust me, the self-projected modernity or tradition of a woman doesn't determine her progressive values. Conservative feminists are many in India. Even while they benefit from the radical feminist politics that has come before, they may align themselves with socio-culturally acceptable or normative ideas of femininity. In a society that is obsessed with motherhood and the feminine power to create/destroy, it makes complete sense to use the same ideas to achieve one's (feminist) goals. These women aren't victims of patriarchy. They are repositories of untold power.

The women I look up to the most in my life are those in my family. My grandmothers, mother, and aunts. To the appraising feminist eye, they may appear conservative at first glance. Dressed in saris, observing fasts, and perpetuating tradition. But that's only one part of the story. They are also doctors, businesswomen, teachers, bankers, and matriarchs. Women with steely eyed ambition. Not only did they defy all odds to create lives of dignity for themselves, but they also dared to dream beyond feminine convention. This has deeply impacted the way I see tradition and modernity. I do not see these two sets of values as contradictory or mutually exclusive. It is every woman's choice to take what she likes from different schools of thought to create her own unique blend. As feminists, as women, I think it is our duty to respect such female choice and grit.

A Matter of Faith

'My relationship with God was always on and off,' says Maria Josephine Divya. 'I come from a strict Catholic family that diligently went to mass every Sunday. But still somehow I felt disconnected to God.' An engineer by training, Chennai-born Divya went against the norm and married a Hindu. She says she didn't think about God until the day she delivered her son. Due to complications at birth, her son was rushed to the NICU where he was diagnosed with rheumatism. 'They let me see my son when he stabilized. I stayed with him for two minutes but couldn't stay there longer. I ran out of the NICU and cried. Back in my room, I knelt down and prayed, my legs still hurting from severe oedema. I didn't pray to Jesus. But to Mary. Maybe because she is a mum too?' Divya tells me she cannot put into words what she felt that day. However, since that moment, she spoke to Mother Mary every day that she spent in the hospital, while her son was fighting for his life. 'One day when the doctor said that it's very difficult for the child to survive, and that we should prepare for the worst, I prayed to Velankanni Matha that I would shave my head. I felt I had to humble myself.' Two hours later, her son stabilized. 'If you ask me whether my son survived because I prayed to shave my hair[12], I wouldn't be able to

---

[12]And she did shave her hair later.

answer that. But I think some divine power was at work. Perhaps I hung on to God as a last strand of hope.'

Faith is a highly personal affair. Millions of Indian women believe in a transcendental power that permeates all life. Some pray to it, others seek it, many waver in their devotion. Yet, for secular feminists, may they be atheist, agnostic, or nihilist, religious faith is a nemesis. They wonder how any woman would choose to be part of a creed that curses philandering ladies to be afflicted with evil diseases,[13] dictates that arrogant wives be beaten[14] or ordains that women be silent altogether[15]?

No religion is eminently feminist or egalitarian (at least, not by the parameters of the twenty-first century). But this is a moot point. Because religion and faith are essentially two different things. Faith is a private matter. It is what one believes irrespective of whether or not others agree. Religion is organized faith. We must wonder now, why is it that women who pursue faiths that aren't as rad as hippie Buddhism are considered complicit in perpetuating misogyny? I'm sure you know that certain paths of divine contemplation are considered woke: (Western and Indian) feminists have no qualms with those who are 'spiritual but not religious' as they seek nirvana through a multireligious approach that (in all possibility) centres around Buddhist thought—because it is considered the most feminist religion of them all. Only, Buddhism isn't exempt from misogyny. Yes, the Buddha allowed women to become monks, but only with a hundred more rules[16] for them to follow, to make sure that they rejected their female sexuality altogether. The Buddha, who abandoned his wife to find enlightenment, is known to have remarked on many

---

[13]Manusmriti (3.159n.) 'By being unfaithful to her husband, a woman becomes disgraced in the world, takes birth in a jackal's womb, and is afflicted with evil diseases.'

[14]Quran (4:34) 'But those [wives] from whom you fear arrogance—advise them; [then if they persist], forsake them in bed; and [finally], strike them.'

[15]Bible (Timothy 2:12) 'I do not permit a woman to teach or to have authority over a man, she must be silent.'

[16]In the Vinaya Pitaka, bhikkunis have 331 rules to follow, while bhikkus have 227.

occasions about the lethal charms of women. To say the least, feminists seem to be celebrating Buddhism with rose-tinted glasses. The lot of contemporary Buddhist nuns in Southeast Asia is a case in point. The inequality they face in the monastic order doesn't overshadow Buddhism's global appeal as a progressive faith, while Hinduism, Islam, and Christianity are often written off as corrupt religions due to their present-day cloistral scandals.

Since the patriarchy has been coded into much of organized religion, male chauvinism has been written into most major religions, in every possible way. There is much need for feminist scrutiny into the diktats of problematic and fundamentalist scriptures. However, does this mean (feminist) women must give up on the idea of the divine altogether (whether this entity be a he, she or they) if all religion is retrograde? Why do we assume that every self-identified Hindu, Muslim, Christian, Jain, Parsi or Sikh woman is a naïve believer who'd follow her religion down to the t of fundamentalism? Why is it so hard for us to imagine that these women may be battling the norm to recontextualize their orthodox faiths to align with their modern lifestyles?

'As a Christian, feminism is a reality check on the gospel message of equality among all people in the eyes of God,' Rev Winnie Varghese, an Episcopal priest in New York, told *Huffington Post* in an interview. 'If we believe we are equal in the eyes of God, we have to work to make that equality a reality in the world we live in.' Hindu feminism is a thing too. On the website of the Women Living Hinduism and Islam Project[17], the idea is explained by a scholar as follows: 'how do we, women, find a source of strength in a spiritual tradition? ...The Divine Feminine[18] rests on diversity, it does not

---

[17]This is an international and interdisciplinary collaborative research network of scholars from India, Bangladesh, Pakistan, and the United States.

[18]First mentioned in the Rig Veda's Devi Suktam, the feminine aspect is much revered in Hindu tradition. There are several texts devoted to goddesses, with the Devi Mahatmayam (400–600 CE) glorifying the feminine power as the supreme creator of the universe—conflating femininity with the Brahman for the first time.

create a road-roller homogeneity. There are so many forms of the goddess, no one form subsumes the other. So, it is a wonderful model to understand human diversity, indeed bio diversity, it is a very positive way of looking at the world. It is lila, the world of god's play.' Islamic feminists proclaim that the Quran has many interpretations, and that the original version of the divine text was wholly gender egalitarian. Sociologist Fatima Mernissi holds that in the Islamic community the Prophet Muhammad established, 'women had their place as unquestioned partners in a revolution that made the mosque an open place and the household, a temple of debate.'

From a radically rationalist point of view, none of this talk about faith matters. Ideas that can't be proven scientifically or incidents that can't be confirmed materially, for all practical purposes, don't exist. While most people presume that this sort of modern thinking is the antipathy of religious belief, it helps to look back at history (which many ancient cultures believe is cyclical). Rationalist lines of enquiry existed even back in the day. In Indian antiquity, the Lokayata[19] school of thought challenged Vedic philosophy on very scientific grounds. Now, talking about anything from ancient India with any amount of pride is ill-advised, for one'd be branded anti-science, but I'll do it nevertheless. While I'm not so sure if ancient India had internet or magical cows, I can certainly say that several metaphysical ideas from that period were rooted in science. Quantum physics tells us today that reality is what we make of it, an idea that is at the core of ancient Indian religions (remember Maya[20]?). Several research papers[21] have been written about the uncanny similarities between these theories. Meanwhile, scientists are increasingly beginning to listen

---

[19]Philosophical skeptics, empiricists and atheists, the Lokayatas (600 BCE) questioned the Vedas, ritualism, and supernaturalism.
[20]Maya is a powerful force that creates the cosmic illusion that our phenomenal world is real.
[21]Read Emeritus Professor of Physics Kashyap Vasavada to discover the mind-boggling similarities between modern physics and ancient Indian philosophy.

to indigenous communities, to gain knowledge about their nature gods, and possibly reverse the ecological damage that industrialization has caused to Mother Earth.

But, it isn't the existence of a superhuman power (or lack thereof) that secular feminists contend. Their primary problem with religion is to do with viscerally regressive practices that are sanctioned either through faith, custom, or law. And in a country like India, such practices are many. From sati to female genital mutilation, child marriage to widow ostracization, the list is long. Secular women's movements have done much to hinder such practices from being propagated among various religious communities, and fought for women's legal rights. However, in the absence of a uniform civil code, religious laws apply in several personal matters like marriage and divorce. This results in complicated situations where personal laws cannot be reformed easily because they're tied to religious customs and culture—promptly positioning feminism against religion[22].

'Legal pluralism can lead to gender justice,' argues Dr Gopika Solanki[23], an associate professor of political science at Carleton University. 'Critical feminism,' she adds 'aids in this endeavour.' She points to what the Indian women's movement did in the 1990s: it 'realigned its ideologies and practise, dropped its longstanding demands for uniform civil laws...and advanced gender equality within the framework of legal pluralism.' Further, she holds that a 'shared adjudication model'[24] facilitates interreligious dialogue between Hindu and Muslim women's organizations, secular women's groups, litigants, and lawyers from both communities. Dr Solanki's position

---

[22]'Those who supported the demand for a uniform civil code (UCC) or common civil code that would supersede religious law were posited as secular, modern, and pro-women,' write Laxmi Murthy and Rajashri Dasgupta in *Our Pictures, Our Words*, 'while those opposing the UCC were viewed as orthodox, communal, obstructionist, and anti-women.' This bifurcation remains to this day. Those who support the UCC do not see merit in women who seek to reform religious laws from within the fold.

[23]I had a lengthy email conversation with Dr Solanki regarding the ideas quoted.

[24]Which is the current Indian model, where legal recognition is granted to culturally plural versions of what constitutes marriage, divorce, and family.

exists in sharp contrast to the feminist scholars keen to bring in a uniform civil code and end the tensions between gender equality and cultural autonomy once and for all.

In a time of great political turmoil, when religious diversity is under threat, you know something is amiss when the party promoting Hindutva is hell bent on passing a bill to end the triple talaq practice of the Muslim community, in a bid to protect Muslim women. Meanwhile, the secular feminist group that has been campaigning for this to happen for ages, is left in an awkward position. The bulk of Muslim women themselves, on the other hand, aren't as invested in this issue and demand other things altogether. Indian Muslim women's groups[25] want to 'move beyond looking at Muslim women's issues as consisting only of *purdah* (veiling and segregation), polygamy, and triple talaq, which have been the main tropes through which "Muslim women" have been constructed and understood as a category in the Indian context,' writes sociologist Nida Kirmani in *openDemocracy*. She points out that Muslim women seek to draw attention instead 'to problems related to violence against the community as a whole, and women in particular, as well as addressing issues related to the targeting of Muslims by the state apparatus. This does not mean that the issue of personal laws is forgotten, but rather, that...[Muslim] networks are attempting to contextualize the multiple disadvantages and insecurities faced by Muslim women in a broader pattern of economic, social political exclusion.'

But, but, to be a secular nation, everyone must follow the same rules, no? Except, what secular nation is truly secular? Even the most secular state of them all, France, is really a post-Christian nation that hasn't entirely shed its medieval prejudices against Islam. French secularism has demonized and ghettoized the Muslim community because the latter insists on holding on to its beliefs and practices. Not only are burqas banned in France, but burkinis too (it's like the

---

[25]Muslim Women's Rights Network (MWRN) and BMMA challenge the authority of the male-dominated All India Muslim Personal Law Board and the bias of mainstream secular women's groups.

French government's saying to Muslim women: you either expose more skin to prove your secularism or don't swim in our oceans). In India, meanwhile, secularism isn't so much anti-religion, but more about the equality of all faiths (at least on paper). In reality, secularism has been about keeping religious communities segregated for the sake of vote bank politicking. The Congress gifted itself the job of protecting India's religious minorities, while the BJP took on the role of fighting for the Hindu majority. In all this hullabaloo, the matter of secularism—or the equality of all religions—has metamorphosed into a scheme where the Hindu majority either protects or piques minority communities. While the (secretly Hindu) Congress promotes progress and human rights, the BJP (for whom Hindutva is an ideology of nationhood) seeks to Hinduize everyone.

The hypocrisy of Indian political parties with regard to secularism became public knowledge in the aftermath of Sabarimala. After the Supreme Court passed a verdict allowing women of menstruating age to enter the Sabarimala temple, secular feminists everywhere cheered. Political parties snivelled and sympathized with Hindu believers who created a violent ruckus in protest (something political parties won't condone when perpetrated by Muslim or Christian believers). The communists, meanwhile, built a Women's Wall to pledge gender equality, which historian and social critic J. Devika decried as duplicitous: leftist parties used 'women's bodies as bricks in a wall to ostensibly guard Kerala from Hindutva's efforts to "drag it back into tradition"…built by modern patriarchy against pre-modern patriarchy….' For secular feminism though, the Sabaramila ruling (and the wall) became a symbolic triumph over Brahmanical Hinduism's sexist and discriminatory practices: which largely considers menstruating women impure. Then again, not all Indian feminists agreed.

'I don't think this issue, the way it has been propagated, has anything to do with gender equality,' says leading columnist Neelima Menon, who writes about culture and film for the *Indian Express*, *Firstpost*, and *Huffington Post*, among others. 'This has become a war zone between believers and non-believers instead.' Talking specifically about Kerala, she states that 'Opinions are always divided here, and there is also the matter of faith. There are men and women who equally abhor and protest this new rule, as they feel their faith is being derided. I have read so many Facebook posts, trolls and memes trivializing and smirking at Lord Ayyappa's chastity and I find it disrespectful.' Menon doesn't mince words when talking about sexism either. She tells me that she is squarely against gender-based discrimination. Denying women entry into a temple, she explains, 'does sound archaic, offensive, and regressive but this is also not how it should be handled. This is extremist behaviour from both sides—believers and non-believers. The government is also turning this into a planned political propaganda, trying to convert this into votes...' In any case, she argues, it all boils down to one's choice. 'Something as basic as visiting a place of worship. Should it be based on your gender? No! Should it be based on the Supreme Court order? No! Does the thought of visiting Sabarimala while I am menstruating give me a sense of empowerment? Not at all.... Don't manipulate every social issue as a fight for gender equality. Live and let live.'

The women who fought against all odds to enter the Sabarimala temple are feminist heroines, but are they devotees? Possibly not. They entered the shrine to make a point, to exercise their legal right, not to gain the blessing of the brahmacharya god. Now, one may wonder why Sabarimala had such a weird rule in the first place—well, because the temple deity is an eternal celibate. Male devotees who make the pilgrimage to Sabarimala undertake forty-one days of penance and refrain from sexual thoughts in order to gain control over all their energies. So, it's all very sacrosanct. Women of menstruating age aren't meant to enter the shrine lest they bring their sexual energies with them and distract the god as well as his devotees. Now, before non-believers blow their top over the misogyny inherent in Hinduism, let me tell you about some other Hindu temples—where men aren't allowed. The Attukal Bhagavathy temple in Kerala is on the Guinness Book of World Records 2009, for attracting over 2.5 million female devotees to its Pongala celebrations, and not a single man is allowed in. At the Kanya Kumari temple in Tamil Nadu, the goddess is said to be in perpetual sanyas, so married men are not allowed to enter so as not to disturb her meditational state. Then, are we to see these shrines as feminist temples or as places that perpetuate gender inequality by barring men?

In any case, Hinduism's depressing record in keeping gender and caste purity[26] doesn't elicit sympathy from secularists when it comes to the matter of hurting religious sentiment, because caste Hindus take offence quite easily, to begin with.

So, eighteen steps to Sabarimala's sanctum sanctorum, a giant leap for feminism in India? 'For the life of me, I do not understand how "patriarchy" is attacked when women devotees bow down before male priests and a male celibate god,' wonders Asha Kotwal, the general secretary of the All India Dalit Mahila Adhikar Manch, in an article for *The Wire*. 'Where in this spectrum lies the end of misogyny? So can somebody please explain to me how and why is the savarna women-led feminist movement in India claiming this to be a historic win for women rights?'

Secular Dalit feminists reject Hindu religion altogether, and fairly so (for most of its codified customs are discriminatory and sexist, especially against Avarna women). Since caste and Hinduism are so inextricably intertwined, it's almost impossible to view the Hindu way of life without also cringing at its obsession with caste purity. However, I argue that it is unfair to charge every practising Hindu woman with the crime of abetting caste. For one thing, Hinduism isn't built on one text alone. Not everybody follows the *Manusmriti* in their spiritual or daily lives. Hinduism, after all, is an amalgamation of varied beliefs and customs from across the subcontinent. More often than not, our religious philosophies are what we learn from our foremothers. Faiths and traditions

---

[26]Avarna believers are still denied entry into several temples in India. In the few temples where they can enter, there are known instances of priests performing purification rites after their visit.

are passed down generation after generation through women. It would seem that female religiosity isn't always a consequence of Brahminism, but can have other roots too.

For perspective, let me give you a personal example. My matriarchal Dalit great-grandmother was a devout woman. In fact, she built a temple in her village for Goddess Amman, the malevolent aspect of the Divine Mother—our family deity. The temple still stands, as does my faith in the primeval energy of Shakti. What's interesting is that it was in my great-grandmother's time that the Dravidian Self-Respect Movement grew in Tamil Nadu.[27] She and the women after her must've been inspired by the anti-caste crusade (and the nascent feminism) that enveloped the state. However, despite the movement's atheistic underpinnings, they continued to believe. They opposed caste and sexist bigotry, but still propagated their faith in the divine. Perhaps this is to do with keeping their female traditions. Of course, this is one story of one family. Not all Dalit women are believers, several are agnostic or atheist. Many have consciously left casteist Hinduism to convert to other more egalitarian faiths, for there's no denying the obnoxious side of caste Hinduism. As a result of varnashrama, the practices of upper-caste groups are venerated as superior to others. I've been witness to this too as a member of an inter-caste family, where every traditionally conducted wedding ceremony requires months of negotiation to ensure that nobody's caste rituals are undermined (because by default Brahmins expect their rituals to take precedence over others).

Feminism is suspicious of rituals in any case. Women's practices that are rooted in religious tradition are seen as regressive. Obviously, there are several customs that are incompatible with our modern

---

[27]'For women who…opposed caste, their new sense of self came to hinge on two aspects of consciousness: reason and mutuality', writes V. Geetha about women self-respecters. 'Reason was interpreted by women to mean an aspect of a probing, curious and active intelligence and one which would enable them to unravel the meaning of all those rituals, customs and everyday practices which bound them to a life of unknowing and domestic servitude.'

lives or are altogether cruel. However, there must be some nuance even when considering rituals, because some religious practices can be empowering too. 'The hijab/burqa stands for freedom,' proclaims Sidra Binte Islam. 'The freedom to practice one's religion, symbolic of our obedience to Allah. It means modesty, it is an outer manifestation of our inner modesty. There's a very common misconception about the hijab that it has only been imposed on women when in reality, men too have been asked to lower their gaze, grow a beard and to guard their modesty.' Theologist Vijaya Rettakudi Naragarjan explores the agentive and transformative power in women's ritual behaviours in the book *Women's Lives, Women's Rituals in the Hindu Tradition*. Naragarjan suggests that the ritual placement of kolams, designs on the threshold of homes, and pottus, decorative dots on women's foreheads, are external markers of internal auspiciousness. They allow women to participate in the creation of their own moral status, a self-determined identity that they project into the public sphere.

The Paradox of Choice

'I heard a talk by a senior academician once, who spoke of mythology and language, and she said: "the reason I took up these studies so late is because for the last forty years I was keen on taking care of my family and my children." She did not say it with regret, but as a declaration to answer any questions that would come up. She considered herself a successful woman through and through. It stuck with me,' recounts Prarthana Patil, the co-country director for None in Three at India, where she collaborates with local groups to address the concepts of patriarchy, feminism, myth, and ethical dilemma. 'If a woman wants to enjoy family life, there is nothing "non-progressive" about it. I feel we need to look at what is it that we want to pursue as women. Success is a misleading term, because its meanings are seeped deep in patriarchal thought. What if we were to not look at anything as "success" or "achievements"? Take it out of the equation and we are left with simply living the way we choose to. Biologically, one cannot take away the fact that we are wired differently. At the same time, are we choosing a career or a lifestyle only to prove a point? Or are we doing it because "I want to?"'

Success is a relative term. There's no winning if a woman pays heed to every criticism that's levelled against her. This is why the postfeminist idea of choice works for many millennial and Gen Z women. They're not declaring that patriarchy has ended, but proclaiming that they aren't its victims any more as they consciously make self-empowering choices in their lives. They do not see feminism as an (unachievable) goal that one eternally struggles for, but something that can be tangibly achieved within the confines of their own existence. More so, in their minds.

Alas, the ceaseless wrath of self-righteous feminism endures. Recently, Kashmiri actress Zaira Wasim (of *Dangal* and *Secret Superstar* fame) announced that she was quitting Bollywood because it interfered with her imaan: faith in god. She wrote on social media that the film 'indeed brought a lot of love, support, and applaud my way, but what it also did was lead me to a path of ignorance...while I kept trying to convince myself that what I was doing is okay and isn't really affecting me, I lost all the Barakah from my life.' Barakah, as she explains, is to do with emotional stability, which she felt was being depleted by her line of work. Now, self-righteous feminists (and trolls of the far-right) concluded that her choice was a reaction to the (sexist) trolling from fellow Muslims that Wasim is routinely subjected to. However, why can't we imagine, for one moment, that her decision to quit was guided by an inner compass? That she's not a victim who fell in line because religious hardliners wanted her to, but that she changed her life's path to find peace as a self-empowering young woman. Choice, for the conservative Indian woman, is a double-edged sword.

'I found choice feminism, or the idea that any choice a woman makes is a feminist one, quite absurd,' writes well-known journalist Pallavi Aiyar in *Babies & Bylines: Parenting on the Move*, with regard to the choice women make to quit their jobs and become full-time mums. 'Feminism is a political stance not just a lifestyle. If choice becomes the yardstick by which to determine gender justice, deep structural change becomes a casualty. An emphasis on choice responds to available options rather than highlighting the need to widen those options.' While it is true that an emphasis on choice doesn't necessarily serve to diversify options, it doesn't mean that anyone who chooses between the options available is setting themselves up for permanent incarceration in a patriarchal prison. Their children will grow, new opportunities will knock on their doors, and women will reassess their lives to find new purpose. But remember, high-achieving feminists who make such judgements about other women are also often their own vicious critics. The fact that they've widened their options doesn't necessarily mean they're happier. Armed with sharp feminist jargon, most feminists jab at themselves relentlessly.

'Since many millennials and Gen Z have the feeling that women shouldn't be restricted to home and they need to perform equally as men, they unknowingly put on a lot of pressure on themselves,' says Dr Mareena Wesley, who teaches psychology at Bengaluru's Christ University. 'They also consider it as a weakness on their part if they have to ask for help or to accept their condition. Many put up a false mask of "I can do anything."' Dr Wesley has published several papers on bipolar disorder, depression, and trauma. She has also done exceptional research in the matter of existential dilemmas. So, what happens when women aren't able to take the pressure? 'They try their best, put in a lot of effort, but still, when they feel mentally or physically incapable of reaching their goals, they break down.' What about social support systems? 'In spite of having thousands of virtual friends, I have come across many who suffer from extreme loneliness; they feel trapped in their own golden cage of feminism. Many of them don't really know their actual potential and identity. They end up confused and struggle to make a meaningful existence. This existential crisis, with identity confusion and high expectations, poses a high vulnerability to anxiety and stress.'

Choice has its consequences, but we cannot really complain about that. Because the lack of choice has even direr consequences.

In 2018, every day, sixty-three housewives died by suicide across India. Imagine a life where you do not have a choice at all because of social or familial convention. Despite the existence of a number of women's legal rights and protections, most women aren't able to utilize them. This doesn't mean they all don't know what opportunities lie outside their homes. Many a time, the fact that they know of the free choices they could be making but are unable to, pushes them to the edge. How can we change our society? Sensitization drives and welfare schemes are numerous, but nothing seems to change patriarchal mindsets. Perhaps, instead of pursuing one-size-fits-all feminist advocacy, we should twist and turn our language to inspire different communities, drawing out pre-feminisms from our own histories to stimulate change.

I often wonder, by banning traditional practices like the convention of bridal dowry, are we strengthening women's position within communities or making them more vulnerable? While there are several cases of women being tortured by their in-laws for more dowry, (don't kill me for saying this) the original idea behind the tradition was to provide brides financial protection after marriage (especially true for women who don't have a career). But sadly, the groom's family appropriates the dowry. By making dowry illegal we haven't ended the practice; many families still give 'gifts'. Except, since they're not called dowries any more, brides aren't even entitled to it because it's all hush hush. This doesn't strengthen a woman's position, but weakens it right at the beginning of a marriage. Honestly, more often than not, marriage is an economic proposition in India. Why should we shy away from that reality? Why not work to empower women within that institution? Instead of fighting against the idea of dowry altogether, maybe it would make more sense to legalize a woman's right to wealth—protecting the wealth she brings from her family and the wealth she is entitled to through marriage. It was only in 2005 that daughters were granted the equal right to inherit as sons do (something feminists fought for tooth and nail). Except, many women sacrifice their right to inheritance because their families spend large amounts of money for their weddings. However, 2019 saw a sharp rise in women claiming their inheritance in various parts of India. Before you applaud it as a feminist win, you must know that gender experts like Prem Chowdhry suspect that these women are making the choice to claim their rights because of pressure from their husbands or fathers-in-law—with rising property prices, which patriarch will let wealth slip away from his hands?

While Indian feminism observes the everyday lives of women through statistics or idealism, it often misses the mark on cultural and emotional understanding. Take the matter of death penalty for rape. Even as feminism rages against patriarchal injustice, it is equally outraged by women's rage. When the Hyderabad encounter[28] happened, young women across the country celebrated the suspected rapists' death. Proper feminists, of course, were appalled (because as expounders of textbook feminism, they take their humanist credentials so seriously, to the point that they often end up fighting for the rights of rapists). They wrote several letters condemning the killings. 'There is no short cut to justice and safety,' read a statement issued by over 400 feminists, including lawyer Indira Jaising, scholar Nivedita Menon, activist Lalita Ramdas, and women studies scholar Mary E. John. 'The death penalty often becomes a short cut when, in fact, there is a need to focus on long term social change, and the State's failure to ensure the security of women.... the State is trying to... distract us by creating an "illusion of justice", by selectively hanging people even as it protects others responsible for similar crimes.' While this is true, it didn't sit well with women who are already suspicious of self-righteous feminism. And to make matters worse, on the eve of the approaching execution of the Delhi gang rapists, feminist advocate Indira Jaising advised Asha Devi (on Twitter) to forgive the men who raped and brutally killed her daughter. Clearly, (humanist) feminism is out of touch with the pulse of India's women. When

---

[28]In the aftermath of the rape and murder of a Hyderabad veterinarian, the police conducted extra-judicial killings, executing the accused rapists at the spot of the crime.

the Delhi rapists were finally hung, righteous feminists criticized the penalty while everyday women rejoiced.

While it may be (humanist) feminists' choice to forgive rapists, they aren't entitled to counsel other women to do the same. Especially when this is done with an obvious show of being holier-than-thou. Most postfeminist women want to see all rapists hanged. Call it revenge. Bloodthirst. Young women are angry as hell. They want justice, right here, right now. In the face of systemic apathy, women have no patience left. Even in 2018, case disposal rates of police and the courts was extremely poor across Indian states.[29] In this scenario, when feminists come in the way of hanging even the few rapists who have been convicted, it hardly bodes well for its image.

In a world filled with hate, I believe love for humanity is what we should all strive for. When we consider the idea of humanism through the prism of equality (of empowering historically marginalized communities) and reason (to prevent ancient and medieval prejudices from poisoning our modern lives), it appears to be the most progressive ideology one could follow. In that sense, the fact that mainstream feminism has now metamorphosed into humanism is a very welcome development. Nonetheless, problems arise when feminist advocates of humanism use the doctrine not to include more people in its fold, rather to exclude all those who don't agree with their version of humanist feminism. After all, even humanism has its varieties: secular humanism, religious humanism, socialist humanism, and humanistic capitalism, to name a few. Women are free to choose what they want to be. While all humanists are feminists, the reverse does not need to be true.

I'm opening a Pandora's box here for myself, I know. Because if all feminists are not humanists, does this mean that non-violence is not mandatory? Is a self-empowered woman who instigates or perpetrates violence a feminist? Where does postfeminism draw the line? Personally, I'm tempted to draw a line here and announce that

---

[29]Mizoram, M.P., and Chhattisgarh fared better than other states.

anyone who crosses the contour of non-aggression isn't entitled to feminism because in my ideal world, created with tolerance, human rights, and freedom at the centre, violence against any individual is unacceptable. For a radical Hindu nationalist, Muslim extremist, or a Naxalite (post)feminist, violence is not off-limits. As India slowly turns into Bharat, a nation fighting historical and ideological blood feuds, women are rising up in arms to make their point. On university campuses, violent clashes between students from the right and the left are becoming an everyday spectacle across the country. There have been reports of women dragging their adversaries by their hair. We've all seen the images of the masked woman armed with an iron rod threatening to strike,[30] and videos of another woman, allegedly a student president, leading mobs through a university complex. I shudder to imagine an India where violence is normalized. Women at each other's throats. Everyone running around with trishools, bombs, daggers, and guns, apart from legal notices and black magic, to take revenge. And as we all know, rape is also a weapon.

Am I allowed to still assume that all women are good in some form (deep, deep inside)? That, apart from a handful of extremists, most women are civil and don't want others harmed physically or psychologically? That they have integrity? Or, am I deluding myself? Either way, allow me to spray on some of that lavender (post)feminist perfume and feel excited about a feminist future where women rule the world—despite all their differences. Clearly, our oppositional ideologies will remain as they are, even in a post-patriarchal world. Only, I'd like to imagine that when women are in charge, they'd resolve their differences through conversation and compromise, not carnage.

---

[30]At the height of a political stand-off between leftist student groups and the RSS-affiliated ABVP at Jawaharlal Nehru University in New Delhi, a masked mob, including a young woman with a rod, attacked students and vandalized hostels. Later, it was reported that they belonged to the ABVP.

CONCLUSION
THE FUTURE IS FEMALE

Once upon a time, feminism helped us locate our oppressed position in the superstructure. It gave us tools with which to assess our victimhood. It made us aware of our lack of choice. It compelled us to fight against misogynistic violence, gendered discrimination, and bias. Today, as inheritors of that grand proposition, we are empowered in our thoughts and in our lives. Indian women across the spectrum are forging ahead against all odds, individually and collectively. Irrespective of our identities, we're not playing victim any more, but being the creators of our own destinies. As Madame Gandhi brilliantly raps in her feminist music album, *'I'm not every day tryna turn up to the sound of my own oppression, you feel me? We always assume our powerlessness but never own our power.'*

As I write this, the realities of anthropogenic climate change are becoming evident. The Covid-19 pandemic has spread across the world leaving behind death and destruction in its wake, disrupting our routines, and forcing us to reassess our lives. Many women have lost their jobs, most are struggling to manage work and childcare, and we have *all* lost our minds. But this pandemic has also shown us our grit. Our resilience. In India, women have been at the forefront fighting against the Covid-19 threat—among them fearless doctors, nurses, scientists, ministers, government officers, police officers, journalists, technicians, and housekeeping staff. We've also come to realize that across the globe, in countries led by women, the strategy to handle the crisis has been swifter and more considerate, taking into account all sections of society. Not only is their response grounded in data, but is also centred on concern. As several historical studies show, women have played a key role in transforming nations in times of crisis. So, when the time comes to make amends, to renegotiate our politics and rebuild our world, we must remember that patriarchal superstructures are created to exclude, disenfranchise, and exploit. Perhaps, this is the time for women to take over. Imagine a new world. A feminine (and feminist) world.

Society will continue to call us names. Mock our power. Our intuition, our charm. Scoff at our masculinity; the ambiguities of our bodies and minds. Let them. Rise above. Don't give up on your subjectivity. Your sexuality. You are capable of seeing through the illusions and leading with vision. Remember your foremothers, those women of tenacity and wisdom. Their suffering and transcendence. Reclaim all that is yours. Never mind if they think you're a narcissist— love yourself in your own way. You are the burning fire. The silvery water that quenches the ire. You are air, light, and bliss.

The feminist future is within our grasp. We already know that this isn't a dull, monochromatic future; each woman will live on her own terms. Your approach may not align with another woman's, her choices may not appeal to you. I implore: don't judge. Seek to understand why women make the choices they make. Set aside your idealism for a little while. Then, perhaps, we can find some (un)common ground.

ACKNOWLEDGEMENTS

This book exists because of my wonderful editor Pujitha Krishnan. She has inspired me and pushed me to explore every tangent of feminist thought and, as a result, expand the scope of my work. I am eternally grateful for her pointed feedback, suggestions, and patience.

I'm thankful to Aleph Book Company for trusting me with this book. I'd also like to thank my copy editor, Kanika Praharaj, for closely reading my work and providing valuable inputs to improve the narrative.

I've researched and written this book over the course of three years. In this time, I have spoken to hundreds of women about what feminism means to them and how the patriarchy affects their everyday lives. Many of their interviews are included in this book, while many others have influenced my opinion. I am thankful to everyone who has shared their thoughts with me. Without your diverse ideas, I couldn't have constructed this narrative.

I'm deeply indebted to all the knowledge experts, academics, and activists who engaged with me in conversation. Your experiences, theories, and analyses have enriched the pages of this book and deepened my understanding of various positions. I'm especially thankful to Professor Ranu Uniyal, Dr Murli Desai, Smita Naidu, Devanshi Shah, and Sejal Dand for introducing me to new ideas and some incredible people. I'd also like to thank Neeta Hardikar, co-founder of ANANDI, for facilitating and translating interviews with women from the interior of Gujarat. To all my friends who helped me translate from various languages—nandri.

Finally, I'd like to thank all the amazing women who helped me care for my daughter while I spent hours writing. I started this book just after my daughter was born and I owe every minute that I got to focus on it to her teachers, nannies, and my friends. Special thanks to Aria's teachers Nidhi Bagaria, Sanjana Laha, Jeany Tudio, and Beth Stevens; and her nannies Soni Thokale and Shabnam. My friends Patrizia Zanetti and Kriti Sharma have taken care of Aria as their own—thank you.

My parents, sister, Nandita, and partner, Sushant, have been pillars of strength while I wrote this book, aiding me in every possible way. I am glad they exist in my life.

REFERENCES

Author's Note

ix   **Footnote 3: 'What I call collective reflexivity can be seen':** Maithree Wickramasinghe, *Feminist Research Methodology: Making Meanings of Meaning-making*, New Delhi: Zubaan, 2014, p. 64.

x   **'The vocabulary of Feminism today is':** Vibhuti Patel and Radhika Khajuria, 'Abstract', *Political Feminism in India: An Analysis of Actors, Debates and Strategies*.

x   **Feminist idol Germaine Greer has called:** Alison Flood, 'Germaine Greer criticises 'whingeing' #MeToo movement', *The Guardian*, 23 January 2018.

x   **Gloria Steinem has made multiple:** Sarah Grey, 'An Open Letter To Gloria Steinem On Intersectional Feminism', *Medium*, 8 February 2016.

xi   **'There is no *original* or *authentic* postfeminism':** Stephanie Genz, *Postfeminisms in Popular Culture*, London: Palgrave Macmillan, 2009, p. 20.

xi   **Feminist scholar Imelda Whelehan mockingly wonders:** Imelda Whelehan, *Modern Feminist Thought: From the Second Wave to 'Post-Feminism'*, Edinburgh: Edinburgh University Press, 1995, p. 216.

Introduction

1   **Footnote 1: A woman was raped every six hours:** National Crime Records Bureau, *Crime in India 2018*, New Delhi: Ministry of Home Affairs, 2018.

1   **Footnote 1: But when Thomson Reuters declared:** Belinda Goldsmith, Meka Beresford, 'India most dangerous country for women with sexual violence rife - global poll', Thomson Reuters Foundation, 2018.

1   **Footnote 2: most of whom are Dalit:** Rajiv Kumar, 'On an Average, India Reported 10 Cases of Rape of Dalit Women Daily in 2019, NCRB Data Shows', *CNN-News 18*, 3 October 2020.

1   **Footnote 2: or Adivasi:** Shoaib Daniyal, 'The Daily Fix: Why do reports of mass rape of Adivasi women by the police fail to elicit outrage?', *Scroll.in*, 11 January 2017.

1   **Footnote 2: Remember Hathras?:** Sowjanya Tamalapakula, 'Dear upper caste Indians, Hathras is not another Nirbhaya. It is a Khairlanji', *The Print*, 24 October 2020.

1   **Footnote 2: As of 2018, our parliament and:** PTI, '48 MPs, MLAs Have

Cases of Crime Against Women, 12 Belong to BJP', *The Quint,* 20 April 2018.

2   **Footnote 3: Twentieth-century philosopher and existentialist Simone de Beauvoir:** Simone de Beauvoir, *The Second Sex,* New York: Vintage Books, 1974, p. 301.

2   **Footnote 4: Mahatma Gandhi considered women's ability:** Madhu Kishwar, 'Gandhi on Women', *Economic and Political Weekly,* 1985.

2   **Footnote 4: 'Woman has to be ready to suffer':** Rabindranath Tagore, 'Was Rabindranath Tagore a feminist? Read his essay 'Woman and Home' from 1922 to find out', *Scroll.in,* 9 May 2017.

3   **Footnote 6: The archetypal divine mother seems to:** Asko Parpola, 'Fertility Cults in Folk Religion', *The Roots of Hinduism: The Early Aryans and the Indus Civilization,* New York: Oxford University Press, 2015.

3   **Footnote 6: It appears that when patrilineal:** J. F. Hewitt, 'The Pre-Aryan Communal Village in India and Europe', *The Journal of the Royal Asiatic Society of Great Britain and Ireland,* 1899, pp. 329–356.

3   **Footnote 9: The masculine (purusha) and feminine (prakrti) principles:** Vandana Shiva, *Staying Alive: Women, Ecology and Development,* London: Zed Books, 1989, p. 39.

6   **'strong implicit bias in various scientific fields':** Isabelle Régner, Catherine Thinus-Blanc, Agnès Netter, et al., 'Committees with implicit biases promote fewer women when they do not believe gender bias exists', Nature Human Behaviour, Vol. 3, 2019, pp. 1171–1179, <https://doi.org/10.1038/s41562-019-0686-3>.

6   **Footnote 15: Known as the 'Matilda effect':** Sara McLaughlin Mitchell, Michelle L Dion, Jane Lawrence Summer, 'Replication Data for: Gendered Citation Patterns across Political Science and Social Science Methodology Fields', *Harvard Dataverse,* 2018.

6   **Footnote 17: women's brains are highly connected across:** Ragini Verma, Alex Smith, Drew Parker, et al., 'Sex differences in the structural connectome of the human brain', *Proceedings of the National Academy of Sciences of the United States of America,* 14 January 2014, <https://doi.org/10.1073/pnas.1316909110>.

7   **work in freezing office temperatures:** Petula Dvorak, 'Frigid offices, freezing women, oblivious men: An air-conditioning investigation', *Washington Post,* 23 July 2015.

7   **Footnote 20: They are consequently at a major risk:** Vidhya Venugopal, K. Manikandan, 'Heat stress and inadequate sanitary facilities at workplaces–an occupational health concern for women?', *Global Health Action,* 2016.

8   **women have a higher threshold for pain:** Loren J Martin, Erinn L Acland, Chulmin Cho, et al., 'Male-Specific Conditioned Pain Hypersensitivity in Mice

and Humans', *Current Biology*, Vol. 29, No. 2, 2019, pp. 192–201, <https://doi.org/ 10.1016/j.cub.2018.11.030>.

8   **Footnote 21: Diseases such as endometriosis:** Gabrielle Jackson, 'Why don't doctors trust women? Because they don't know much about us', *The Guardian*, 1 September 2019.

8   **Footnote 21: Meanwhile, several women are misdiagnosed:** 'Cardiology's problem women', *The Lancet*, 9 March 2019.

8   **Footnote 21: Women with autism often aren't diagnosed:** 'The Autism Dilemma for Women Diagnosis', *Organization for Autism Research*, 26 October 2018.

8   **Santhi Soundarajan, an Olympian:** Samantha Shapiro, 'Caught in the middle', *ESPN*, 24 July 2012.

8   **Footnote 23: With every passing year, the medical:** Stephen R Hammes, Ellis R Levin, 'Impact of estrogens in males and androgens in females', *The Journal of Clinical Investigation*, 2019, pp. 1818–1826.

11   **'[t]he history of silence is central to women's history':** Rebecca Solnit, 'Silence and powerlessness go hand in hand—women's voices must be heard', *The Guardian*, 8 March 2017.

12   **their virtual bodies become 'sites of dissent':** Padmini Ray Murray, 'Bringing Up the Bodies: The Visceral, the Virtual and the Visible', *Bodies of Information: Intersectional Feminism and Digital Humanities*, Elizabeth Losh and Jacqueline Wernimont (eds.), Minneapolis: University of Minnesota Press, 2018, <https://dhdebates.gc.cuny.edu/projects/bodies-of-information>

12   **Footnote 35: There are more men on the internet than women in India:** Sandhya Keelery, 'Distribution of internet users in India 2016–2020 by gender', *Statista*, 2020.

14   **'But their kind of feminism has come from':** Peter Griffin, 'Grappling with different feminisms: Urvashi Butalia on the diversity of the women's movement', *The Hindu*, 14 February 2019.

17   **'that is all but inaccessible to the uninitiated':** Rene Denfeld, *The New Victorians: A Young Woman's Challenge to the Old Feminist Order*, New York: Grand Central Publishing, 1995, p. 5.

17   **She's constantly dissed for her 'double entanglement':** Angela McRobbie, *The Aftermath of Feminism: Gender, Culture and Social Change*, London: Sage, 2008, p. 21.

17   **'abjectifying attitudes and conceptions of her':** Lesa Lockford, *Performing Femininity: Rewriting Gender Identity*, Lanham: AltaMira Press, 2004, p. 54.

17   **'humour and irony are central themes':** Fien Adriaens, and Sofie Van Bauwel, '*Sex and the City*: A Postfeminist Point of View? Or How Popular Culture Functions as a Channel for Feminist Discourse?', *The Journal of Popular Culture*,

Vol. 47, No. 1, 2011, p. 14.

18   **In 2016, the gender pay gap narrowed:** Arundhati Ramanathan, 'Level to level, women earn almost as much as men in India: survey', *Live Mint*, 25 May 2016.

18   **A survey by PWC found that 76 per cent:** 'The female millennial: A new era of talent', *PwC*, 2015.

18   **The World Bank warns that millions:** Luis A. Andres, Basab Dasgupta, George Joseph, 'Precarious Drop: Reassessing Patterns of Female Labor Force Participation in India', *South Asian Region*, World Bank Group, 2017.

18   **The average age of a woman:** 'Median age at first pregnancy among married women in India 2015–16 by age group', *Statista Research Department*, 2020.

18   **But also, 25 per cent of women quit:** '25% of First-Time Mothers in India Quit Jobs to Raise Children: Survey', *NDTV Profit*, 9 May 2015.

18   **Sociologist Michèle Barrett notes that:** Michèle Barrett and Anne Phillips, *Destabilizing Theory: Contemporary Feminist Debates*, Redwood City: Stanford University Press, 1992, p. 201.

21   **Anthropologist Rama Srinivasan called this:** Rama Srinivasan, 'The right identity: Evolving feminist narratives in India must resolve the fault lines that have emerged', *Indian Express*, 30 October 2018.

21   **Many DBA feminists left the women's collective:** Shradha Lama, Sabah Maharaj, 'Statement: Why we decided to leave Pinjra Tod', *Round Table India*, 20 February 2019.

22   **Footnote 49: In a panel discussion, 'members were invited':** Jennifer C. Nash, 'The Intersectionality Wars: Does the Term Even Mean Anything Anymore?', *Literary Hub*, 7 January 2019.

24   **'unlike the state where the citizen is':** Shilpa Phadke, 'Thirty Years On: Women's Studies Reflects on the Women's Movement', *Economic and Political Weekly*, October 2003, pp. 4575.

24   **Footnote 54: 'On one hand, Sandberg and her ilk':** Cinzia Arruzza, Tithi Bhattacharya, and Nancy Fraser, *Feminism for the 99%: A Manifesto*, Brooklyn, New York: Verso, 2019, p. 2.

24   **Footnote 55: As of 2020, India's richest 1 per cent:** 'Time to Care', Oxfam India, 2020.

25   **'If patriarchy considers women to be':** Alka Shukla, 'Pushpa, I Love Tears: How to Counter Dick Bosses with Some Weeping,' *Arré*, 7 May 2018.

26   **'Feminism is a cool sisters' club online':** Vandana Shukla, 'Is #feminism elitist in India?', *The Tribune*, 5 March 2017.

27   **As philosopher Gayatri Chakravorty Spivak points out:** Gayatri Chakravorty Spivak, as cited in Mary Eagleton, *Feminist Literary Criticism*, New York: Routledge, p. 14.

27   Footnote 59: 'a whole range of issues—from "eve teasing"': Srila Roy, Whose Feminism Is It Anyway?, *The Wire*, 1 November 2017.

28   'The one person Savarnas traditionally cannot stand': Mimi Mondal, 'A Dalit woman's thoughts on #MeTooIndia', *Indian Express*, 14 April 2018.

28   there 'is nothing about being "female"': Donna Haraway, 'A Manifesto for Cyborgs', *The Norton Anthology of Theory & Criticism*, Vincent B. Leitch (ed.), London and New York: W. W. Norton & Company, Inc., 2010, pp. 2040.

28   '[i]t has become difficult to name one's feminism': Ibid., p. 2067.

29   Footnote 62: She argues that we should strive towards: Sue Ruddick, 'Towards a Dialectics of the Positive', *Environment and Planning A: Economy and Space*, 2008, pp. 1588–2602.

30   Footnote 63: depressive disorders accounted for: Savita Malhotra, Ruchita Shah, 'Women and mental health in India: An overview', *Indian Journal of Psychiatry*, 2015, pp. 205–211.

30   Footnote 63: Anxiety disorders and psychological distress: Ibid.

30   Footnote 63: Suicide attempts and deliberate self-harm: Ibid.

30   Footnote 65: '[w]ith its intense reformist streak and': G. Arunima, 'Sex and the Feminist', *Economic & Political Weekly*, 27 October 2012.

31   '[t]o have a right-wing guy go down': Anonymous, 'Saffron in the Streets, Woke in the Sheets: My brief liaison with a polyamorous man of the right', *Vice*, 26 July 2018.

31   Footnote 67: 'prostitution is work, both in terms of': Geetanjali Gangoli, 'Prostitution as Livelihood: "Work" or "Crime"?', *Livelihoods and Poverty Reduction: Lessons From Eastern India*, September 2001, <http://www.anthrobase.com/Txt/G/Gangoli_G_01.htm>.

31   Footnote 67: the '"choice" to do sex work is no more or less': Nivedita Menon, *Seeing Like A Feminist*, Gurgaon: Penguin Random House India, 2012, p. 183.

31   Footnote 68: '[s]ex work and sexual exploitation are two': Nalini Jameela, *The Autobiography of a Sex Worker*, Chennai: Westland Ltd., 2007, <https://www.goodreads.com/work/quotes/3123711-the-autobiography-of-a-sex-worker>.

32   'understanding the multiple ways of being a feminist': Shelley Budgeon, 'Emergent Feminist(?) Identities: Young Women and the Practice of Micropolitics', *European Journal of Women's Studies*, Vol. 8, No. 1, 2001, p. 26.

On Beauty

33   country with more than 656 million women: Central Statistics Organization, *Women and Men in India*, New Delhi: Ministry of Statistics and Programme Implementation, 2005.

33   is growing at 16 per cent CAGR: India Women's Cosmetics Market Forecast

and Opportunities, 2020, *TechSci Research*, June 2015.

34 **'[t]he concept of "beauty capitalism" best describes':** Meeta Jha, *The Global Beauty Industry*, London: Routledge, 2005, p. x.

34 **Footnote 1: In India and around the world, independent organic beauty:** Hena Desai, 'The 'Woke' Beauty Bag: All The Brands Millennials Are Currently Loving', *Grazia*, 22 October 2020.

35 **who complained that the people of Hindustan:** Ziya Us Salam, 'What Baburnama Says', *Frontline*, 6 December 2019.

35 **Footnote 3: As Neha Mishra specifies:** Neha Mishra, 'India and Colorism: The Finer Nuances', *Washington University Global Studies Law Review*, 2015, pp. 725–750.

36 **Times Most Desirable Women 2019:** 'Meet the Times 50 Most Desirable Women 2019', *Times of India*, 29 August 2020.

36 **Footnote 5: 100 tribal girls were trained to be airhostesses:** Saif Khalid, 'Fighting India's ugly fancy for fair skin', *Al Jazeera*, 2 October 2013.

37 **Footnote 7: 'Dear Taslima Nasreen, I'm sorry you':** Khatija Rahman (khatija. rahman), Instagram post, 15 February 2020, <https://www.instagram.com/p/B8jzyv4lKTT/>

38 **'the burqa offering a refuge from sexual harassment':** 'Between the Burqa and the Beauty Parlor? Globalization, Cultural Nationalism, and Feminist Politics', *Postcolonial Studies and Beyond*, Ania Loomba, Suvir Kaul, et al. (eds.), Durham: Duke University Press, 2005, pp. 206–230.

40 **women are required to be 'aesthetic entrepreneurs':** Ana Sofia Elias, Rosalind Gill, and Christina Scharff, *Aesthetic Labour: Rethinking Beauty Politics in Neoliberalism*, London: Palgrave Macmillan, 2017, p. 174.

41 **'why are you dressed like a parachi':** Christina Dhanraj (caselchris1), Tweet, 19 March 2018, <https://twitter.com/caselchris1/status/975763436054355968>.

41 **wearing a burqa is 'sinister':** Nabeela Jamil, 'Why I Choose to Wear Hijab: An Open Letter from A Tired Muslim Feminist', *Feminism in India*, 5 October 2018.

42 **'When I posted a picture in [a] Western outfit':** Kiruba Munusamy, 'Intersection of Identities: Online Gender and Caste Based Violence', *GenderIT. Org*, 7 June 2018.

43 **'I would always make sure that I carry':** Srijoni Roy, 'How Does the Male Gaze Affect Your Everyday Dressing? We Ask 5 Women', *iDiva*, 8 July 2019.

43 **'They think all short-haired people are lesbians.':** Maroosha Muzaffar, 'An Informal Survey Reveals Deep Homophobia in Indian Schools', *Vice*, 17 May 2018.

43 **society 'locates masculinity in females as abhorrent':** Judith Halberstam, 'The Good, the Bad, and the Ugly: Men, Women and Masculinity', *The Norton*

Anthology of Theory & Criticism, Vincent B. Leitch (ed.), New York: W. W. Norton & Company, Inc., 2010, pp. 2,527–28.

44 **'Fashion is important to express one's identity':** Vatsala Chhibber, 'Durga Gawde: Fashion is important to express one's identity', *Live Mint*, 14 December 2018.

44 **'As a good millennial feminist':** Kahini Iyer, 'Goodbye 2010's: The Decade We Embraced Fleabag Feminism', *Arré*, 24 December 2019.

45 **'Whilst individuals may be invested in':** Elias, Gill, and Schraff, *Aesthetic Labour*, p. 19.

45 **Footnote 16: 'In an absurdist take on a classic':** Elias, Gill, and Schraff, *Aesthetic Labour*, p. 19.

46 **74 per cent of Indian women believe:** IANS, 'Beauty brand launches 'let's break the rules of beauty' campaign following the findings of a survey', *The Weekend Leader*, 9 May 2016.

46 **proposes the idea of 'contradictive femininity':** Gitte Marianne Hansen, *Femininity, Self-harm and Eating Disorders in Japan*, London: Routledge, 2016, p. 4.

47 **'if u r a fat person and':** Priyanka Paul (artwhoring), Instagram post, 22 December 2020.

48 **'female body could be experienced as both':** Meenakshi Thapan, 'Gender, Body and Everyday Life', *Social Scientist*, Vol. 23, No. 7/9, 1995, p. 33.

48 **'important for a woman to see her body':** Ibid.

48 **'It is true that make-up can be empowering':** Manasi Pant, 'Choice Feminism: A Self-Imposed Barrier To Progress?', *Feminism in India*, 17 September 2019.

49 **A few years ago, researchers conducted:** Jean-Luc Jucker, Tracey Thornborrow, and Martin J. Tovee, 'The effect of the thin body ideal in a media-naïve population', 14 August 2017, < https://www.biorxiv.org/content/10.1101/176107v1.full>.

51 **'To lose confidence in one's body is':** Simone de Beauvoir, as cited in Karen Bridson, *The Secrets of Skinny Chicks*, New York: McGraw-Hill Education, 2010, p. 15.

52 **'Upper caste equals fair skin equals':** Tannishtha Chatterjee, 'The Indian Hatred for Dark Skin Comes From Caste Bias', *The Wire*, 28 September 2016.

53 **The fairness cream market is projected:** 'India Fairness Cream & Bleach Market Overview, 2018–2023', *Research and Markets*, 2018.

53 **Only recently has the Health Ministry proposed five years:** Nidhi Sharma, 'Govt proposes 5-year jail, Rs 50-lakh fine for ads promoting fair skin', *Economic Times*, 6 Feb 2020.

54 **In today's India, women possess 85 per cent:** Ritu Mody Kamdar, 'The evolution of Indian women as consumers', *Fortune India*, 29 December 2018.

56 **'some form of aesthetic labour is increasingly demanded':** Elias, Gill, and

Schraff, *Aesthetic Labour*, p. 38.

56 **'new sexual contract':** Angela McRobbie, 'TOP Girls? Young women and the postfeminist sexual contract', *Cultural Studies*, 2007, p. 2.

56 **'"Flexibility" has been stressed as':** Sofie Van Bauwel, 'Representing Gender Benders: Consumerism and the Muting of Subversion', *At the Interface: Continuity and Transformations in Culture and Politics*, E. Siapera and J. Hands (eds.), Oxford: Rodopi Press, 2004, pp. 17–38.

56 **Footnote 32: '[M]ajor aspects in the culture of Victorianism':** Maitrayee Chaudhuri, 'Feminism in India: The Tale and its Telling', *Revue Tiers Monde*, Vol. 209, No. 1, 2012, p. 19.

57 **'[W]e really need to start worrying when one':** Suchetana Sinha, 'The Headless Women of Bollywood: A Look into the Industry's Blatant Sexual Objectification', *ScoopWhoop*, 27 May 2016.

57 **'Madhuri Dixit's bosom heaving sensuously':** Manjima Bhattacharya, 'Book Excerpt: Mannequin: Working Women in India's Glamour Industry', *Godrej India Culture Lab*, 7 February 2019, <indiaculturelab.org/blog/excerpt-mannequin-manjima-bhattacharya>.

57 **Footnote 35: 'the fetishistic fragmentation of the figure via':** Preminda Jacob, *Celluloid Deities: The Visual Culture of Cinema and Politics in South India*, Lanham: Lexington Books, 2009, p. 127.

58 **'I embrace nudity as I have nothing to hide':** TNN, 'I embrace nudity as I have nothing to hide: Swastika', *Times of India*, 12 January 2017.

58 **'Instagram is a part of my life':** Ashraya Kannan, 'Movies are for entertainment', *Deccan Chronicle*, 1 June 2018.

59 **Footnote 36: The cover for Malayalam magazine *Grihalakshmi* triggered sexism:** TNM Staff, '"Obscenity lies in eyes of beholder": Kerala HC on Grihalakshmi breastfeeding cover', *News Minute*, 21 June 2018.

60 **'powerful industries…have arisen from the capital':** Naomi Wolf, 'The Beauty Myth', *Equity in Schools and Society*, Judy M. Iseke-Barnes and N. Nathani Wane (eds.), Toronto: Canadian Scholars' Press Inc., 2000, p. 306.

62 **It is expected to generate 1.42 crore jobs:** Virendra Pandit, 'Beauty, wellness sector will be a job puller by 2022', *Hindu Business Line*, 12 March 2018.

63 **the 'sense of being a woman is internalized':** Veena Das, as cited in Meenakshi Thapan, *Living the Body: Embodiment, Womanhood and Identity in Contemporary India*, New Delhi: Sage Publications, 2009, p. 167.

63 **'I'm happy to say this is my life':** Aakanksha Raghuvanshi, '"This Is My Life, My Face": Shruti Haasan On Body Shaming, Plastic Surgery And Hormonal Pain', *NDTV*, 28 February 2020.

64 **'beauty sick':** Renee Engeln, *Beauty Sick: How the Cultural Obsession with Appearance Hurts Girls and Women*, New York: Harper, 2017, p. 10.

65 Footnote 45: She writes that while second-wave feminists: Lena Dunham, 'Why Red Lipstick is Feminism's New Calling Card', *Vogue*, 1 June 2017.

Ishq in the Times of Tinder

66 'all romantic experiences are essentially caste experiences': Kavya, 'All Romantic Experiences are Essentially Caste Experiences'–In Conversation with Jyotsna Siddharth, *Feminism in India*, 20 May 2019.

68 'The time has come to think about sex': Gayle Rubin, 'Thinking Sex: Notes for A Radical Theory of the Politics of Sexuality', *The Norton Anthology of Theory & Criticism*, Vincent B. Leitch (ed.), pp. 2373–2377. New York: W. W. Norton & Company, Inc., 2010, p. 2195.

68 'Incels aren't looking for sex': Jia Tolentino, 'The Rage of the Incels', *The New Yorker*, 15 May 2018.

68 It's crucial to undo 'the false impression': Jennifer Baumgardner and Amy Richards, as cited in A. Susan Owen, Sarah H. Stein and Leah R. Vande Berg, *Bad Girls: Cultural Politics and Media Representations of Transgressive Women*, Bern: Peter Lang Publishing, 2007, p. 115.

69 'Sexuality is integral to women's political': Hawkins, K., Cornwall, A., and Lewin, T., 'Sexuality and Empowerment: An Intimate Connection, Pathways Policy Paper', *Pathways of Women's Empowerment Research Programme Consortium*, Brighton: Pathways of Women's Empowerment, IDS, 2011.

70 their highest-selling product among: HT Correspondent, 'Punjabi women buy most sex toys, sales go up during Navratri in Gujarat: Survey', *Hindustan Times*, 9 August 2017.

70 millennial couples have far less sex: Janet Burns, 'Millennials Are Having Less Sex Than Other Gens, But Experts Say It's (Probably) Fine', *Forbes*, 16 August 2016.

70 it is 'an egalitarian understanding of': Ashley Fetters, 'Why William and Kate Are a "Fairy Tale" but Harry and Meghan Are "Couple Goals"', *The Atlantic*, January 2020.

71 'I am learning how to love': Rupi Kaur, *Milk and Honey*, New Delhi: Simon & Schuster India, 2017, p. 55.

72 'Certainly, people fell in love during': Stephanie Coonz, *Marriage, a History: How Love Conquered Marriage*, London: Viking Penguin, 2005, p. 8.

72 Ninety-two per cent of marriages in India: Pankaj Madan, and Mark Alexander Friedrich, 'Attitudes, Anxieties and Aspirations of India's Youth: Changing Patterns', Delhi: Centre for the Study of Developing Societies (CSDS) and Konrad-Adenauer-Stiftung, 2016.

73 'I don't want to sound like a snoot': Moni Basu, 'Why these Indian millennials are choosing arranged marriage', *CNN*, 24 March 2018.

74 **'I believed that no man, no husband':** Namita Bhandare, 'When home is a prison: Meena Kandasamy's story of domestic abuse', *Live Mint*, 2 June 2017.

74 **More than 30 per cent of Indian women:** 'National Family Health Survey - 5 (2019-2020)', Mumbai: International Institute of Population Sciences, 2020.

74 **India has the lowest divorce rate:** Arushi Kapoor, 'India Has The Lowest Divorce Rate In The World, Here's Why It Isn't Necessarily A Good Thing', *ScoopWhoop*, 2019.

75 **10 awesome tricks you must try:** Namrata Arora, '10 Awesome Tricks You Must Try To Make Your Husband Obey You Always', *BollywoodShaadis.com*, 13 February 2015.

75 **there has been a spike online:** Special Correspondent, 'Demand for divorce and family lawyers has increased, Chennai tops, says new study', *The Hindu*, 17 December 2019.

77 **Even in the twenty-first century, not much seems:** Charmy Harikrishnan, 'Indian youth is a strange mix of conservative and liberal attitudes: Survey', *Economic Times*, 23 April 2017.

77 **'The merest expression of same-sex desire':** Amritananda Chakravorty, 'Pride and Prejudice: The Desires of Indian Queer Women', *Live Wire*, 30 June 2018.

77 **Footnote 11: 'With stress levels high when':** Joanna Sydra, 'Men feel stressed if their female partners earn more than 40% of household income – new research', *The Conversation*, 20 November 2019.

78 **'We fight like every other couple':** Sreemoyee Piu Kundu, 'Heartwarming Story of a Married Lesbian Couple,' *DailyO*, 5 March 2016.

78 **'Forget meet cutes in bars':** Dipannita Saha, 'Tinder is no place for dating for queer women in India. So where are all the lesbians supposed to go?', *OddNaari*, 30 March 2017.

78 **On Tinder, there is a 'very curious trend':** Smita Vanniyar, 'How Queer Are Your Dating Apps?', *TARSHI*, 15 June 2017.

79 **'Being able to own every emotion':** Tracy Ann, 'Forgive Yourself, Falling Out of Love with a Long Term Partner is Only Human', *iDiva*, 13 February 2019.

79 **announce the end of their marriage:** Shepali Bhatt, 'Happily Divorced: Indian women are breaking stigma around separation like never before', *The Economic Times*, 27 January 2019.

80 **'we've also learned that we cannot':** Ayushi Murli, 'Open Letter to the Man Who Sexually Abused Me. And Never Got Reported', *Arré*, 8 October 2018.

81 **'One morning, when I was home and':** India Today Web Desk, 'Niharika Singh: Nawazuddin Siddiqui is a sexually repressed man with toxic male entitlement', *India Today*, 10 November 2018.

81 **'There is a man's reputation involved':** IANS, 'Why shouldn't I stand by Nawazuddin, asks Kubbra Sait', *Outlook*, 13 November 2018.

81 **'For men, there seems to be no concept of mind':** Anoo Bhuyan, 'Women Remember, Men Don't', *Outlook*, 22 October 2018.

83 **'Consent becomes a little bit of a grey area':** Sayani Gupta (interviewed by Kirti Kulhari), India Today Conclave 2019.

83 **Footnote 16: 'If a trans woman is abused and harassed':** Pallavi Pundir, 'Transgender People Tell Us Why India's Newly Proposed Rape Laws are Discriminatory', *Vice*, 11 September 2019.

84 **'One of the most common misconceptions about kink':** Shreya Ila Anasuya, '"A twist in a straight line": inside India's kinky networks', *Deep Dives*, 22 December 2015.

86 **'Patriarchal hook-up culture treats consent like':** Kamayani Sharma, '#MeToo: Understanding Consent and Sex-Positivity in a Patriarchal Society', *Firstpost*, 12 November 2018.

87 **'In India, feminism is and has to be':** Shubha Tiwari, 'Rooting Feminism to India', *Boloji.com*, 5 November 2017.

87 **Footnote 19: 'My choice, to marry or not marry':** Deepika Padukone – "My Choice", Directed by Homi Adajania, for *Vogue* India, 2015.

88 **'The conflict of the Protection of Children':** Adrija Bose, 'How India's Most Important Law for Children's Safety is Leading to Unsafe abortions Among Teenagers', *News18*, 23 October 2019.

88 **In fact, 95 per cent of Indian men:** Mukesh Rawat, 'Indian men have a problem, they hate condoms. This is what it results in', *India Today*, 11 July 2019.

90 **'The women of Avanti hate kissing':** Sir Richard F. Burton, *Kama Sutra "Aphorism of Love" Vatsayana (Improvised Edition)*, Pradeep Thakur (ed.), Ludhiana: Pradeep Thakur & Sons, pp. 82–83.

90 **'This practice, extraordinarily rich and inventive':** Hélène Cixous, 'The Laugh of the Medusa', Keith Cohen and Paula Cohen (tr.), *Signs*, Vol. 1, No. 4, 1976, p. 876.

91 **'Self-love is important because':** Mandovi Menon, 'Five Young Indian Women Get Real About Masturbation,' *Homegrown*, 28 March 2017.

92 **'Porn can also turn upside down':** Jaya Sharma, 'Porn, Not Erotica', *TARSHI*, 1 July 2019.

92 **Footnote 23: 'Back when I first came across':** Nadika Nadja, '"I knew I was home": A transwoman's journey through porn', *Deep Dives*, 17 November 2016.

93 **'Over the past few years I have not only':** Samcha Lowang, 'What's The First Thing You Think Of When You See A Person From The North East?', *Youth Ki Awaaz*, 29 March 2019.

93 **Footnote 24: '[e]rotica has artistic and literary value':** Richa Kaul Padte, 'From Judy Blume to the Sexy Internet: What Counts as Erotica?', *TARSHI*, 1 July 2019.

94 '[y]ou don't have to worry about your': Joanna, '10 Reasons Why It Is Amazing To Date A Northeast Girl', *Daily Moss*, 30 November 2017.

94 'LOVE having a great time': Shreya Aachar, 'What are the perks of dating a Northeast Indian woman?', *Quora*, 9 March 2017.

94 **Sexual violence and harassment are disproportionally:** Tanika Godbole, 'Why India's Dalit women are vulnerable to sexual violence', *DW*, 28 October 2020.

95 **'It is right that they think that':** Aparna Ragupathi, 'Panel on Indian feminism, caste system gives Rutgers new perspectives', *Daily Targum*, 11 March 2019.

95 **'Can someone whose neck barely moves':** Soumita Basu, 'Can we ever have a conversation about desire without centering my disability', *Skin Stories*, 17 December 2018.

97 **women are given the 'husband stitch':** Carrie Murphy, 'The Husband Stitch Isn't Just a Horrifying Childbirth Myth', *Healthline*, 27 September 2018.

98 **Woman 'itself is a term in process':** Judith Butler, *Gender Trouble*, New York: Routledge, 1999, p. 43.

98 **'I'm not sure if this is a phase':** Shruti B., 'Lessons in Self-Exploration: Discovering My Bi-Curiosity', *Gaysi*, 14 November 2018.

98 **As a 'queer demisexual trans man in India':** Jamal Siddiqui, '5 Things To Know About Dating Trans Men in India', *Youth Ki Awaaz*, 6 August 2017.

100 **'Sex is empowerment, sex is gendered':** Paromita Vohra, 'ishq & Ice Cream: Because Too Much of a Good Thing can be Wonderful', *Desi Writers' Lounge*.

100 **'We talk about all the things that can':** TARSHI Team, 'Interview: Paromita Vohra – Part I', *TARSHI*, 1 August 2018.

100 **'In actuality we should have numerous':** Ibid.

101 **tantric sex originated in this subcontinent:** David B. Gray, 'Tantra and the Tantric Traditions of Hinduism and Buddhism', *Oxford Research Encyclopedias*, 5 April 2016.

102 **'The Mahabharata warns that women become':** Arti Dhand, *Woman as Fire, Woman as Sage: Sexual Ideology in the Mahābhārata*, New York: State University of New York Press, 2008, p. 184.

103 **'I think homosexuals and bisexuals are not':** Sneha Sharma, 'What is it like to be a lesbian in India?', *Quora*, 16 November 2016.

103 **Footnote 33: High Court ruled in favour of:** 'India court rules lesbian couple can live together', *BBC*, 25 September, 2018.

104 **Footnote 35: 'Queer Pride is about celebrating':** Laxmi Murthy and Rajashri Dasgupta, *Our Pictures, Our Words: A Visual Journey Through The Women's Movement*, New Delhi: Zubaan, 2011, p. 110.

105 **'by admitting that there is a "natural" division':** Monique Wittig, 'One Is Not Born a Woman', *The Lesbian and Gay Studies Reader*, Henry Abelove (ed.), London: Routledge, 2012, p. 104.

105 **Footnote 36: '[i]n our present day culture':** Margaret Mead, 'Preface', *Sex and Temperament: In Three Primitive Societies*, New York: The New American Library, 1950.

106 **'societies where female sexuality is not shamed':** Kate Lister, 'Sex in Our Strange World: Why the Matriarchy Means Better Sex and a Better Society', *Vice*, 7 March 2019.

Women at Work

107 **are trying to cut women out of the workplace:** Kim Elsesser, 'The Latest Consequence Of #MeToo: Not Hiring Women', *Forbes*, 5 September 2019.

107 **women account for only 19.9 per cent:** 'Labor force, female (% of total labor force): India', The World Bank, 29 January 2021.

107 **In fact, we could add US$ 770 billion:** Anu Madgavkar, Jonathan Woetzel, and Kevin Sneader, 'The power of parity: Advancing women's equality in Asia Pacific', McKinsey & Company, 23 April 2018.

107 **'apart from the problem of unsafe working spaces':** Nishtha Satyam, and Francine Pickup, 'To Reverse Decline of Women in Labour Force, India Must Make Its Working Spaces Safe', *The Wire*, 2 December 2018.

107 **Footnote 1: In 2013, a Mumbai photojournalist:** 'Mumbai photojournalist gang-raped on assignment', *BBC*, 23 August 2013.

107 **Footnote 1: In 2017, an Infosys techie was:** 'Chennai: Techie found dead in Infosys dorm, family members suspect murder', *New Indian Express*, 31 May 2017.

107 **Footnote 1: In 2018, an Ola driver molested a:** Deepika, 'Karnataka: Ola driver takes detour, molests woman passenger in Bengaluru', *One India*, 6 June 2018.

108 **'women with more education marry':** Esha Chatterjee, Sonalde Desai, and Reeve Vanneman, 'Indian paradox: Rising education, declining women's employment', *Demographic Research*, Vol. 38, No. 31, 2018.

108 **In fact, 34.7 per cent of urban women:** Janaki Shibu and Rosa Abraham, 'More women are self-employed in India, fewer hold salaried jobs', *Business Standard*, 2 July 2019.

108 **A majority of female entrepreneurs, 51.2 per cent:** 'Women & Entrepreneurship In India 2019', *Women's Web*, 16 July 2019.

108 **Footnote 2: direct employment for 50 to 60 million:** 'Women Entrepreneurship in India', New Delhi: Bain & Company and Google, 2019.

109 **40 per cent of working mothers:** '1/4th working women & 40% working mothers intend to quit job: Survey', ASSOCHAM, 7 March 2016.

110 **Footnote 5: Women in India do almost ten times:** Nita Bhalla, 'High share

of care work keeps Indian women out of economy—McKinsey', *Reuters*, 3 November 2015.

111 **'They have chosen to leave':** Hana Schank and Elizabeth Wallace, 'Opting out of a career doesn't make you less ambitious', *Quartz*, 20 June 2018.

114 **'To put it another way, if women':** Mary Beard, *Women & Power: A Manifesto*, New York: Liveright, 2017, p. 83.

114 **Footnote 7: 'Matriarchal values grow out of':** Peggy Reeves Sanday, 'Matriarchal Values and World Peace: The Case of the Minangkabau', *Societies of Peace—2nd World Congress on Matriarchal Studies*, 2005, <http://www.second-congress-matriarchal-studies.com/sanday.html>.

115 **'women hold views at odds with the':** Ann Mari May, David Kucera, and Mary G. McGarvey, 'Mind the Gap', *Finance & Development*, Vol. 55, No. 2, June 2018, p. 1.

116 **64 per cent of Indian businesses have adopted:** PTI, 'India's ranking improves in gender diversity: Report', *The Economic Times*, 8 March 2018.

116 **According to Monster India, a popular job site:** Avishek Rakshit, 'Gender pay inequality decreases by only a per cent in 2018: Monster India', *Business Standard*, 7 March 2019.

117 **'Gender equality is a critical component':** Lucy Lamble, 'Only six countries in the world give women and men equal legal work rights', *The Guardian*, 1 March 2019.

117 **'[W]omen must learn how to question':** Germaine Greer, *The Female Eunuch*, London: 4th Estate, 1970, p. 17.

117 **Feminist movements in the last era:** Sohela Nazneen, and Maheen Sultan, *Voicing Demands: Feminist Activism in Transnational Contexts*, London: Zed Books, 2014, p. 2.

117 **Footnote 8: 'If you spread your legs because':** 'Germaine Greer criticises 'whingeing' #MeToo campaigners', *The Week*, 23 Jan 2018.

118 **Today, Iceland is the most gender-equal:** 'Why is Iceland the world's global leader in gender equality?', *Women Political Leaders*, 24 March 2014.

118 **During this time each parent is entitled:** Maternity and Paternity Leave, *Work in Iceland*, <https://work.iceland.is/living/maternity-and-paternity-leave>.

118 **equality 'won't come about by itself':** Jon Henley, '"Equality won't happen by itself": how Iceland got tough on gender pay gap', *The Guardian*, 20 February 2018.

118 **It's illegal in Iceland now:** 'In Iceland, it's now illegal to pay men more than women', *Al Jazeera*, 1 January 2018.

120 **'for women by introducing new social rights':** Marijan Pavčnik, 'Human Rights, Minority Rights, Women's Rights', *Proceedings of the 19th World Congress of the International Association for Philosophy of Law and Social Philosophy*, New

York: Franz Steiner Verlag Stuttgart, 2001.

120 **Footnote 12: 'Dalit men are the most discriminatory':** Aishwarya Rao, 'Dalit Women in Politics: Aishwarya Rao on why disabled women must be included in mainstream dialogues', *Firstpost*, 6 March 2019.

122 **'biological difference between the male and female':** Lois McNay, *Foucault: A Critical Introduction*, Cambridge: Polity Press, 1994, p. 99.

122 **Footnote 14: 'Shameless women are a powerful force':** Suzanne Moore, 'Ocasio-Cortez has shown 'shameless' women are a powerful force', *The Guardian*, 10 January 2019.

123 **Femininity 'here is powerful, playful and narcissistic':** Rosalind Gill, 'Culture and Subjectivity in Neoliberal and Postfeminist Times', *Subjectivity*, 2008, pp. 432–445, <https://openaccess.city.ac.uk/id/eprint/4113>.

124 **'The idea that women are irrational':** Jenna Baddeley, 'On the "irrationality" of women (and men)', *Psychology Today*, 3 November 2010.

124 **Footnote 18: Research suggests that having more:** Denis Yanov, 'How Gender Diversity Affects Team Productivity?', *TMETRIC*, 2 August 2020.

125 **There's a reason why women:** Divya J. Shekhar, 'Women hold 17% of board positions in corporate India, but only 11% leadership roles', *Forbes India*, 8 December 2020.

126 **'I hate that most workplaces in the country won't':** Sonali Kokra, 'How I Shamefully Benefitted from Patriarchy', *Arré*, 14 January 2019.

127 **'it has become somewhat fashionable':** Uma Shashikant, 'Why women need to work', *Economic Times*, 30 September 2019.

127 **'dented and painted':** Sabyasachi Dasgupta, 'Delhi protests are by "dented and painted" women: President Pranab's son', *NDTV*, 27 December 2012.

127 **'Affluent stay-at-home mothers are':** Rachel Sherman, 'A sociologist explains why wealthy women are doomed to be miserable', *Quartz*, 9 November 2017.

128 **Footnote 20: An army chief publicly said:** Ghazala Wahab, 'Women in Combat: The Navy Chief Spoke Sense but the Army Chief Did Not', *The Wire*, 21 December 2018.

129 **'positive sentiments are disseminated through':** Gill, 'Culture and Subjectivity'.

131 **gender diverse organizations are known to:** Vivian Hunt, Dennis Layton, and Sara Prince, 'Diversity Matters', McKinsey & Company, 2 February 2015.

131 **'The current feminist narrative of corporate India':** Christina Thomas Dhanaraj, 'Dalit Women in Corporate India are Being Left Behind', *The Wire*, 2 March 2017.

132 **Ninety-four per cent of top jobs:** Ashish Gupta, 'Caste: Why it's still an issue for India Inc.', *Fortune India*, 14 October 2016.

132 **'Most of my shaming came from senior':** Prachi Sibal, 'Chinmayi Sripaada's Relentless Fight Against Sexual Harassment In The Tamil Film Industry',

Huffington Post, 6 June 2019.

133 **Footnote 23: In 2018, a nun from the:** The Hindu Net Desk, 'Bishop Franco Mulakkal and Kerala nun rape case: the story till now', *The Hindu*, 15 October 2018.

134 **Women with children are known to outperform:** Matthias Krapf, Heinrich W. Ursprung, and Christian Zimmermann, 'Parenthood and productivity of highly skilled labor: Evidence from the groves of academe', *Journal of Economic Behavior & Organization*, Vol. 140, August 2017, pp. 147–175.

135 **A survey of 1,700 fathers across:** Team Flipkart Stories, 'How India's "Penguin Dads" Are Redefining Fatherhood', 1 March 2018.

136 **women did the bulk of housework and childcare:** Sanchari Basu Chaudhuri, 'Lockdown Humour and Domestic Work: Perpetuating Gender Roles', *EPW Engage*, 17 February 2021.

138 **'confidence, resilience, and positive mental attitude':** Gill, 'Culture and Subjectivity'.

139 **'the self-indulgent mumbo-jumbo':** Barkha Dutt, 'I'm a feminist. Giving women a day off for their period is a stupid idea', *Washington Post*, 4 August 2017.

139 **Footnote 27: A college in Gujarat even:** India Today Web Desk, '68 Bhuj college women forced to remove underwear, prove they weren't on period', *India Today*, 14 February 2020.

140 **'narcissistic reflexive thought process':** Jessa Crispin, *Why I Am Not a Feminist: A Feminist Manifesto*, February 2017, p. xiii.

140 **'Of all the terrible things that have happened':** Veena Venugopal, 'Feminists Have Killed Feminism', *Hindu Business Line*, 10 March 2018.

140 **'[i]n our culture both men and women':** Madhu Kishwar, 'Why I do not call myself a feminist', *Feminism in India*, Maitrayee Chaudhuri (ed.), New Delhi: Kali for Women & Women Unlimited, 2004, p. 31.

142 **'We are at the brink of a gender equal world':** Akansha Gupta, 'We Are At The Brink Of A Gender Equal World, The Big Change Is Social Media', *SheThePeople.tv*, 30 May 2018.

143 **'Borders between countries are marked out':** Tripti Lahiri, *Maid in India: Stories of Inequality and Opportunity Inside Our Homes*, New Delhi: Aleph Book Company, 2017, p. xii.

143 **'Two-thirds of all domestic help':** Ibid., p. 3.

145 **'such interventions are designed and delivered':** Andrea Cornwall, Elizabeth Harrison, and Ann Whitehead (eds.), *Feminisms in Development: Contradictions, Contestations and Challenges*, London: Zed Books, 2007, p. 30.

147 **'I really feel proud to be a woman in prostitution':** Haclyon Pictures,

'The Power of the Collective' [video], Vimeo, 12 April 2012, <https://vimeo.com/40236081>.

147 **'VAMP members don't want to be "saved"':** Andrea Cornwall, 'Indian sex-workers are a shining example of women's empowerment', *The Guardian*, 26 July 2012.

148 **Surrogate mothers earned between:** Pallavi Pundir, 'It Will Soon Be Illegal to Get Paid as a Surrogate Mother in India', *Vice*, 6 August 2019.

Demystifying the Feminine

150 **'This prejudice against feeling is sustained':** Leela Gandhi, *Postcolonial Theory: A Critical Introduction*, New York: Columbia University Press, 1998, p. 57.

151 **'Within the male centred conception of the':** Karen Green, 'Femininity and Transcendence', *Australian Feminist Studies*, Vol. 4, No. 10, 1989, pp. 85–96.

151 **'consists in refusing to be "the Other"':** Mary Daly, 'Glory to God the Verb', *Ms.*, No. 3, December 1974, p. 64.

151 **Footnote 3: 'their otherness to masculinity, women are':** Bronwyn Davies, 'The Concept of Agency: A Feminist Poststructuralist Analysis', *Social Analysis: The International Journal of Social and Cultural Practice*, Vol. 30, 1991, p. 44.

152 **Footnote 4: 'In one of her most intriguing ideas':** Josephine Donovan, *Feminist Theory*, New York: Bloomsbury Academic, 2012, p. 41.

153 **'Draupadi deconstructed the notions of chastity':** Jasbir Jain, as cited in Vandana Shrivastava, 'Feminism in India', Global Journals Inc., Vol. 16, No. 6, 2016, p. 1.

153 **'the later Brahmin imaginary greatly played':** Wendy Doniger, *The Hindus: An Alternative History*, New York: Viking Penguin, 2009, p. 232.

155 **Philosopher Judith Butler argues that gender is:** Judith Butler, 'Performative Arts and Gender Constitution: An Essay in Phenomenology and Feminist Theory', *Theatre Journal*, Vol. 40, No. 4, 1988, pp. 519–531.

156 **'the confluence of two significant factors in':** Niharika Dinkar, 'Framing Women: Gender and Modernity in Colonial India', *Marg*, Vol. 62, No. 4, 2011, p. 12.

157 **'[s]he takes femininity out of the bedroom':** Lockford, *Performing Femininity*, p. 54.

158 **'This coinciding expectation and undervaluation of':** Shwethaa S. Ballakrishnen, 'She gets the job done: Entrenched gender meanings and new returns to essentialism in India's elite professional firms', *Journal of Professions and Organization*, Vol. 4, No. 3, October 2017, pp. 324–342.

159 **spaces like call centres 'female ghettos':** Vicki Belt, 'A female ghetto? Women's careers in call centres', *Human Resource Management Journal*, Vol. 12, No. 4, 2002, pp. 51–66.

159 'steady and shifting structures of gender differentiation': Mathangi Krishnamurthy, *1-800-Worlds: The Making of the Indian Call Centre Economy*, New Delhi: Oxford University Press, 2018, p. 6.

159 'Even as gender discourses are conduits for the': Ibid.

160 performativity constituted by 'expressions': Judith Butler, *Gender Trouble: Feminism and the Subversion of Identity*, London and New York: Routledge, 1990, p. 25.

160 'complicating processes of shifting masculinities': Sunaina Arya and Aakash Singh Rathore, *Dalit Feminist Theory: A Reader*, New Delhi: Routledge India, 2019, p. 187.

162 'It is about time we reflect on the all': Rekha M. Shangpliang, '"Mother Earth": Just A Metaphor Or A Spiritual Context?', *East India Story*, 6 March 2021.

164 'dilemma that has been projected upon': Royona Mitra, 'Living a Body Myth, Performing a Body Reality: Reclaiming the Corporeality and Sexuality of the Indian Female Dancer', *Feminist Review*, Vol. 84, 2006, p. 67.

165 'lay at the centre of all early Indian religions': Nupur Dasgupta, *In Search of Pasts? History, Women's Movements and Women's Studies*, Secundrabad: Indian Association for Women's Studies, 2000, p. 25.

166 'listen with another ear, as if hearing an': Luce Irigaray, 'This Sex Which Is Not One', tr. Claudia Reeder, in *New French Feminisms*, Elaine Marks and Isabelle de Courtivron (eds.), New York: Cornell University Press, 1981, pp. 99–106.

166 'identifications in process: as multiple, dynamic': Shirley Anne Tate, *Black Skins, Black Masks: Hybridity, Dialogism, Performativity*, New York: Routledge, 2017, p. 8.

167 Footnote 13: The values 'of the Internet, like': Sadie Plant, as cited in Subhadra Channa, *Encyclopedia of Feminist Theory*, Vol. 1, New Delhi: Genesis Publishing Pvt. Ltd., 2004, p. 181.

168 'being myself' is the top priority: 'For India's youngest adults, marriage is no longer the first priority', *Quartz*, 9 January 2019.

173 'rejection of motherhood as a pre-requisite': Gerda Neyer and Laura Bernardi, 'Feminist Perspectives on Motherhood and Reproduction', *Historical Social Research*, 2011, pp. 164–165.

173 'Giving birth becomes a moment in which': J. Devika, *Womanwriting = Manreading?*, New Delhi: Zubaan-Penguin Books, 2013, pp. 83–148.

175 'we are living in a male power structure': Anne Koedt, Ellen Levine, and Anita Rapone (eds.), 'Politics of the Ego: A Manifesto for N.Y. Radical Feminists', *Radical Feminism*, New York: Times Books, 1973, p. 380.

181 'Relying on the imagery of men's lives in': Carol Gilligan, *In a Different*

Voice, Cambridge, Massachusetts: Harvard University Press, 2003, pp. 24–39.

181 **'Women have served all these centuries as':** Virgina Woolf, *A Room of One's Own*, London: Penguin Books, 2000, p. 29.

181 **Take the Mahatma for instance, who:** Rita Banerji, as cited in Michael Connellan, 'Women suffer from Gandhi's legacy', *The Guardian*, 27 January 2010.

183 **'When we assert intuition, we are':** Clarissa Pinkola Estés, *Women Who Run With the Wolves: Myths and Stories of the Wild Woman Archetype*, New York: Ballantine Books, 1989, p. 3.

185 **'She can be jarred out of ambivalence':** Gloria Anzaldúa, *Borderlands/La Frontera: The New Mestiza*, San Francisco: Aunt Lute Books, 2007, p. 101.

Society, Sanskar, and Choice

186 **It's not very encouraging to know that domestic violence:** Shalu Nigam, 'COVID-19: India's Response to Domestic Violence Needs Rethinking', *South Asia Journal*, 2020.

186 **Footnote 1: Uttarakhand's (male) CM recently criticized:** Kautilya Singh, 'Not against jeans, only ripped jeans, says Uttarakhand CM Tirath Singh amid furore', *Times of India*, 20 March 2021.

186 **Footnote 2: In 2016, a twenty-two-year-old Hindu woman:** India Today Web Desk, 'Hadiya's marriage restored, Supreme Court says no love jihad', *India Today*, 2018.

188 **Footnote 4: 'Feminism is not a "pure" ahistorical ideal':** Maitrayee Chaudhuri, *Feminism in India*, New Delhi: Kali for Women and Women Unlimited. 2004, p. xvii.

189 **'Purdah, in certain western feminist analyses':** Rajeshwari Sundar Rajan, *Real and Imagined Women: Gender, Culture and Postcolonialism*, London and New York: Routledge, 1993, p. 70.

189 **'feminism as a mode of analysis':** Nancy Hartsock, 'Fundamental Feminism: Prospect and Perspective', *Building Feminist Theory*, Charlotte Bunch (ed.), New York: Longman, 1981, p. 40.

189 **'operating from the vantage of strategic resistance':** Karlene Faith, 'Resistance. Lessons from Foucault and feminism', *Power/Gender, Social Relation in Theory and Practise*, H. Loraine Radtke and H. J. Stam (eds.), London: Sage, 1994, p. 39.

189 **'Freedom, choice, and self-responsibility':** Suvi Salmenniemi, 'New Heroines of Labour: Domesticating Post-feminism and Neoliberal Capitalism in Russia', *Sociology*, 2015, pp. 88–105.

191 **'emphasised that Indian culture places':** Elizabeth Jackson, *Feminism and Contemporary Indian Women's Writing*, London: Palgrave Macmillan, 2010, p. 11.

191 **'Stop asking the worn-out question':** Monica Pierce, 'I'm Not Failing Anyone by Leaning Out. I Just Want More Time with My Family', *Working Mother*, 6 December 2018.

193 **'new demands for feminist "caring"':** Mary Beth Mills, 'Gender and Inequality in the Global Labor Force', *Annual Review of Anthropology*, 2003, p. 54.

196 **Footnote 6: 'However, they may kill for the sake of izzat':** AP, 'India records huge spike in honour killings in 2015', *Live Mint*, 7 December 2016.

197 **salwar kameez paired with pinned dupattas:** Express News Service, 'No jeggings, leggings or jeans is first lesson at Medical college in Chennai', *New Indian Express*, 5 September 2017.

197 **'Pinjra Tod is an organisation of Savarna Hindu women':** Lama and Maharaj, 2019.

197 **'Acknowledge your privilege and stop occupying':** Divya Kandukuri, 'Is The Feminism We See Really Intersectional?', *Buzzfeed India*, 2019.

198 **Only 11 per cent of marriages in India:** Kumuduni Das, Kailash Chandra Das, Tarun Kumar Roy, et al., 'Inter-caste marriage in India: has it really changed over time?', European Population Conference 2010, <https://epc2010.princeton.edu/papers/100157>.

198 **Footnote 9: over 80 per cent of SC/ST/OBC students:** Scroll Staff, 'NEET results: Over 80% of SC, ST and OBC students who qualified cleared general category cut-off', *Scroll.in*, 6 June 2019.

198 **Footnote 9: while Dalits top the UPSC exams:** Bharti Jain, 'Dalit IIT-B graduate tops UPSC exam, 10 women in top 25', *Times of India*, 6 April 2019.

198 **Footnote 9: Meanwhile, the upper-caste (lower-class):** ET Online and Agencies, 'Modi govt announces 10 per cent quota for economically backward in general category', *Economic Times*, 7 January 2019.

199 **'Most often we are seen as victims':** Pradnya Jadhav, 'From Victimhood to Power: Dalit Mahila Swabhiman Yatra at Hyderabad', *Round Table India*, 21 April 2015.

203 **Footnote 11: As the civil rights activist and feminist Audre Lorde:** BlackPast, '(1981) Audre Lorde, "The Uses of Anger: Women Responding to Racism"', *BlackPast.org*, 12 August 2012.

204 **'Conservative feminists rarely identify themselves':** Sanya Dhingra, 'Smriti Irani's Amethi act and the rise of palatable feminism in India', *The Print*, 27 May 2019.

208 **Footnote 13: 'By being unfaithful to her husband':** Shreyashi Gosh, 'Manusmriti: The Ultimate Guide To Becoming A "Good Woman"', *Feminism in India*, 11 January 2018.

208 **Footnote 14: 'But those [wives] from whom you fear':** Your Vibe, 'Analysing

the so-called 'Wife Beating Verse': 4:34 of the Holy Quran', *The Muslim Vibe*, 20 January 2019.

208 **Footnote 15: 'I do not permit a woman to teach':** Bible Ref, '1 Timothy 2:12 Parallel Verses', *Bible Ref*, <https://www.bibleref.com/1-Timothy/2/1-Timothy-2-12.html>.

209 **'As a Christian, feminism is a reality check':** Carol Kuruvilla, '15 Christian Women Get Real About The Role Of Women In The Church', *Huffington Post*, 30 March 2016.

209 **'how do we, women, find a source of strength':** 'Reflections on Hindu Feminism', *Women Living Hinduism and Islam Project*, 2020, <https://www.cpp.edu/~wlhip/hindu-feminism.html>.

210 **'women had their place as unquestioned':** Fatima Mernissi, *The Veil and the Male Elite: A Feminist Interpretation of Women's Rights in Islam*, New York: Addison-Wesley, 1991, p. 11.

210 **Meanwhile, scientists are increasingly beginning to listen:** George Nicholas, 'When Scientists "Discover" What Indigenous People Have Known For Centuries', *Smithsonian Magazine*, 21 February 2018.

211 **'realigned its ideologies and practise':** Gopika Solanki, 'Beyond the Limitations of the Impasse: Feminism, Multiculturalism, and Legal Reforms in Religious Family Laws in India', *Politikon*, Vol. 40, No. 1, 2013, p. 83.

211 **'shared adjudication model':** Gopika Solanki, *Adjudication in Religious Family Laws: Cultural Accommodation, Legal Pluralism and Gender Equality in India*, New York: Cambridge University Press, 2011, p. 41.

211 **Footnote 22: 'Those who supported the demand for a uniform civil code':** Murthy and Dasgupta, *Our Pictures, Our Words*, p. 123.

212 **Indian Muslim women's groups want to 'move beyond':** Nida Kirmani, 'Mobilising for Muslim women's rights in India', *openDemocracy*, 14 January 2011.

213 **who created a violent ruckus:** '1,400 arrested for violence during Sabarimala protest', *The Hindu*, 25 October 2018.

213 **leftist parties used 'women's bodies as bricks in a wall':** J. Devika, 'A feminist view: Why I cannot celebrate the success of Kerala's women's wall', *Scroll.in*, 14 January 2019.

214 **The Attukal Bhagavathy temple in Kerala is:** PTI, 'Thousands perform 'pongala' ritual at Attukal temple', *Times of India*, 19 February 2011.

215 **'For the life of me, I do not understand':** Asha Kotwal, 'There's No Reason for Women to Celebrate their Entry to Sabarimala', *The Wire*, 24 January 2019.

215 **Footnote 26: Lower-caste believers are still denied entry:** Srawan Shukla, 'UP temple purified with Gangajal after visit of Dalit woman BJP MLA',

DNA India, 30 July 2018.

216 **Footnote 27: 'For women who…opposed caste':** V Geetha, 'Periyar, Women and an Ethic of Citizenship', *Economic and Political Weekly*, Vol. 33, No. 17, 1998, WS9–WS15.

217 **'The hijab/burqa stands for freedom':** Sidra Binte Islam, 'I Am A Hijabi Feminist', *Huffington Post*, 6 October 2017.

218 **'I found choice feminism, or the idea':** Pallavi Aiyar, 'Why women aren't empowered just because they can choose', *Scroll.in*, 1 May 2016.

220 **In 2018, every day sixty-three housewives:** Kapil Kajal, 'The reasons why 63 Indian housewives killed themselves every day in 2018', *Scroll.in*, 19 February 2020.

221 **However, 2019 saw a sharp rise in women:** Rina Chandran, 'As property prices rise, more Indian women claim inheritance', *Reuters*, 13 March 2019.

221 **Footnote 28: the police conducted extra-judicial killings:** 'Hyderabad case: Police kill suspects in rape and murder of Indian vet', *BBC News*, 6 December 2019.

222 **Footnote 29: Mizoram, M.P., and Chhattisgarh fared better:** Vignesh Radhakrishnan, 'Data | How States dealt with crimes against women', *The Hindu*, 22 January 2020.

223 **masked woman armed with an iron rod:** 'Masked Woman In JNU Video Suspected To Be From Delhi University: Sources', *NDTV*, 13 January 2020.

223 **videos of another woman, allegedly a student:** 'Left students led by JNU Students Union president Aishe Ghosh behind violence, say cops', *Hindustan Times*, 11 January 2020.

223 **Footnote 30: Later, it was reported that they belonged:** 'JNU violence: Police name masked woman in video, ABVP admits she is a member', *Scroll.in*, 15 January 2020.

Conclusion: The Future is Female

225 **We've also come to realize that across the globe:** Gillian Tett, 'Have countries led by women coped better with Covid-19?', *Financial Times*, 2 December 2020.

SELECT BIBLIOGRAPHY

Adriaens, Fien, and Bauwel, Sofie Van, '*Sex and the City:* A Postfeminist Point of View? Or How Popular Culture Functions as a Channel for Feminist Discourse?', *The Journal of Popular Culture*, Vol. 47, No. 1, 2011, pp. 1–22.

Aiyar, Pallavi, *Babies & Bylines: Parenting on the Move*, New Delhi: HarperCollins, 2016.

Anasuya, Shreya Ila, '"A twist in a straight line": inside India's kinky networks', *Deep Dives*, 22 December 2015.

Anzaldúa, Gloria, *Borderlands/La Frontera: The New Mestiza*, San Francisco: Aunt Lute Books, 2007, p. 101.

Arif, Yasmeen, *Life, Emergent: The Social in the Afterlives of Violence*, Minneapolis: Minnesota University Press, 2016.

Arruzza, Cinzia, Bhattacharya, Tithi, and Fraser, Nancy, *Feminism for the 99%: A Manifesto*, Brooklyn, New York: Verso, 2019.

Arunima, G. 'Sex and the Feminist,' *Economic & Political Weekly*, Vol. 47, Issue 43, 27 October 2012.

Arya, Sunaina, and Rathore, Aakash Singh, *Dalit Feminist Theory: A Reader*, New Delhi: Routledge India, 2019.

Baddeley, Jenna, 'On the "irrationality" of women (and men)', *Psychology Today*, 3 November 2010.

Ballakrishnen, Shwethaa S., 'She gets the job done: Entrenched gender meanings and new returns to essentialism in India's elite professional firms', Journal of Professions and Organization, Vol. 4, No. 3, October 2017, pp. 324–342.

Banerji, Rita, *Sex and Power: Defining History, Shaping Societies*, New Delhi: Penguin Books, 2009.

Barrett, Michèle, *Women's Oppression Today: Problems in Marxist Feminist Analysis*, London: Verso, 1980.

Barrett, Michèle, and Phillips, Anne, *Destabilizing Theory: Contemporary Feminist Debates*, Redwood City: Stanford University Press, 1992.

Bartlett, Elizabeth, *Liberty, Equality and Sorority: Contradiction and Integrity in Feminist Thought and Practice*, Brooklyn, NY: Carlson Publishers, 1994.

Baumgardner, Jennifer, and Richards, Amy, *Manifesta: Young Women, Feminism, and the Future*, New York: Farrar, Straus and Giroux, 2000.

Bauwel, Sofie Van, 'Representing Gender Benders: Consumerism and the Muting of Subversion', *At the Interface: Continuity and Transformations in Culture and Politics*, E. Siapera and J. Hands (eds.), Oxford: Rodopi Press, 2004.

Beard, Mary, *Women & Power: A Manifesto*, London: Profile Books, 2017.

Beauvoir, Simone De, *The Second Sex*, New York: Vintage Books, 1974, p. 301.

Bhandare, Namita, 'When home is a prison: Meena Kandasamy's story of domestic abuse', *Live Mint*, 2 June 2017.

Bhattacharya, Manjima, *Mannequin: Working Women in India's Glamour Industry*, New Delhi: Zubaan, 2018.

Bhuyan, Anoo, 'Women Remember, Men Don't', *Outlook*, 22 October 2018.

Bose, Adrija, 'How India's Most Important Law for Children's Safety is Leading to Unsafe Abortions Among Teenagers', *News18*, 23 October 2019.

Brooks, Ann, *Postfeminisms: Feminism, Cultural Theory, and Cultural Forms*, London: Routledge, 1997.

Budgeon, Shelley, 'Emergent Feminist(?) Identities: Young Women and the Practice Of Micropolitics', *European Journal of Women's Studies*, Vol. 8, No. 1, 2001, pp. 7–28.

Butler, Judith, 'Judith Butler: the backlash against "gender ideology" must stop', *New Statesman*, 21 January 2019.

———, 'Performative Arts and Gender Constitution: An Essay in Phenomenology and Feminist Theory', *Theatre Journal*, Vol. 40, No. 4, 1988, pp. 519–531.

———, *Gender Trouble*, New York: Routledge, 1999.

Chakravorty, Amritananda, 'Pride and Prejudice: The Desires of Indian Queer Women', *Live Wire*, 30 June 2018.

Chatterjee, Esha, Desai, Sonalde, and Vanneman, Reeve, 'Indian paradox: Rising education, declining women's employment', *Demographic Research*, Vol. 38, No. 31, 2018, pp. 855–878.

Chaudhuri, Maitrayee, 'Feminism in India: The Tale and its Telling', *Revue Tiers Monde*, Vol. 209, No. 1, 2012, pp. 19–36.

———, *Feminism in India: The Tale and its Telling*, New Delhi: Kali for Women & Women Unlimited, 2004.

Cixous, Hélène, 'The Laugh of the Medusa', *The Norton Anthology of Theory & Criticism*, Vincent B. Leitch (ed.), London and New York: W. W. Norton & Company, Inc., 2010, pp. 1938–1959.

Coonz, Stephanie, *Marriage, a History: How Love Conquered Marriage*, London:

Viking Penguin, 2005.

Cornwall, Andrea, 'Indian sex-workers are a shining example of women's empowerment', *The Guardian*, 26 July 2012.

Cornwall, Andrea, Harrison, Elizabeth, and Whitehead, Ann (eds.), *Feminisms in Development: Contradictions, Contestations and Challenges*, London: Zed Books, 2007.

Daly, Mary, 'Glory to God the Verb', *Ms.*, No. 3, December 1974, pp. 58–62.

Dasgupta, Nupur, *In Search of Pasts? History, Women's Movements and Women's Studies*, Secundrabad: Indian Association for Women's Studies, 2000.

Das, Veena, 'Language and Body: Transactions in the Construction of Pain', *Deadalus*, Vol. 125, No.1, 1996, pp. 67–91.

Davies, Bronwyn, 'The Concept of Agency: A Feminist Poststructuralist Analysis', *Social Analysis: The International Journal of Social and Cultural Practice*, Vol. 30, 1991, pp. 42–53.

De Beauvoir, Simone, *Extracts from The Second Sex*, London: Vintage, 2015.

Denfeld, Rene, *The New Victorians: A Young Woman's Challenge to the Old Feminist Order*, New York: Grand Central Publishing, 1995.

Devika, J., *Womanwriting = Manreading?*, New Delhi: Zubaan-Penguin Books, 2013.

Dhanaraj, Christina Thomas, 'Dalit Women in Corporate India are Being Left Behind', *The Wire*, 2 March 2017.

Dhand, Arti, *Woman as Fire, Woman as Sage: Sexual Ideology in the Mahābhārata*, New York: State University of New York Press, 2008.

Dhingra, Sanya, 'Smriti Irani's Amethi act and the rise of palatable feminism in India', *The Print*, 27 May 2019.

Dinkar, Niharika, 'Framing Women: Gender and Modernity in Colonial India', *Marg*, Vol. 62, No. 4, 2011, pp. 12–15.

Doniger, Wendy, *The Hindus: An Alternative History*, New York: Viking Penguin, 2009.

Donovan, Josephine, *Feminist Theory: The Intellectual Traditions, Third Edition*, New York: Continuum, 2006.

Dutt, Yashica, *Coming Out as Dalit*, New Delhi: Aleph Book Company, 2019.

Elias, Ana Sofia, Gill, Rosalind, and Scharff, Christina, *Aesthetic Labour: Rethinking Beauty Politics in Neoliberalism*, London: Palgrave Macmillan, 2017.

Estés, Clarissa Pinkola, *Women Who Run With the Wolves: Myths and Stories of the Wild Woman Archetype*, New York: Ballantine Books, 1989.

Faith, Karlene, *Unruly Women: The Politics of Confinement and Resistance*, New York: Seven Stories Press, 2011.

Gandhi, Leela, *Postcolonial Theory: A Critical Introduction*, New York: Columbia University Press, 1998.

Gangoli, Geetanjali, 'Prostitution as Livelihood: "Work" or "Crime"?', *Presented at the conference Livelihoods and Poverty Reduction: Lessons From Eastern India*, 25–27 September 2001, <http://www.anthrobase.com/Txt/G/Gangoli_G_01.htm>.

Genz, Stephanie, *Postfeminisms in Popular Culture*, London: Palgrave Macmillan, 2009.

Gilligan, Carol, *In a Different Voice*, Cambridge, Massachusetts: Harvard University Press, 2003.

Gill, Rosalind, 'Culture and Subjectivity in Neoliberal and Postfeminist Times', *Subjectivity*, Vol. 25, 2008, pp. 432–45.

Green, Karen, 'Femininity and Transcendence', *Australian Feminist Studies*, Vol. 4, No. 10, 1989, pp. 85–96.

Greer, Germaine, *The Female Eunuch*, London: 4th Estate, 1970.

Hakim, Catherine, *Erotic Capital: The Power of Attraction in the Boardroom and the Bedroom*, New York: Basic Books, 2011.

Halberstam, Judith, 'The Good, the Bad, and the Ugly: Men, Women and Masculinity', *The Norton Anthology of Theory & Criticism*, Vincent B. Leitch (ed.), New York: W. W. Norton & Company, Inc., 2010, pp. 2635–2654.

Hansen, Gitte Marianne, *Femininity, Self-harm and Eating Disorders in Japan*, London: Routledge, 2016.

Happonen, Tove, 'Making the political personal: how psychology undermines feminist activism', *Feminist Current*, 21 December 2017.

Haraway, Donna, 'A Manifesto for Cyborgs', *The Norton Anthology of Theory & Criticism*, Vincent B. Leitch (ed.), London and New York: W. W. Norton & Company, Inc., 2010, pp. 2187–2220.

Hartsock, Nancy, 'Fundamental Feminism: Prospect and Perspective', *Building Feminist Theory*, Charlotte Bunch (ed.), New York: Longman, 1981, pp. 32–43.

Hawkins, K., Cornwall, A., and Lewin, T., 'Sexuality and Empowerment: An Intimate Connection, Pathways Policy Paper', *Pathways of Women's Empowerment Research Programme Consortium*, Brighton: Pathways of Women's Empowerment, IDS, 2011.

Irigaray, Luce, 'This Sex Which Is Not One', tr. Claudia Reeder, in *New Feminisms*, Elaine Marks and Isabelle de Courtivron (eds.), New York: Cornell University Press, 1981.

Jackson, Elizabeth, *Feminism and Contemporary Indian Women's Writing*, New York: Palgrave Macmillan, 2010.

Jacob, Preminda, *Celluloid Deities: The Visual Culture of Cinema and Politics in South India*, Lanham: Lexington Books, 2009.

Jadhav, Pradnya, 'From Victimhood to Power: Dalit Mahila Swabhiman Yatra at Hyderabad', *Round Table India*, 21 April 2015.

Jain, Jasbir, 'Daughters of Mother India in Search of a Nation: Women's Narratives about the Nation', *Economic and Political Weekly*, 29 April 2006, pp. 1654–1664.

———, *Indigenous Roots of Feminism: Culture, Subjectivity and Agency*, New Delhi: Sage, 2011.

Jameela, Nalini, *The Autobiography of a Sex Worker*, Chennai: Westland Ltd., 2007.

———, *Romantic Encounters of a Sex Worker*, Noida: Om Books International, 2018.

Jha, Meeta, *The Global Beauty Industry*, London: Routledge, 2015.

Jolly, Susie, Cornwall, Andrea, and Hawkins, Kate, *Women, Sexuality and the Political Power of Pleasure*, New York: Zed Books, 2013.

Kadambari, V., *Gender Studies: A Primer*, Sriperumbudur: Rajiv Gandhi Institute of National Development, 2009.

Kannan, Ashraya, 'Movies are for entertainment', *Deccan Chronicle*, 1 June 2018.

Kathuria, Poonam, and Bhaiya, Abha, *Indian Feminism: Individual and Collective Journeys*, New Delhi: Zubaan, 2018.

Kavya, 'All Romantic Experiences are Essentially Caste Experiences' – In Conversation with Jyotsna Siddharth, *Feminism in India*, 20 May 2019.

Kirmani, Nida, 'Mobilising for Muslim Women's Rights in India', *openDemocracy*, 14 January 2011.

Kishwar, Madhu, 'A Horror of Isms', *The Woman's Question*, Mary Evans (ed.), London: Sage Publications, 1994.

Koedt, Anne, Levine, Ellen, and Rapone, Anita (eds.), 'Politics of the Ego: A Manifesto for N.Y. Radical Feminists', *Radical Feminism*, New York: Times Books, 1973.

Kokra, Sonali, 'How I Shamefully Benefitted from Patriarchy', *Arré*, 14 January 2019.

Kowtal, Asha, 'There's No Reason for Women to Celebrate Their Entry to Sabarimala', *The Wire*, 24 January 2019.

Krishnamurthy, Mathangi, *1-800-Worlds: The Making of the Indian Call Centre Economy*, New Delhi: Oxford University Press, 2018.

Lahiri, Tripti, *Maid in India: Stories of Inequality and Opportunity Inside Our Homes*, New Delhi: Aleph Book Company, 2017.

Lama, Shradha, and Maharaj, Sabah, 'Statement: Why We Decided to Leave Pinjra Tod', *Round Table India*, 20 February 2019.

Lister, Kate, 'Sex in Our Strange World: Why the Matriarchy Means Better Sex and a Better Society', *Vice*, 7 March 2019.

Lockford, Lesa, *Performing Femininity: Rewriting Gender Identity*, Lanham: AltaMiraPress, 2004.

Madan, Pankaj, and Friedrich, Mark Alexander, 'Attitudes, Anxieties and Aspirations of India's Youth: Changing Patterns', Delhi: Centre for the Study of Developing Societies (CSDS) and Konrad-Adenauer-Stiftung, 2016.

Malhotra, Savita, and Shah, Ruchita, 'Women and mental health in India: An overview', *Indian Journal of Psychiatry*, Vol. 57, No. 2, 2015, pp. 205–211.

Mani, Lata, *Contentious Traditions: The Debate on Sati in Colonial India*, Berkeley: University of California Press, 1998.

Mann, Patricia, *Micro-politics: Agency in a Postfeminist Era*, Minneapolis: University of Minnesota Press, 1994.

McNay, Lois, *Foucault: A Critical Introduction*, Cambridge: Polity Press, 1994.

McRobbie, Angela, *The Aftermath of Feminism: Gender, Culture and Social Change*, London: Sage, 2008.

McRobbie, Angela, 'TOP GIRLS? Young women and the postfeminist sexual contract', *Cultural Studies*, Vol. 21, Nos. 4–5, 2007, pp. 718–737.

Mead, Margaret, *Sex and Temperament: In Three Primitive Societies*, New York: Harper Perennial, 2001.

Menon, Madhavi, *Infinite Variety: A History of Desire in India*, New Delhi: Speaking Tiger Books, 2018.

Menon, Mandovi, 'Five Young Indian Women Get Real About Masturbation,' *Homegrown*, 28 March 2017.

Menon, Nivedita, 'Between the Burqa and the Beauty Parlor? Globalization, Cultural Nationalism, and Feminist Politics', *Postcolonial Studies and Beyond*, Ania Loomba, Suvir Kaul, et al. (eds.), Durham: Duke University Press, 2005.

———, *Seeing Like A Feminist*, Gurgaon: Penguin Random House India, 2012.

Mernissi, Fatema, *The Veil and the Male Elite: A Feminist Interpretation of Women's Rights in Islam*, tr. Mary Jo Lakeland, New York: Addison-Wesley, 1991.

Mills, Mary Beth, 'Gender and Inequality in the Global Labor Force', *Annual Review of Anthropology*, Vol. 32, 2003, pp. 41–62.

Mishra, Neha, 'India and Colorism: The Finer Nuances', *Washington University Global Studies Law Review*, 2015.

Mitra, Royona, 'Living a Body Myth, Performing a Body Reality: Reclaiming the Corporeality and Sexuality of the Indian Female Dancer', *Feminist Review*, Vol. 84, 2006, pp. 67–83.

Mondal, Mimi, 'A Dalit woman's thoughts on #MeTooIndia.' *The Indian Express*,

14 April 2018.

Moore, Suzanne, 'Ocasio-Cortez has shown "shameless" women are a powerful force.' *The Guardian*, 10 January 2019.

Mukhoty, Ira, *Daughters of the Sun: Empresses, Queens & Begums of the Mughal Empire*, New Delhi: Aleph Book Company, 2018.

Munusamy, Kiruba, 'Intersection of Identities: Online Gender and Caste Based Violence', *GenderIT.Org*, 7 June 2018.

Murli, Ayushi, 'How Do We Sustain India's #MeToo movement?', *Arré*, 24 October 2018.

Murthy, Laxmi, and Dasgupta, Rajashri, *Our Pictures, Our Words: A Visual Journey Through the Women's Movement*, New Delhi: Zubaan, 2011.

Murray, Padmini Ray, 'Bringing Up the Bodies: The Visceral, the Virtual and the Visible', *Bodies of Information: Intersectional Feminism and Digital Humanities*, Elizabeth Losh and Jacqueline Wernimont (eds.), Minneapolis: University of Minnesota Press, 2018, <https://dhdebates.gc.cuny.edu/projects/bodies-of-information>.

Naragarjan, Vijaya Rettakudi, 'Threshold Designs, Forehead Dots and Menstruation Rituals', *Women's Lives, Women's Rituals in the Hindu Tradition*, Tracy Pintchman (ed.), New York: Oxford University Press, 2007.

Nazneen, Sohela, and Sultan, Maheen, *Voicing Demands: Feminist Activism in Transnational Contexts*, London: Zed Books, 2014.

Padte, Richa Kaul, 'From Judy Blume to the Sexy Internet: What Counts as Erotica?', *TARSHI*, 1 July 2019.

Pant, Manasi, 'Choice Feminism: A Self-Imposed Barrier To Progress?', *Feminism in India*, 17 September 2019.

Patel, Vibhuti, and Khajuria, Radhika, 'Political Feminism in India: An Analysis of Actors, Debates and Strategies', New Delhi: Friedrich-Ebert-Stiftung India Office, 2016.

Pavčnik, Marijan, 'Human Rights, Minority Rights, Women's Rights: Proceedings of the 19th World Congress of the International Association for Philosophy of Law and Social Philosophy. New York, June 24–30, 1999', Stuttgart: Franz Steiner Verlag Stuttgart, 2001.

Phadke, Shilpa, 'Thirty Years On: Women's Studies Reflects on the Women's Movement', *Economic and Political Weekly*, 25–31 October 2003, pp. 4567–4576.

Pierce, Monica, 'I'm Not Failing Anyone by Leaning Out. I Just Want More Time with My Family', *Working Mother*, 6 December 2018.

Piu Kundu, Sreemoyee, 'Heartwarming Story of a Married Lesbian Couple,' *DailyO*,

5 March 2016.

Plant, Sadie, *Zeros + Ones*, New York: 4th Estate, 1997.

Pundir, Pallavi, 'Transgender People Tell Us Why India's Newly Proposed Rape Laws are Discriminatory', *Vice*, 11 September 2019.

Rajan, Rajeshwari Sundar, *Real and Imagined Women: Gender, Culture and Postcolonialism*, London and New York: Routledge, 1993.

Rippon, Gina, *The Gendered Brain: the new neuroscience that shatters the myth of the female brain*, London: The Bodley Head, 2019.

Riviere, Joan, 'Womanliness as a masquerade,' *International Journal of Psycho-Analysis*, Vol. 9, 1929, pp. 303–13.

Roy, Srila, 'Whose Feminism Is It Anyway?', *The Wire*, 1 November 2017.

Rubin, Gayle, 'Thinking Sex: Notes for A Radical Theory of the Politics of Sexuality', *The Norton Anthology of Theory & Criticism*, Vincent B. Leitch (ed.), New York: W. W. Norton & Company, Inc., 2010, pp. 2373—2377.

Salmenniemi, Suvi, and Adamson, Maria, 'New Heroines of Labour: Domesticating Post-feminism and Neoliberal Capitalism in Russia', *Sociology*, Vol. 49, No. 1, 2015, pp. 88–105.

Sanday, Peggy Reeves, *Women at the Center: Life in a Modern Matriarchy*, New York: Cornell University Press, 2013.

Sandhu, Nupur, *NUMI: The Guarded Loop*, New Delhi: Blue Rose Publishers, 2019.

Satyam, Nishtha, and Pickup, Francine, 'To Reverse Decline of Women in Labour Force, India Must Make Its Working Spaces Safe', *The Wire*, 2 December 2018.

Schank, Hana, and Wallace, Elizabeth, *The Ambition Decisions: What Women Know About Work, Family, and the Path to Building a Life*, New York: Penguin, 2018.

Scott, Joan Wallach, *Sex and Secularism*, Princeton and Oxford: Princeton University Press, 2018.

Sharma, Jaya, 'Porn, Not Erotica', *TARSHI*, 1 July 2019.

Sharma, Kamayani, '#MeToo: Understanding Consent and Sex-Positivity in a Patriarchal Society', *Firstpost*, 12 November 2018.

Shashikant, Uma, 'Why Women Need to Work', *The Economic Times*, 30 September 2019.

Sherman, Rachel, *Uneasy Street: The Anxieties of Affluence*, New Jersey: Princeton University Press, 2017.

Shiva, Vandana, *Staying Alive: Women, Ecology and Development*, London: Zed Books, 1989.

Shugart, Helene, Waggoner, Catherine Egley, and Hallstein, D. Lynn O'Brien, 'Mediating Third-Wave Feminism: Appropriation as Postmodern Media Practice',

Critical Studies in Media Communication, Vol. 18, No. 2, 2001, pp. 194–210.

Shukla, Vandana, 'Is #feminism elitist in India?', *The Tribune*, 5 March 2017.

Sinha, Suchetana, 'The Headless Women of Bollywood: A Look into the Industry's Blatant Sexual Objectification', *ScoopWhoop*, 27 May 2016.

Skeggs, Beverley, *Formations of Class and Gender: Becoming Respectable*, London: Sage Publications, 1997.

Solanki, Gopika, *Adjudication in Religious Family Laws: Cultural Accommodation, Legal Pluralism and Gender Equality in India*, New York: Cambridge University Press, 2011.

Solnit, Rebecca, 'Silence and powerlessness go hand in hand—women's voices must be heard', *The Guardian*, 2017.

Spivak, Gayatri Chakravorty, 'A Literary Representation of the Subaltern: Mahasweta Devi's Stanadāyini', *Indian Literary Criticism: Theory and Interpretation*, G. N. Devy (ed.), Hyderabad: Orient Blackswan Private Limited, 2009, pp. 220–58.

Srinivasan, Rama, 'The right identity: Evolving feminist narratives in India must resolve the fault lines that have emerged', *The Indian Express*, 30 October 2018.

Sripaada, Chinmayi, 'Chinmayi Sripaada's Relentless Fight Against Sexual Harassment in the Tamil Film Industry', *Huffington Post India*, 17 June 2019.

Tagore, Rabindranath, 'Was Rabindranath Tagore a feminist? Read his essay "Woman and Home" from 1922 to find out', *Scroll.in*, 9 May 2017.

TARSHI Team, 'Interview: Paromita Vohra—Part I', *TARSHI*, 1 August 2018.

Tate, Shirley Anne, *Black Skins, Black Masks: Hybridity, Dialogism, Performativity*, New York: Routledge, 2017.

Thapan, Meenakshi, *Living the Body: Embodiment, Womanhood and Identity in Contemporary India*, New Delhi: Sage, 2009.

Tilak, Sudha, 'Love, sex and the bhadralok.' *The Hindu*, 16 January 2018.

Tiwari, Shubha, 'Rooting Feminism to India', *Boloji.com*, 5 November 2017.

Tolentino, Jia, 'The Case Against Contemporary Feminism', *The New Yorker*, 8 February 2017.

———, 'The Rage of the Incels', *The New Yorker*, 15 May 2018.

V. Geetha, 'Periyar, Women and an Ethic of Citizenship', *Economic and Political Weekly*, Vol. 33, No. 17, 1998, pp. WS9–WS15.

Vanita, Ruth, *Queering India: Same-Sex Love and Eroticism in Indian Culture and Society*, New York: Routledge, 2002.

Vanniyar, Smita, 'How Queer Are Your Dating Apps?', *TARSHI*, 15 June 2017.

Vatsyayana, *The Kamasutra of Vatsyayana*, Toronto: Penguin Random House Canada, 2002.

Vavrus, Mary Douglas, *Postfeminist News: Political Women in Media Culture*, New York: State University of New York Press, 2002.

Venugopal, Veena, 'Feminists Have Killed Feminism.' *The Hindu Business Line*, 10 March 2018.

Whelehan, Imelda, *Modern Feminist Thought: From the Second Wave to 'Post-Feminism'*, Edinburgh: Edinburgh University Press, 1995.

Wickramasinghe, Maithree, *Feminist Research Methodology: Making Meanings of Meaning-making*, New Delhi: Zubaan, 2014.

Wolf, Naomi, *The Beauty Myth*, New York: Harper Perennial, 2002.

Woolf, Virginia, '[Androgyny]', *The Norton Anthology of Theory and Criticism*, Vincent B Leitch (ed.), New York & London: W. W. Norton & Company, Inc., 2010, pp. 900–05.

———, *A Room of One's Own*, London: Penguin Books, 2000.

Wittig, Monique, 'One Is Not Born a Woman', *The Norton Anthology of Theory and Criticism*, Vincent B Leitch (ed.), New York & London: W. W. Norton & Company, Inc., 2010, pp. 1,904–12.

INDEX

Dark is Beautiful campaigns, 53–54
fairness, 52, 53, 131, 156
ideal, 36, 40, 46, 49, 50
organic products of, 34n1
parlour, 38, 48
products, 34, 34n1
routines, 33, 39, 48, 56
Bharathi, Rachelle Chandran, 160–161
Bharatiya Janta Party (BJP), 20, 204, 213
Bharatiya Muslim Mahila Andolan (BMMA), 20n45, 212n25
Bhattacharjya, Manjima, 57, 57n34
Bhattacharya, Trisha, 169–170
Bhuyan, Anoo, 81
Bible, 152n4, 208n14
biological essentialism, 105, 122, 206
bisexuality, 4, 67, 69, 99n31
Biswas, Shrinjita, 178–179
BJP, 204, 213
black feminism, 22n49
body politics, 59, 83, 84, 122
body positivity, 47, 50, 61
Bollywood, 16n43, 35, 52, 52n23, 57, 57n35, 58, 73, 103, 218
Brahmanical patriarchy, 2, 3n8, 95, 175, 199, 213
British colonialism, 10n28, 178, 188
B., Shruti, 98
Buddhism, 29n62, 208, 209
Budgeon, Shelley, 32
burqa, 36, 37n7, 38, 41, 42, 205, 212–213, 217
Butalia, Urvashi, 14, 14n38
butch 4, 4n11, 43, 99
Butler, Judith, 99n30, 155

campaigns in social media
#BelieveWomen, 81
#DalitWomenFight, 12, 12n34
#DalitWomenThrive, 200
#HappyToBleed, 12, 50n21
#IWillGoOut, 12, 195
#mentalhealthawareness, 82
#mentalhealthmatters, 82
#MeToo, x, xiii, 12, 12n33, 80, 81, 86, 87, 107, 117n8, 122, 125, 132, 141, 187
#PinjraTod, 196, 196n7, 197
#PrideNotPrejudice, 12
#QueerIndia, 12
#SmashBrahmanicalPatriarchy, 12
#TimesUp, 12
#WhyLoiter, 12
'Dark is Beautiful', 53, 54
capitalism, 15, 19, 23, 23n51, 23n52, 24, 25, 31n67, 34, 45n17
career, 110, 111, 126, 135, 139
caste, 2, 3n8, 19, 23n51, 24, 41, 197
apartheid, 12n34
-based bias, 131
-based discrimination, 12n34
Celluloid Deities (Preminda Jacob), 57n35
Chakraborty, Mimi, 123
Chakravorty, Amritananda, 78
Chand, Dutee, 78
Chatterjee, Tannishtha, 52
childbirth, 8, 97, 173, 173n16, 174, 183
Chiramel, Dhanya Sijo, 52
Chitnis, Suma, 191
Choo, Jimmy, 34, 89n20
Chopra, Priyanka, 37
Chowdhry, Prem, 221
cinema/film/movie(s)
Bala, 52n24
Dangal, 58, 218
Kabir Singh, 73

Manogaran, Elavarasi, 142
Manusmriti, 3n8, 94, 208n13, 215
marriage, 36, 66, 66n1, 75, 77
  intra-caste and arranged, 72–73
Marxist feminists, 21, 150
masculine/masculinity, 1, 3n9, 4, 6,
  12, 47, 68, 172, 180, 226
  dominant, 102
  idealistic, 177
  toxic, 73
  traits, 158
masturbation, 70, 90, 91, 98
Maternity Leave Act, 135n24
Matilda effect, 6n15
Maya, 210, 210n20
McRobbie, Angela, 56
Medical Termination of Pregnancy
  (MTP) Act 1972, 88
Medical Termination of Pregnancy
  (Amendment) Bill, 2020, 13
Menon, Mandovi, 91
Menon, Neelima, 213
Menon, Nivedita, 31n67, 38, 221
menopause, 8
menstrual leave, 110n4
menstruation, 8, 51n21, 183
mental health, 82, 110, 129
Mernissi, Fatima, 210
micropolitics, 10n28, 12, 14, 22
millennials, 12, 31, 33, 44, 71, 136,
  138, 139, 167, 219
Ministry of Women and Child
  Development, 82n15, 137
misogyny, 1, 35, 36
Mitra, Royona, 164
Mody, Anvi, 55
Mondal, Mimi, 28
Moses, Beulah, 121–122
motherhood, 16, 96, 108, 139,
  152n4, 153, 166, 173, 173n16,

174, 186, 205, 206
Mufti, Mehbooba, 38–39
Mukherjee, Sree, 78
Mukherjee, Swastika, 58
Munusamy, Kiruba, 42
Murli, Ayushi, 80
Muslim Women's Rights Network
  (MWRN), 212n25

narcissism, xiii, 9, 10, 64, 64n44,
  140, 180–185
National Commission for Women
  (NCW), 1n1, 137
neoliberalism, 19, 189
neo-liberalism, 189
non-binary, 161, 161n9
Northeast, 93, 94, 162,
Nicollet, Sharmila, 123
nudity, 38, 38n8, 50, 58, 102
NUMI: The Guarded Loop (Nupur
  Sandhu), 168

Obama, Michelle, 138
1-800 Worlds (Mathangi
  Krishnamurthy), 159
organic beauty, 34n1, 62, 62n42

Padukone, Deepika, 36n4, 58, 87,
  87n19
Pandey, Anuja, 156–157
Pant, Manasi, 48
parenthood, 97, 99, 118, 135, 137,
  174
Patil, Prarthana, 217
patriarchy, xiii, 7–10, 12, 15–17,
  19–20, 30, 32, 43, 53n27, 67,
  83, 102, 114–116, 118, 120, 182,
  190, 209, 217. *See also* Femininity;
  Feminism
  Brahmanical, 175